Option Choice

Option Choice:
A question of equal opportunity

John Pratt, John Bloomfield and Clive Seale

A study sponsored by the Equal Opportunities Commission

NFER-NELSON

Published by The NFER–NELSON Publishing Company Ltd.,
Darville House, 2 Oxford Road East, Windsor, Berkshire SL4 1DF

First published 1984
© John Pratt, John Bloomfield and Clive Seale
ISBN 0-7005-0528-8
Code 8171 02 1

All rights reserved, including translation. No part of this publication may be reproduced or transmitted in any form or by any means, electronic or mechanical, including photocopying, recording or duplication in any information storage and retrieval system, without permission in writing from the publishers.

Filmsetting by Vantage Photosetting Co. Ltd
Eastleigh and London
Printed by Billing and Sons Ltd., Worcester

Contents

Acknowledgements

	Page
1. THE RESEARCH STUDY	
Sources	3
'Postal survey'	3
Case studies	4
National statistics	5
Attitude surveys	5
2. CONTEXT	
Sex differences in take up of subjects	6
Reasons to do with educational provision and school organisation	10
3. THE LETTER AND SPIRIT OF THE ACT	
The letter of the law	19
The spirit of the Act	20
4. PATTERNS OF CURRICULUM CHOICE	
Subject differentiation	26
Subject take up 1973 and 1980–1	32
Examinations – entries and passes	33
Careers aspirations and achievements	45
Subject take up and careers	46
Subject take up and further and higher education	48
Conclusions	53
5. SCHOOL POLICY	
Local authority commitment	55
School policy	56
Formal discussion	56

     Special responsibility   57
     Policy statements   58
     Other policy documents   61
     Comments on equal opportunities policy   62
     Single-sex schools   66
  Equal opportunities practices   67
     Single-sex schools   73
  School background and policy   74
     Combined indicators of good practice   76
  Relationship of policy to subject take up   78
  Conclusions   82

6. OPTION SYSTEMS
  Tests of option schemes   86
     Test results   87
     Option schemes and subject take up   93
  Institutional influences   99
     The user's views   99
     Teacher influence   104
     Linked subjects   105
     Ability grouping   107
     Rotational Craft Timetables   109
  Option forms   113
     Alternative considerations   119
  Conclusions   121

7. ORGANIZATION AND TEACHING OF SUBJECTS
  The overall picture   125
  Sciences   127
     Case study schools   129
     Single-sex schools   134
  Vocational subjects   135
     Case study schools   144
     Design and technology   149
     Single-sex schools   150
  Other subjects   152
  Careers Teaching   154
     Single-sex schools   163
  Links between subjects and jobs   165
  Conclusions   167

8. TEACHER ATTITUDES
  Teacher attitude scales   175
     Basic beliefs   179

Commitment to equal opportunity	181
The role of careers education	185
Physical sciences and technical subjects	187
Stereotyped subjects	189
Encouragement of non-traditional choice	192
School organization	197
Role of parents	203
Teachers and the idea of 'neutrality'	205

9. PUPIL ATTITUDES

Pupil attitude scales	210
Agreement with EOC policy on good practice 'Score P'	212
Boys and girls in school	213
Outside influences	217
Jobs and careers	218
Men and women	220
Family and home	222
Combating stereotypical influences	223

10. CONCLUSIONS 225

Appendices

1. Response rate and representativeness of samples	239
2. Good practice in schools	242
3. Aspirations, destinations and hobbies of pupils from case study schools	246
4. Classification of non-traditional subjects, careers and hobbies	253
5. Categorization of subjects for option tests	255
6. Careers associated with subjects in option booklets in mixed schools	256
7. Teacher attitudes: statements about school	264
8. Pupil attitudes: items on careers, home life and personality characteristics	265
Reference list	267
Further reading	271
Index	273

Acknowledgements

This book reports the findings of a research study undertaken by the Centre for Institutional Studies at the Anglian Regional Management Centre, North East London Polytechnic.

The study was commissioned by the Equal Opportunities Commission and we are grateful not only for this financial support but also for the encouragement of the Commission's officers, particularly Christine Jackson and Lynda Carr, and of former Commissioner Eric Robinson who was especially helpful in the formative stages of the project. The project was advised by a steering group established by the Commission and we are grateful to members of this, Dr Ann Robinson, Judith Whyte, Richard Knight and Miss M. Goodfellow. Despite their best efforts, none of the above can be held responsible for the detail of this book or the opinions expressed in it.

The project could not have proceeded without help of all kinds from within the Centre and the Polytechnic, especially the secretarial and administrative support of Jill Sweeney and Barbara Knight (both lost to us before the end of the project because of public expenditure cuts) and the criticism and advice of our colleagues, particularly Michael Locke.

Most importantly of all, however, the project could not have begun without the cooperation of teachers and pupils in schools. To all those who completed questionnaires, answered our questions and revealed, deliberately or inadvertently, their views on equal opportunities we offer our thanks and the hope that they will get as much from our visits as we did.

John Pratt
John Bloomfield
Clive Seale

Stratford
March 1984

CHAPTER 1

The research study

Although Her Majesty's Inspectors stated that 'the school curriculum is the key to pupils' achievement' (GB.DES, 1977), it has been repeatedly found that the curriculum offered to boys and girls differs substantially. The last national survey of these differences was conducted in 1973 and published two years later (GB.DES, 1975). It was found that differences appeared even in the curriculum in primary schools, but by the time of option choice in the fourth and fifth years of secondary school, there were striking differences in the subjects studied by boys and girls. The authors of the survey were sufficiently impressed to comment that

> It may be that society can justify the striking differences that exist between the subjects studied by boys and girls in secondary schools, but it is more likely that a society that needs to develop to the full the talents and skills of all its people will find the discrepancy disturbing.

Since that survey, the Sex Discrimination Act (1975) has made sex discrimination in education (with certain exceptions) unlawful, but there have been no national studies of the position.

This book records the findings of a study commissioned in 1980 by the Equal Opportunities Commission into curricular differences in secondary schools. The Commission presented three aims for the study.

1. Appraise the current situation in a sample of secondary schools. The sample should be as large as possible and should include schools covering all types of organizational pattern, and all age ranges, together with a range of socio-economic backgrounds and geographical areas.
2. Study the extent to which the Sex Discrimination Act is being implemented, both in letter and spirit, and the effects it is having in secondary schools.

2   *Option choice*

3. Identify and assess the practical problems which it is said preclude a free choice of curricular options by both sexes, and to examine possible solutions.

To undertake our first research task, to appraise the current situation in a sample of secondary schools, we attempted to establish the national picture of subjects taken by boys and girls after option choice, the extent of differences between them and the changes, if any, since the HMI survey conducted in 1973 (GB.DES, 1975). This we did in two main ways: by a survey of subjects taken by pupils in a sample of secondary schools; and by examination of especially commissioned tabulations of examination entries from DES statistics. This information was supported by detailed statistics on pupil subject choices from selected case study schools. We were able to go further, however, than subjects studied or taken for examination; we gathered information from schools, careers offices and DES statistics on the future educational or career destinations or aspirations of pupils, and so to examine the issue of the relationship between educational opportunity and future careers.

This aspect of the study might be regarded as concerned with the 'outcomes' of the education process, though undoubtedly these result also from a number of other factors, such as the prejudices and preferences of pupils, parents, employers and teachers.

The second aspect of our study, therefore, was concerned with the educational process. We attempted to determine the extent of good or bad practice, and to investigate whether practice was associated with outcome. This involved detailed investigation into organization and teaching in case study schools. This aspect of the study is clearly problematical. As Chapter 2 shows, there are several candidates for the most important influence on pupils' choice of options (if indeed this is the right way of putting it, since the importance of influence surely varies from pupil to pupil) and variations on the extent to which schools are behaving in accordance with the Act.

Some progress towards estimating the extent to which pupils are influenced by various factors can be made by seeing whether variations in an influencing factor are associated with variation in subject take up. Thus, it is possible to see whether different ways of grouping subjects for option schemes is associated with differences in take up; whether the overall stress which a school gives to equal opportunities as a policy (as measured by various items on the survey questionnaire and combined into a score) is associated with variation in subject take up. Variation in teacher attitudes from school to school (as measured on an attitude scale) can be compared with subject take up in the schools. The study also gathered evidence from survey schools about how option subjects are presented to pupils and parents in school literature, and various other potential influences have been examined; these include staffing patterns in schools, differences in punishments; ways in which subjects can be presented to either encourage or discourage the non-traditional sex to opt for them.

The study also collected information about extra-school factors. Pupils were asked in interviews about the extent to which teachers, their peers or parents influenced their choice. Visits to careers offices and interviews with careers teachers have occasionally provided us with information about the expectations of local employers. Data on the linkage between subjects taken and career advice derived from DES statistics and careers office records can be regarded as showing the influence of the job market on option choice (as well as the influence of option choice on the job market as mentioned earlier).

Sources

In order to investigate all these issues, the study had to collect different kinds of data from different sources. There were four main approaches: a postal survey; case studies of selected schools; analysis of national statistics; attitude surveys.

Postal survey

During the academic year 1980–81, two samples of secondary schools were sent questionnaires. The questionnaire asked for basic information about the school (age range, catchment area etc.), and about organization and practices concerned with equal opportunities (e.g. if there was a member of staff with special responsibility for this issue). The rationale for the questions was derived from the EOC booklet *Do You Provide Equal Opportunities?* (GB.EOC, 1979) and a general principle that the questionnaire embodied was that information should be gained as far as possible from existing school records or from various enclosures (such as prospectuses) asked for. The first sample of schools, the *nominated* sample, consisted of 139 schools in 63 of the Local Education Authorities in England and Wales. All Chief Education Officers in England and Wales were asked to nominate one or more schools in their authority that, in their view, were examples of good practice in the area of equal opportunities. A summary of the chief recommendations in the Equal Opportunities Commission's commentary (GB.EOC, 1979) was provided to assist their choice. The second sample, a *cluster* sample, consisted of all the 216 secondary schools of six LEAs, including one from Scotland.

The purpose of choosing two samples like this was to compare what it was hoped were the best examples (the nominated sample) of good practice with a sample more representative of the state of affairs in the country as a whole (the cluster sample). Taken together the samples represent 7·27 per cent of secondary schools in England, Wales and Scotland. Excluding Scotland, the samples represent 7·61 per cent of English and Welsh schools. Details of the representativeness of the sample and response rates are found in Appendix 1.

Case studies

Fourteen schools were selected for detailed case study visits during 1981 and 1982. One of the guiding factors in choosing these schools was to visit some examples of very good practice and some of very bad. We also aimed to choose one from each of the cluster authorities. In terms of age range, geographical location and type of school, we aimed to choose a cross-section. Brief details of each school are given in Appendix 1. Of the cluster schools, each came from a different authority, except in the case of the two single-sex schools which came from the same authority, and the two Scottish schools which came from the same authority.

Previous to our visits to these schools two pilot case studies had been carried out, whose general aim was to construct a relatively standard procedure for case studies. It became clear early on that local careers offices could provide us with much of the information we sought. However, there were sometimes problems of access to records, and sometimes records were not complete.

Interviews with pupils were developed during pilot visits and were further refined in practice interviews with volunteer children. While the original aim was to interview pupils doing non-traditional subjects, it became clear that some pupils doing traditional subjects might usefully be included in the sample.

Case studies were conducted over a period of about three days for each school, by either one or two members of the research team. Interviews with teachers did not follow set questions, except for a few standard questions asked of careers teachers and they were usually tape recorded, if the teacher permitted. Immediately after a visit a report was written, describing what we had been told at the school, and sent to the school for comment as to its accuracy. Any comments of this nature were noted in the final analysis of case study material. These reports were deliberately uncritical, and so are not included here.

For ease of reference in the rest of this report we have given the schools pseudonyms. These identify the kind of school, either by its location, educational nature (e.g. comprehensive) or the reason it was selected (such as its commitment to equality of opportunity). Obviously these titles reflect our initial impressions about the schools overall, but they are designed to help in identification, and are not the basis on which the schools' practices were judged: often the practices belied the appearance.

National statistics

We commissioned special tabulations from the Department of Education and Science of statistics from the 1980 school-leaver survey. These showed the numbers of pupils entering and passing school-leaving examinations in selected subjects and groups of subjects and their post-school destinations. The results are analysed in Chapter 4.

Attitude surveys

In 1981 and 1982 we undertook studies of the attitudes of teachers and pupils towards equal opportunities. Our teacher sample consisted of 850 teachers in 50 schools in England and Wales. The results are shown in Chapter 8. The pupil sample consisted of nearly 1,000 pupils in the fourth or fifth year of secondary school. The results are shown in Chapter 9.

CHAPTER 2

Context

We begin by examining what has been recorded so far about the pattern of differentiation in the curriculum in secondary schools.

Sex differences in take up of subjects

The HMI survey (GB.DES, 1975) documented differences in the subjects studied by boys and girls.

At the fourth-form option stage, boys were found mostly in physics and chemistry and girls in biology; more boys than girls were taking two science subjects; in languages (French and German) girls predominated. A slightly higher proportion of boys than girls took geography and more girls than boys took history; proportionately more girls than boys were studying music. The survey commented that the predominance of boys in physics and chemistry raised 'important questions about the content of scientific studies followed ... by boys and girls.... Again, the preponderance of girls taking French and German suggests ... boys may equally miss opportunities in the field of modern languages.'

The survey also found that home economics and commerce were predominantly girls' subjects and technology predominantly boys'. A number of cases were quoted of pupils choosing non-traditional subjects, though these were more of boys entering an area traditionally associated with female roles than vice versa.

Courses designed mainly for early school-leavers also tended to be sex differentiated. The courses offered to boys included agriculture, accounts, building, catering, electronics, engineering design, fashion design and surveying. Of these, accounts, catering, electronics and fashion design were also offered to girls. Child care and home-making were usually 'regarded as the province of girls'. Integrated courses, such as citizenship, humanities, environmental studies, urban studies or social education, were taken by more girls than boys. Linked courses with colleges of further education appeared to disadvantage girls in England, though not in Wales.

At sixth-form level, the survey found further differentiation. In most of the subjects in which there were differences at fourth- and fifth-form level the gap had widened by the sixth.

Sex differences in subject take up at secondary-school level are also illustrated by exam results. Girls predominate in O-level and CSE passes in French and biology, and boys in physics and chemistry. In craft subjects, boys dominate CSE passes in technical drawing, metalwork and woodwork, while girls do so in domestic and commercial subjects. (GB.DES, 1981)

The pattern of examination results has changed over time. But as Wardle (1978) shows, while the overall pass rate at O-level has become more equal over the years, sex differences in entries according to subject remain. Murphy (1980), examining trends between 1951 and 1977, observed that in later years the imbalance in physics and chemistry O-level entries has lessened, while in English and French at A-level the number of girls' entries has risen dramatically to overtake that of boys. Murphy (1980) claims that overall boys are more likely to enter A-levels than girls, while the larger numbers of boys at O-level only reflects their larger numbers in the population. Blackstone (in Mitchell and Oakley, 1976), Lobban (1978) and Murphy (1980) all note that the pass rate of girls in O-levels and A-levels is better than that of boys, although Miles (1979) observes that this is not true of chemistry and physics at A-level.

Behind the figures are some interesting differences. Harding (in Deem, 1980) shows that girls in mixed comprehensives (as opposed to single sex or grammar schools) are at a particular disadvantage in science exams, and she also supports Murphy (1980) in finding that boys do better on objective tests than extended written responses. Wood (1976) as well as Sharma and Meigham (1980) investigated question topics within mathematics exams where there are sex differences in achievement. Sharma and Meigham (1980) also found that girls taking mathematics at O-level do as well as boys, if they have also taken courses in physics or in technical drawing.

The reasons for the differences between the sexes in the take up of subjects and performance within them may be described as lying in two main areas: reasons to do with the pupils, their expectations, attitudes and abilities; and reasons to do with educational provision and school organization. This distinction is offered in full awareness of the fact that pupils' views are influenced by factors outside their control.

Reasons to do with pupils

It is not proposed here to review literature on differences in abilities between the sexes. Suffice to say that differences that have been found are greater between members of the same sex than between the two sexes. Further, by the stage of secondary school it is virtually impossible to say the extent to which differences in ability have been caused by innate differences or are the result of earlier socialization. Finally on this, it does not follow, as Brierley (1975) seems to think, that the existence of inherited differences constitutes an imperative to emphasize those differences in school or family life.

Research on the processes of subject choice at secondary-school level rarely refers to sex differences, but there are some relevant studies. Firstly, though, something may be said about the general situation of girls and jobs, since the nature of the job opportunities may be a strong influence on subject choice.

Smith (in Love *et al.*, 1980) claims that 40 per cent of women at work are involved in clerical and related work. Of women in manual work, 52 per cent are in catering, cleaning, hairdressing and other personal services, and 18·7 per cent are involved in painting, assembling, inspecting and packing. Of all non-manual jobs in which women are involved, 55·2 per cent are in education, welfare and health (Ashton and Maguire, in Deem, 1980). In a study of 250 recent school-leavers Sawdon *et al* (1981) found that 83 per cent of girls' jobs could be fitted into one of four categories: clerical, shop assistant, sewing, factory work. Girls changing jobs, in this study, were found rarely to change to a higher status job, whereas boys often did so.

It is frequently stated in literature on women and education that until the basic economic structures that lead to this job distribution are altered, changes in the course of study and school experience of girls and boys can have only a limited effect in providing less sex stereotyped career patterns. Examples of debate in this area are Love *et al* (1980), Kuhn and Wolpe (1978) and Nava's (1980) criticisms of the work of Byrne (1978) for underemphasizing economic factors that perpetuate the sexual division of labour.

Given this distribution of jobs, it is hardly surprising that the expectations of girls with regard to their future employment are similarly sex stereotyped. Coleman (1977) has reviewed American literature on girls' career expectations and found that 'women do on the whole identify with lower levels of occupational achievement than men do, and ... work itself is of less importance to them'. Sharpe (1976) also asked a sample of girls what jobs they wanted and found that three quarters of the choices were office work, teaching, nursing, retailing, banking (clerical), reception work, nursery nursing, hairdressing and air hostessing.

It is reasonable to expect that job aspiration or expectation is a significant influence on subject choice. However, there are other expectations of pupils which influence their subject choice. Keys and Ormerod (1977) have shown that girls are more influenced in their 13-plus choice by perception of subject difficulty than boys. While both the boys and girls in their sample had similar perceptions of subject difficulty — traditionally male subjects such as the physical sciences and mathematics being seen as most difficult — girls were more likely to avoid subjects on the grounds of difficulty. A recent HMI study of girls and science (GB.DES, 1980) draws similar conclusions as does Kelly's (1976) review of the literature on women and science. Kelly found that girls are also discouraged by an image of science as having had bad effects on society. Many girls studying science in the sixth form record aspirations to medical careers as a solution to the conflict between their desire to help the community and the perceived negative effects of science. The relatively low aspirations of girls, reversing as it does trends before puberty, has received much comment. Accounts of the process based on participant observation studies appear in the work of Sharpe (1976), Wolpe (1977), McRobbie (in CCCS, 1978), Davies (1978) and Llewellyn (in Deem, 1980). Numerous American studies at college level show a similar phenomenon. Frazier and Sadker (1973) refer to some of these.

Rauta and Hunt's (1975) survey of the hopes and aspirations of 2,000 fifth-form girls found that girls with low aspirations for their ability, compared to high aspiring girls, were more interested in early marriage and boys, and accepted traditional feminine roles.

Rauta and Hunt (1975) also found that high aspiring girls came from more privileged backgrounds, and this suggests the influence of social class on the sex differentiation in subject choices. Sharpe (1976) observes that 'unless girls belong to the minority (mainly middle class) that move upwards into higher education, they tend to fall back on the familiar expectations of feminine roles'. Thus for girls '"feminine" ideology becomes more infused into the curriculum the lower down the "ability" level we look' (Smith, in Love *et al*, 1980). Davies's (1978) study found that higher-stream girls were discouraged from doing child care, and top-stream boys discouraged from taking metalwork and woodwork. In one of the schools that Hurman (1978) studied, top-stream pupils did fewer occupational crafts (e.g. typing and woodwork) and subjects like child care and needlecraft than the average for the school. Lower-stream pupils were less likely than average to be doing scientific and mathematical subjects or languages. In craft and technical courses sex stereotyped choice is more extreme than in more academic subjects.

As well as being of a higher social class than average, girls studying the physical sciences in the sixth form have to go against the social pressures on them to express accepted norms of feminine behaviour. Some research emphasizes – and perhaps reinforces – these pressures. Smithers (1976) found that these girls were 'less sociable', less 'feminine' and less popular than other girls as well as being more ambitious. Pitt (1973) observes that such a girl is, in his personal experience, 'more masculine, a good games player and often a strong advocate of "women's lib"'. Stamp (1979) found that girls studying A-level mathematics, compared with those studying French at the same level, were less feminine, according to his measure, and tended to identify to a greater degree with their fathers.

As well as class and personality variables, there is the possible influence of race on sex differentiated subject choices. This is far less well documented than class influence. Fuller (in Deem, 1980) has studied a (probably unusual) small group of black girls whose attitudes towards school were very negative, although they appreciated the importance of qualifications and sought them eagerly. Sharpe (1976) also has a chapter on black girls. These studies do not, however, contain data on subject choice.

Reasons to do with educational provision and school organization

Government commitment to the goal of equal opportunities between the sexes in education is a recent phenomenon, as Wolpe's (1974) and Love's (in Love *et al*, 1980) accounts of government reports show. Examining the Norwood (1943), Crowther (1959) and Newsom (1963) reports, both writers observe that a curriculum differentiated according to sex is accepted as normal and indeed necessary. In the Newsom Report however, there are the beginnings of a change: it is recognized that employment patterns are changing and that schools may have to adapt curricula to allow for this. Plowden (1967) too, in Love's analysis, shows an increasing awareness of the implication of change in the social and economic conditions of women. Statements by the OECD (1980) stress similar arguments. A most detailed elaboration of the economic argument is contained in Woodhall (1973).

This would seem to lend support to sociologists who stress the economic determinants of school curricula, for example Delamont and Duffin (1978). A number of writers reach conclusions exemplified by Shaw (in Barker and Allen, 1976): 'we can see in the range of choice offered to boys and girls both the means and the expression of economic and social control.'

Sociologists of education tend to emphasize the role of economics in maintaining sex stereotyped curricular patterns. Nava (1980) criticized Byrne (1975) for underemphasizing external economic factors. Sociologists following this line of argument also tend to stress the limited extent to which changes in education can influence the labour market, as we saw earlier. It is on these grounds that the Equal Opportunities Commission has been criticized (see, for example, NUT/EOC, 1980 and Smith, in Love *et al*, 1980) and it is customary for those arguing from this position to rehearse a variety of other criticisms of the EOC. Further to the left, ideologically, are the debates between those who rely more on the analysis of class differences and those who place greater emphasis on the patriarchal nature of society (for those interested in this type of debate, Wolpe, 1977 and MacDonald, in Love *et al*, 1980, are of relevance).

Clearly there is a variety of different ideological positions that are taken by writers on sex differences in education. Some philosophical work that describes these different positions, their problems, conflicts and the practical consequences they imply can be found in Bridges (1974 and 1977), Freeman (1977) and Shaw (1979).

While noting that these debates exist, and the connection between the labour market and school curricula, our concern is with what schools do to encourage sex stereotyped option choices.

One of the effects of past government thinking has been felt in the area of resource allocation to schools which, as Byrne (1978) has shown, has discriminated between the sexes. In a survey of 133 schools she found that girls' schools were deficient in science laboratories and that boys had greater access than girls to laboratories in mixed schools. Biology (predominantly a girls' subject) had fewer laboratory resources than physical sciences (predominantly boys' subjects) and boys' craft subjects were superior in provision to those of girls. One Local Education Authority Byrne (1975) studied gave more money to boys' schools than to girls' schools and she observed that in single-sex schools there were no facilities for studying craft subjects traditionally taken by the other sex. Studies of the processes of resource allocation within schools rather than within LEAs have not been made.

A major factor is simply differentiation within schools. The survey of Benn and Simon (1972) found that 50 per cent of mixed schools restricted some subjects to boys only, and 49 per cent restricted some to girls only. This was greater in Scotland. The HMI survey (GB.DES, 1975) found differential treatment of boys and girls at all levels of school education.

We may identify four aspects of differentiation from the survey. First is simply separation of boys and girls for particular subjects or groups of subjects; second is the differences in patterns of study by boys and girls, particularly in 'traditional' sex differentiated subjects. (Often these two occur together where boys and girls are separated along traditional subject lines.) Third is 'pre-empting', where curriculum in earlier years precludes free choice later; fourth is 'premature specialization'.

The survey found subtle differentiation in primary schools, which increased in some subjects in middle schools. It revealed substantial differences in secondary schools. Of 302 coeducational schools in England, 98 per cent separated boys and girls below the age of 16 for some subjects. In the early years such separation was of two kinds: that which divided the sexes for a particular subject, and that which in effect provided different subjects for boys and girls. Physical education and games belong in the first category; the second included home economics and needlework for girls, and woodwork and metalwork for boys. Separation became more marked by the fourth-form stage, particularly in crafts. Many schools indicated that this was because of timetabling difficulties and the survey commented that 'When facilities for home economics, metalwork, needlework or woodwork are limited, the division of the sexes along traditional lines is regarded as inevitable.'

The survey also reported that over a quarter of its schools revealed 'pre-emptive' curriculum patterns in earlier years. In the first three years, the curriculum pattern produced 'by accident or design, restrictions on what was supposedly a free choice in the fourth year'. The survey cited an example where a 'free' choice in technical drawing was effectively precluded for girls as metalwork had to be taken with it, so that only those pupils who had previously taken metalwork could study it. Pre-empting occurred in crafts, sciences, commerce and languages.

In 'premature specialization', opportunities for boys and girls can be restricted when a course of specialist study makes undue demands on the timetable. And the report says 'early specialization may restrict those involved in it by limiting the range of their experience at a time when it should be extended'. They added that it may also throw out of balance the curriculum for those not involved. Languages, sciences and crafts were the subjects in which premature specialization occurred, and it affected 28 per cent of the survey's schools in England.

The DES survey (GB.DES, 1975) also attempted to examine the extent to which option choice was influenced by the subject's availability and the extent to which choice is due to the pupil's own preferences. These factors were examined for options in the fourth and fifth forms. They show that in most cases the differences in take up between boys and girls are more attributable to the pupils' choices than availability of the subjects, though if the figures are examined, availability of subject did affect the differences in take up in many subjects. For example, if physics had been available to the same percentage of girls in single-sex schools as boys (85 per cent), and the same proportion of girls still chose the subject, the take up would have increased to 20 per cent of all girls, though this is still a long way below the boys' figure of 51 per cent.

The survey found marked differences in the curricular patterns of single-sex and mixed schools. Girls were more likely to choose a science and boys a language in single-sex schools. If we consider the difference that equal provision *could* have made, then the picture is somewhat different. Differences of provision appear to affect pupils more in single-sex schools than in mixed schools.

The DES survey (GB.DES, 1975) concludes with a number of outspoken conclusions (for government publications): while it notes that discriminatory treatment between the sexes may be to the advantage of both girls and boys, and to the extent that this is so, the practices it observed may be expected to continue with the approval of those concerned, the survey says 'the separation of boys and girls for some aspects of physical education at about the age of 11 and afterwards calls for serious thought'. At the third- and fourth-year stage of option choice, the 'question is too often one of "Hobson's choice"' and of the differences in curricular patterns in the fourth and fifth years it says 'it is not possible to study [the tables and the appendix] without asking why it is that physics and chemistry seem to be "boys' subjects" and modern languages "girls' subjects" or why boys seem to have poorer opportunities in art and music ...' Similarly it comments that 'areas of opportunity for girls are restricted' by the availability of composite courses, vocational and similar options and linked courses. Overall the survey concludes that the evidence should be regarded as 'a basis for reconsidering the curricular programme between the ages of 12 and 16, with a view to ensuring that the principal areas of the curriculum are open to all boys and girls in whatever kind of school they happen to be'.

There have been no national surveys of curricular differences between boys and girls since this HMI survey, though King (1981 and 1982) showed a reduction in sex differences in curriculum and organization over a ten-year period, and the national picture of curricular differences in secondary schools was updated to some extent by the publication of an HMI survey (GB.DES, 1979). This was a report of an examination of a 10 per cent structured sample of maintained secondary schools in England (384 schools) visited by HMI between 1975 and 1978, and it concentrated on the last two years of compulsory schooling.

This further survey also collected information on the third-year curriculum as background to the fourth and fifth years. The survey schools numbered 365 for this part of the study, and the large majority of them differentiated in some way in the curriculum according to sex or ability. Only 11 per cent of the schools offered a wholly common curriculum in the first three years. Differentiation by sex took place to a small extent in science, but mainly in craft subjects. Three schools obliged girls to take biology and boys physics, but over 65 per cent of the schools practised some form of sex differentiation in crafts.

Differentiation by sex was markedly less in *fully* comprehensive schools, whereas single-sex schools notably lacked facilities to offer a full range of choice at this age. Some of the larger schools offered 'rotating' craft systems, sometimes including art, in which pupils could take all subjects offered over a period of one or more years.

The major differences in the curriculum followed by girls and boys in the fourth and fifth years were found in science. Most of the 204 schools providing details adopted a policy of expecting or encouraging pupils to take at least one science; in 7 per cent of these schools science was part of the compulsory core and in 12 per cent it was a compulsory option subject. But 9 per cent of all boys and 17 per cent of girls did no science in the fourth and fifth years and about 50 and 60 per cent respectively were studying only one science. The HMI survey regarded these figures as 'a matter for concern'.

Not only did fewer girls than boys study science at this level, they also studied different subjects. Far more boys than girls took physics and more girls than boys took biology. A higher proportion of girls studied physics in single-sex grammar schools. The survey reported that there was no evidence that girls were being deliberately excluded from the physical sciences, although some teachers expressed the view that boys should study physics and girls biology, and that the former was too difficult for girls. Mainly, there was simply no positive encouragement for girls to break out of sex stereotyping, and sometimes grouping of subjects set physics against traditionally girls' subjects. Girls also appeared more reluctant to persevere with physical science if it was not well-taught.

The survey (GB.DES, 1979) did note, however, a great increase in the amount of science studied by girls. 'Almost invariably', the survey says, 'girls and boys follow the same courses up to the end of the third year.' But it goes on:

> the survey revealed ... that traditional attitudes are still prevailing in the fourth and fifth years . . . There are now many more girls choosing physical sciences than there used to be but the number is still small. By not studying the physical sciences beyond a very elementary level, girls are denying themselves skills and knowledge in important areas of the curriculum and are cutting themselves off from many career opportunities in science and engineering. (GB.DES, 1979, p. 199)

As the earlier HMI survey (GB.DES, 1975) found, and other researchers have also described (for example, Keys and Ormerod, 1977), in single-sex schools sex differentiated subject choices are less likely (although not in the area of craft subjects). This has led some (for example, Shaw, in Deem, 1980) to argue that the cause of equal opportunities will be served by the encouragement of single-sex schools. However as Dale (1971) has shown, single-sex schools of both types encourage sexist attitudes about sexual relationships, and a recent document (Women in the NUT, 1980) goes so far as to describe single-sex schools as 'bastions of sexist ideology'.

Kelly (1979) suggests that more girls than boys may be discouraged from science subjects by the system of option groupings in school. An attempt to measure the influence of option groupings or subject choice is being made currently by a group working in Irish education. Hannan *et al* (1981), in a preliminary report of research, suggest that in the case of physics the way in which optional subjects are grouped tends to discourage girls more than boys. Woods (1976) showed that girls' option choices are more often honoured than boys'.

While the formal organization of the school may either contribute to or counteract sex stereotyped patterns, it is also true that much of what goes on in the 'hidden curriculum' of schools contributes. By this is meant both the ideological messages about sex roles contained within schools subjects and careers literature, and those messages conveyed by teacher attitudes and actions.

It is very difficult to find evidence about the extent to which teachers guide pupils into sex stereotyped choices in their verbal interactions with pupils. Hurman (1978) who was not focusing specifically on sex differences in her study of option schemes in two comprehensive schools, noted some occasions where teachers actually told pupils that certain subjects were not appropriate for their sex. Buckley (1979) in her study of a school found that corporal punishment was suffered by boys and not girls, and in the school Davies (1978) studied boys were caned far more than girls. Ricks and Pyke (1973) found that boys were physically punished more, whereas girls were verbally chastized. Deem (1978) lists a variety of ways by which schools convey messages about the separation of sex roles. Examples are: boys are listed separately (and usually first) on registers; boys and girls line up separately; competitions between the sexes are encouraged in class; girls are not allowed to wear trousers. Spender (1981) has recently given much publicity to her finding that teachers tend to spend more time with boys in classroom interaction and that both they and the boys tend to underestimate the amount of the teacher's time that boys receive.

The way in which school subjects and textbooks convey messages about sex roles has also been the subject of comment. Nicholson (1977), Deem (1978), Frazier and Sadker (1973) and the Teachers' Action Alliance (1980) in Eire provide general accounts, and the McGraw-Hill Publishing Company has issued 'Guidelines for Equal Treatment of the Sexes' for authors of their publications to follow.

Lobban's work (1975a and b) is at primary-school level but serves as a good example of work done on textbooks. Taylor (1979) has documented the over-representation of men and boys in science texts, both in the examples used and in the visual illustrations. Kelly (1976) also comments on this as well as Weiner (in Deem, 1980). Parsons in a number of papers (1979, 1980, forthcoming) points out that exam syllabuses in English literature set books usually written by and about men. Dalton (1980) presents an historical study of the role and status of needlecraft in conveying ideological messages about the place of women in the home. Turnbull (in Love *et al*, 1980) accounts for home economics in a similar way. Turnbull and Love observe that their subjects are beginning to be taught to boys, but while for girls the subjects are justified on the grounds that they prepare them for the housework that will be their task in life, for boys the subjects are justified as preparing them for times in life when women are unavailable to do the work (e.g. bachelordom and emergencies in the home), or, in the case of home economics, as a stepping stone to a career as a chef. Wolpe (1977) also notes that these justifications were current among the teachers she studied, and that pupils were in agreement. Studies of this nature of subjects such as child care and technical subjects traditionally done by boys were not found.

Sharpe (1976) discusses history and English and observes that women in history as well as women authors are under-represented in the school curriculum. She also feels that social studies in school should consider the position of women to a greater extent. Acker (1980) records the under-representation of women in the sociology of education.

Physical education too has received some attention. A document produced by Women in the NUT (1980) criticizes the separation of sexes in this subject: Robinson (1973) also argues that the emphasis on strenuous activities for boys and more dance-based activities for girls is unnecessary.

Sex education has been analysed from a feminist point of view. While there is some disagreement among writers, as to whether the sexes should be separated for these lessons, there is agreement that the content often reflects stereotyped views, e.g. Rance (1978); Jackson (1978) and Albert (in Stacey *et al*, 1974).

Careers advice and education has also been the subject of comment. Davies and Meigham (1975) observe that in this area of the school curriculum, unlike others, teachers adopt a passive approach, preferring to aid pupils in following their interests rather than taking the initiative in suggesting careers. Deem (1978) feels that much careers literature contains sex stereotypes. Lobban (in Chetwynd and Hartnett, 1978) reports a study where careers teachers were presented with videotapes of girls talking about their career aspirations. Girls who sought jobs in the non-traditional areas of engineering were judged by the teachers to be in need of more 'guidance' than those choosing traditionally female careers. An ILEA booklet (1975), while showing some confusion as to the amount of stress the authors hope girls would place on their careers rather than families, also observes that careers materials are in need of review to eliminate sex stereotypes.

Finally, on the messages conveyed to pupils about sex roles, is the impression conveyed by the staffing pattern of schools. It is generally recognized that the predominance of male teachers in higher-scale posts and of women in lower or pastoral posts is a pattern which conveys to pupils messages about sex roles. The NUT and the EOC (1980) conducted a study of the reasons for these differential promotion patterns. It is also the case that ancillary staff such as canteen workers (women) and caretakers (men) are generally distributed in jobs according to sex.

CHAPTER 3

The letter and spirit of the Act

The Sex Discrimination Act, 1975, makes sex discrimination in education generally unlawful. Section 22 makes it unlawful, in particular, to discriminate against a woman '. . . in the way that [an educational establishment] affords her access to any benefits, facilities or services, or by refusing or deliberately omitting to afford her access to them . . .' Similarly, Section 23 makes it 'unlawful for a Local Education Authority, in carrying out such of its functions under the Education Acts 1944 to 1975 as do not fall under Section 22, to do any act which constitutes sex discrimination.' Discrimination is defined elsewhere in the Act; direct discrimination arises where a woman is treated, in any circumstances relevant to the Act, less favourably on the ground of her sex than a man; indirect discrimination consists of treatment which may be described as equal in a formal sense, but discriminatory in its effect on one sex. The Act also makes clear that references to the right of women to equal treatment with men also include the right of men to equal treatment with women, and that 'women' and 'men' refer to people of any age.

The aim of examining how far the Act is being implemented is not as straightforward as it sounds. Even identifying how far the letter of the law is being implemented is a complicated task when the pattern of curriculum options in schools is considered. There have been few cases to interpret the Act in this field, and the Equal Opportunities Commission's view of what constitutes unlawful practice thus has yet to be tested in many respects.

When it comes to the spirit of the law, the problem becomes much more complex. It is complicated, as in all matters of discrimination, by the difficulty of distinguishing between discrimination in provision and the differential preferences of those involved. It is complicated, too, by the problem of identifying what might constitute good practice. There is a variety of different, and sometimes conflicting views here, and these are complicated by philosophical issues of what constitutes a balanced curriculum, and the extent to which pupils should have a free choice (which may result in eliminating opportunities later) or be compelled to study a large core curriculum.

The Commission's view on these matters is set out mainly in a commentary (GB.EOC, 1979) on the educational provisions of the 1975 Act. (Although a revised version of the commentary was produced in 1982, our research frame was based on the original version, and so the rest of this section refers to this and our analysis of it.)

The letter of the law

The Commission's commentary (GB.EOC, 1979) discussed the implications of Section 22 of the Act which concerns provision in any one particular educational institution. Thus it said, for example, direct sex discrimination would occur under Section 22 if 'benefits, facilities or services' were not available within a coeducational school because a pupil was a girl (or a boy). The Commission cited the instance of admission to a particular course or class which is reserved mainly or exclusively to boys, or which is made available in a less favourable way because the pupil is a girl (GB.EOC, 1979, paragraph 7.9). The Commission went on to note that, because this section refers only to a particular establishment, discrimination does not occur if, for example, a girl is treated less favourably in one school than boys in another. Nor does the Act prohibit separate facilities for boys and girls within a coeducational school, so long as they provide equal opportunities.

The Commission elaborated what it regards as 'less favourable' treatment elsewhere in its commentary. It said that '... pupils should not be required to make a special application to study a subject which might be described as non-traditional, except in a single-sex school where non-traditional courses are not available'. It went on to say that 'Pupils of both sexes should have equal access to all subjects and if a course is oversubscribed, the pupil's sex must be disregarded when places are being allocated' (GB.EOC, 1979, paragraph 3.6). The Commission similarly cited the exclusion of pupils from visits, community or social service projects and out of school activities solely on grounds of sex as unlawful (GB.EOC, 1979, paragraph 3.7). Visits to commercial or industrial firms, visits by industrial and commercial representatives and school–industry link schemes must all be open to pupils of both sexes. All forms of community or social service undertaken by schools must be open to pupils of both sexes and all recreational and social facilities and out of school activities must be equally available to both sexes. Equally, careers advice, interviews and literature must not be sex discriminatory (GB.EOC, 1979, paragraph 3.9).

Section 23 covers provision by education authorities. The Commission, quoting the White Paper which preceded the Act, explained that this seems to cover the general provision in schools in an authority's area. The Education Act 1944 places on LEAs (in England and Wales) the duty to ensure that there are schools in their area sufficient in number, character and equipment to afford for all pupils opportunities for education as may be desirable in view of their different ages, abilities and aptitudes. Section 23 of the Sex Discrimination Act, in the Commission's view, means that it would be unlawful for an authority to treat girls less favourably than boys, on the ground of sex, in securing the provision of secondary schools. If, for example, an authority provided less-favourable opportunities in its area as a whole for girls than for boys to learn advanced physics, it would be acting contrary to Section 23.

The spirit of the Act

The commentary is clear that, 'if equality of opportunity is to become a reality ... the application of the letter of the law is not sufficient' (GB.EOC, 1979, paragraph 2.3). It goes on to say that:

> The spirit underlying the legislation has to be absorbed by all concerned ... Positive action is needed if equality of opportunity in education for both sexes is to be achieved quickly, and schools should take every opportunity to encourage positively the learning of non-traditional skills by removing any existing barriers and by new courses and developing new teaching materials where appropriate. (GB.EOC, 1979, paragraphs 2.3 and 2.4)

It is sometimes the case that what constitutes good practice in promoting equality of opportunity is not entirely clear; on occasion different views are flatly contradictory. We look now at some of the particular areas that the Commission has highlighted in order to establish what features of school organization can be regarded as good equal-opportunities practice.

The kind of 'positive action' the Commission has in mind is set out in its 'Guidelines for Good Practice in Schools', contained within the commentary (GB.EOC, 1979) on the Act. The Guidelines reflect concern about the kind of differentiation in the curriculum portrayed by HMI (GB.DES, 1975 and 1979) and quote extensively from the 1975 survey.

On secondary school options, the Guidelines express a clear view that 'if pupils are to have a realistic choice of options it is essential that they have experience of as wide a range of subjects as is possible before any choice is made'. They go on to emphasize the importance of this in science, technical and craft areas 'where there has been a tendency to steer girls towards biology rather than physics, office skills rather than technical subjects, and home economics rather than woodwork, metalwork, engineering' (GB.EOC, 1979, paragraph 4.10). The tendency of girls to drop mathematics is also noted. The Guidelines urge schools to 'be particularly careful not to organize the earlier stages of the secondary curriculum in such a way that it prevents a choice of the full range of options at a later stage' by pre-emptive problems in the curriculum, and to offer real opportunities not token gestures to pupils to study non-traditional subjects. The timetabling and grouping of subjects should not discourage choices; content should be attractive to both sexes; and pupils should not have to make special requests to study non-traditional subjects. Schools which have operated a restricted option scheme are urged to consider mounting 'compensatory crash' courses to enable pupils to learn the basic elements of non-traditional subjects, so that, for example, girls might have a second chance to study physics, mathematics and technical subjects (GB.EOC, 1979, paragraph 4.16). The Guidelines also recommend that some form of careers guidance is offered *before* options are chosen in secondary schools, employing an 'integrated' approach, looking at possible careers alongside other aspects of later life such as parenthood, financial problems, etc.

The Commission also sets out guidelines for good practice by Local Education Authorities which reflect these concerns. These suggest that

> Educational provision should be so planned that the staffing and physical resources are sufficient to provide the type, range and level of subjects required so as to ensure that equally favourable opportunities are available to pupils of both sexes with common aptitudes, needs and desires. This may mean a gradual alteration in the distribution of resources. (GB.EOC, 1979, paragraph 5.2)

Authorities which provide single-sex education

> should ensure that the full range of curriculum options is available in each school, or by some other method (e.g. allowing girls to attend classes in boys' schools and vice versa). Any 'other method' should be clearly defined and well publicized among the pupils' parents. (GB.EOC, 1979, paragraph 5.3)

The facilities provided in single-sex schools

> should be no less favourable than those provided at any other single-sex school or any mixed-sex school in the same catchment area (e.g. laboratories, workshops, sports and recreational

facilities), except where such facilities are provided by the other method. (GB.EOC, 1979, paragraph 5.4)

The Guidelines recommend that information given to parents of pupils going on to secondary education should make explicit that all courses are open to all pupils 'as of right' and there will be no need for special requests to be made by pupils wishing to follow 'non-traditional subjects' (GB.EOC, 1979, paragraph 5.5).

Some of these issues are developed in more detail by the Commission elsewhere. For example, core subjects after 13+ option choice in most secondary schools include mathematics, English, physical education and usually some form of non-exam, social education course that includes careers education and sex education. The booklet (Hannon, 1981) suggests that in the areas of physical education and games, segregation is frequently taken as inevitable by schools.

This booklet suggests that more thought should be given to mixed activities, and that syllabuses should be carefully examined to see that what is offered to each sex favours each equally. Some criticism is made of sex-role stereotyping in the different activities that each sex may be given to perform. The Commission's view of sex education is again represented in Hannon (1981, p. 6); sex education should occur, it should include facts about physical development as well as contraception and 'sympathetic small-group discussions about personal relationships' should be available.

Separation of the sexes is not really an issue in relation to mathematics, English and other parts of social education courses, except where schools may teach mathematics to girls separately. This is suggested as good practice by the Commission (GB.EOC, 1979), since the Commission feels that in certain circumstances girls need compensatory teaching in this subject.

The separation of the sexes for teaching the same subject does occur sometimes in craft subjects both before and after option choice. Such separation is often made out of a desire to teach a different syllabus to either sex – which the Commission would no doubt view in a poor light – but on the other hand may sometimes be designed to encourage non-traditional choice (boys-only, home economics classes tend to be popular).

On the general principle of teaching the sexes separately; it is clear that sexist assumptions may sometimes inform such practice and that in other instances separation may be made in order to further an anti-sexist initiative. Teaching dance to girls and games practice to boys will very likely be viewed by the Commission as contrary to the intention, if not the letter, of the Act. A similar view appears to be taken of those schools teaching boys a home economics syllabus geared towards a future catering career, and girls a syllabus geared towards home life (GB.EOC, 1982). In fact, separation in these instances involves the teaching of different material, and so may be regarded as providing unequal access to a subject. A self-defence or women's studies class for girls might be regarded as good practice, though the exclusion of boys from such courses would not be in accordance with the Act.

Thus, under some circumstances separation could work against equality since it can lead to a curriculum differentiated on sex-stereotyped lines. Under other circumstances it can serve to bolster the confidence of girls in a subject (though the effect of single-sex classes on the boys who are presumably left on their own has not been considered by those who advocate the practice).

The restriction of subjects to one sex is clearly unlawful. For example, separation of the sexes for the teaching of craft subjects is unlawful. As noted in the national HMI survey (GB.DES, 1975), it can sometimes be coupled with pre-emptive requirements at option choice stage, thus ensuring continuing discrimination.

The Commission (GB.EOC, 1979, p. 3) view the existence of a special request system as unlawful, since all subjects should be equally open to all. In physical education, however, which under certain circumstances is exempted from the equal access ruling, a special request system may be better than nothing.

A practice the Commission may not have noticed is that followed by many schools where over-subscription of a subject, traditionally associated with one sex, occurs at the option choice stage (e.g. 40 pupils apply for woodwork, which has only 20 places). Giving preference to the traditional sex, on grounds such as 'boys need it more for their careers' is clearly discriminatory. However, the practice in a minority of schools that are keen to promote equal opportunities, of giving preference to the non-traditional sex, is also discriminatory under the Act, since the positive discrimination provisions do not extend to such a case.

In the area of craft subjects the Commission's view seems to go so far as requiring that all subjects be open to all and that syllabuses may be usefully reviewed in order to make material less sex-biased. Making craft subjects open to all in the early years of secondary schooling involves problems of ensuring enough time for a coverage considered adequate by many teachers. On the other hand, the Commission might consider arguments for rethinking some of these subjects in such a way that they are more integrated – perhaps under the heading of 'design'.

The Commission is concerned that girls restrict careers choice through specializing in subjects too early. It is the Commission's view that a physical science (not biology) should be made compulsory for all up to the age of 16. (Memorandum submitted to the Education, Science and Arts Select Committee, 11 May 1981.)

Making a physical science compulsory for all has its problems. Evidence seems to suggest (e.g. from GB.DES, 1980) that boys take this subject more than girls, not because it is interesting to them, but because it is presented to them as necessary for the careers they want. Good practice might consist of making the subject more generally attractive, or that the value of the subject for careers that girls usually desire should be stressed more in school literature. Making it compulsory may lead to girls studying the subject when they don't want to and to discipline problems.

The Commission has tended to stress the importance of scientific qualifications (remedying the disadvantages of girls) but until recently did not place such emphasis on encouraging boys to take up courses in home skills, though it has now argued that home economics is an essential area of experience for all pupils (GB.EOC, 1982). Some mixed schools in our survey made parentcraft compulsory for all; the Commission has not stated that this subject should be a part of the core. Hannon (1981, p. 6) confines herself to recommending that boys should be as strongly involved in parentcraft as girls.

The Commission suggests that schools, which have in the past unfairly disadvantaged one sex, should consider setting up compensatory courses to remedy this (GB.EOC, 1979, p. 12). Clearly, such courses could not be decreed exclusive to one sex without breaking the law.

As well as cases of direct discrimination, the Commission is concerned to encourage a more equal take up of optional subjects. In the area of physical science, as we have seen, the Commission feels the subject is too important to be left to persuasion, but should be made compulsory. To a lesser extent than science and craft subjects the Commission is concerned about the low take up by boys of languages and commercial subjects (in its response to the HMI report GB.DES, 1979).

The Commission feels careers education to be a very important area where equal opportunities may be encouraged. It is considered essential that careers advice should be given before option choice and that at some stage lessons should include discussions of sex roles in work. Materials should be non-discriminatory, and where outside speakers are involved consideration should be given to inviting those in non-traditional roles. Careers staff should be willing to help and encourage pupils expressing an interest in non-traditional areas and should liaise with local employers to ensure they are willing to accept school-leavers in non-traditional areas.

How far careers staff should go in positively encouraging non-traditional choice of career is a point worth considering; the careers service is informed by a philosophy of non-directive counselling which emphasizes that the wishes of clients should be aided in their expression, rather than persuaded that something else is better. Further to this, it may not be a service in a time of high unemployment to encourage a pupil into a non-traditional area where discrimination by employers exists. No doubt a line is drawn by most practitioners between these considerations and the desire to further equal opportunities. Where the line falls will vary from one person to another; at any rate the provision of opportunity during careers lessons to learn about non-traditional careers, to discuss sex roles, to be warned before option choice of the consequences of dropping certain subjects, should not be affected by the considerations above.

This, then, is a summary of the views of the EOC, and others, on what constitutes good equal opportunities practice, and it was against this background that we undertook our research. For day-to-day research in schools, we prepared a working document during the study against which we attempted to assess practice in the schools we studied, which is presented in Appendix 2. It obviously has the drawbacks of a summary, as well as the problem of the occasional internal contradictions of the views of what is good practice. From time to time we had to interpolate or extrapolate the views it implies. But it offered a kind of yardstick. We are able to say that, if this is broadly what is meant by 'good practice', then the following chapters show the extent to which it is, or is not, followed in schools.

CHAPTER 4

Patterns of curriculum choice

In this chapter we examine the combination of subjects that pupils study, and we relate these to the destinations they go to after reaching school-leaving age. We attempt to see if the extent of differentiation has changed in the years since the Sex Discrimination Act was passed, and if pupils taking non-traditional subjects are more likely to pursue non-traditional careers on leaving school. To answer our questions we had to use a variety of sources of data. Figures from our own postal survey of schools tell us about subject choice at 13+ and permit some comparison with the HMI survey (GB.DES, 1975); DES statistics show which subjects pupils entered for and passed in 16+ examinations. But to examine combinations of subjects and the relationship between them and subsequent educational careers we had to commission special tabulations from the DES school-leaver survey. Careers office records examined in the course of our case study visits provide evidence about the relationship of subject choice to actual jobs as well as further education courses. This last source of data also provides information about the spare-time interests and the job aspirations of pupils (as distinct from their actual destinations).

Subject differentiation

The pattern of subjects studied by pupils after option choice can be seen from our survey. A total of 90 mixed schools (59 nominated, 31 cluster) and 12 single-sex schools (5 boys', 7 girls') returned lists of the option subjects individual fourth- or in some cases fifth-year pupils were studying. Numbers of pupils involved are listed in Table 4.1.

Table 4.2 (see page 28) shows the percentage take up by pupils offered each subject. It excludes cases where a subject is made compulsory for all (incidence of this is reported later). In those tables where fewer than three schools offer a subject as optional, take up is not reported.

Table 4.1 Numbers of pupils involved in survey

	Nominated	Cluster	Total
Boys in mixed school	6,313	3,587	9,900
Boys in single-sex school	–	570	570
Total boys	6,313	4,157	10,470
Girls in mixed schools	6,077	3,553	9,630
Girls in single-sex schools	436	586	1,022
Total girls	6,513	4,139	10,652
Total pupils	12,826	8,296	21,122

It will be seen that in mixed schools there is marked differentiation between the subjects studied by pupils. With the exception of biology and human biology, the sciences are dominated by boys. More than three times as many boys as girls study physics, and nearly 50 per cent more study chemistry: a higher percentage of boys study general science. Twice as many girls as boys study biology, and four times as many study human biology. In mathematics options (not mathematics itself as this is the 'core' subject in all our schools) the same pattern continues, with about 50 per cent more boys studying additional mathematics or computer studies, though roughly similar proportions study statistics.

Subjects we have classified as 'commercial' are dominated by girls, with the notable exception of commerce. Hardly any boys study typing, shorthand or office practice subjects, though they outnumber girls in commerce by 50 per cent. In 'home' subjects, girls also predominate. One in a thousand boys study needlework, and not many more child care. A small minority do study home economics, especially when it is solely concerned with cookery.

In languages, girls predominate, though not as much as in the two subject areas above. About twice as many girls as boys study languages, though the gap is smaller in subjects such as French studies – which are usually designed for lower-ability pupils.

Technical subjects are almost wholly boys' subjects; for example, while one in five or one in three boys study engineering or technical drawing, only one in 500 or one in 50 girls does.

In the humanities, aesthetic subjects, social sciences and other subjects, there are on the whole no major disparities between boys and girls in their subject choices. However, the tendency of girls to opt for courses that might be called socially relevant, and for boys to choose technical subjects, is occasionally visible. Religious education, practical living skills, drama, sociology and community education, for example, are studied by girls more than boys. Technical arts, like photography, design and physical education are studied more by boys.

While this pattern of take up is broadly reflected in single-sex schools, there are some important differences. In the sciences, the

28 *Option choice*

Table 4.2 Percentage of pupils taking a subject when offered it

Subject	Mixed schools Boys	Mixed schools Girls	Schools (Number)	Single sex schools Boys	Single sex schools Girls	Boys' schools	Girls' schools
Sciences							
Physics	55	16	88	57	37	3	7
Chemistry	36	26	88	50	41	5	7
Physical science	22	11	12	–	–	2	0
Biology	29	53	87	48	62	4	7
Human biology	6	24	32	–	–	0	2
General science	23	18	58	–	–	1	2
Environmental science	15	8	17	–	–	1	1
Rural studies/science	17	11	22	–	–	1	0
Commercial							
Shorthand	0.06	24	13	–	–	0	0
Typing	1.4	48	66	–	–	1	2
Commerce	32.0	22	39	–	–	1	1
Typing and office practice	2.7	48	7	–	–	0	1
Office practice	0.9	30	33	–	–	0	0
Accounts	9.0	17	12	–	–	1	0
Home							
Needlecraft	0.1	20	79	–	12	1	6
Child care	0.5	30	43	–	–	0	1
Home economics (cookery)	6.0	38	86	–	30	1	7
Home economics (general)	2.3	26	27	–	–	0	0
Languages							
French	23.0	43	89	36	54	4	4
German	8.0	15	66	31	25	3	6
Spanish	3.5	8	14	–	20	1	5

Patterns of curriculum choice

Latin	3.5	6	18	17	13	3	5
Classical studies	7.0	8	4	–	12	0	3
French studies	19.0	21	11	–	–	0	1
Technical							
Technical drawing	38	1.9	84	40	–	3	0
Woodwork	31	1	73	32	–	3	0
Metalwork	30	0.5	71	–	–	2	0
Building	23	0.45	13	–	–	0	0
Motor vehicle engineering	24	0.9	24	–	–	1	0
Engineering	21	0.2	18	–	–	1	0
Electronics	29	1	7	–	–	1	0
Technology	21	0.5	13	–	–	0	1
Design and technology	33	1.5	22	–	–	1	1
Mathematics							
Additional mathematics	32	20	3	–	–	1	1
Statistics	9	8	13	–	–	0	0
Computer studies	19	12	45	–	–	1	2
Humanities							
History	41	45	89	36	57	4	7
Geography	57	43	90	67	54	5	7
Religious education	7	15	51	–	14	0	4
Civics/Government	7	9	3	–	–	1	0
European studies	24	20	15	–	–	1	1
Integrated humanities	24	16	11	–	–	0	0
Practical living skills	14	20	5	–	–	0	0
Aesthetic							
Art	29	29	88	24	30	5	7
Pottery	10	8	14	–	–	1	1
Ceramics	5	6	4	–	–	1	0
Drama	9	14	46	–	–	0	2

30 Option choice

Table 4.2 Percentage of pupils taking a subject when offered it – contd.

Subject	Mixed schools Boys	Mixed schools Girls	Schools (Number)	Single sex schools Boys	Single sex schools Girls	Boys' Schools	Girls' Schools
Media studies	11	7	4	–	–	0	0
Photography	13	6	5	–	–	2	0
Music	3	6	74	3	8	4	7
Design	19	7	13	–	–	0	0
Social science							
Social studies	18	18	22	–	19	1	3
Sociology	9	18	16	–	–	1	1
Economics	15	16	21	–	–	2	0
Miscellaneous							
Community education	11	19	11	–	–	0	1
Physical education	27	18	30	–	–	0	0
Remedial	10	6	13	–	–	0	0
Other English (not remedial)	14	24	16	–	–	1	1
Geology	12	6	15	–	–	1	2
Outdoor pursuits/Recreation	15	12	5	–	–	0	0
Average no. of pupils per school	110	107	90	114	146	5	7

disparities are reduced. For example, roughly the same proportion of boys in mixed and single-sex schools study physics, but girls in single-sex schools study it twice as often as girls in mixed schools. More boys study biology in single-sex than mixed schools.

More pupils in general study languages in our sample of single-sex schools (which probably reflects the selective nature of some of them), but here too the figures suggest that the disparity between girls' and boys' choices is smaller than in mixed schools. Indeed more boys than girls study German, thought this may be because our sample is small.

For most other subjects, there were insufficient figures for analysis, which illustrates one feature of single-sex schools: that they often offer a more limited range of subjects than mixed schools. Figures for single-sex schools should be treated with some caution: there are not very many of them in the sample and they were more likely to make subjects compulsory. Table 4.3 shows how many subjects were made compulsory in the various types of school in the sample.

Table 4.3 Compulsory subjects in mixed and single-sex schools in the sample

Subject	Mixed schools	Boys' schools	Girls' schools
Child development	2	–	–
Design/art	4	–	–
English literature*	1	–	6
Aesthetics	1	–	–
French*	–	1	4
Music	4	–	3
Geography*	2	1	–
History*	1	1	–
Science*	2	–	–
Physics*	–	2	–
Chemistry*	–	1	–
Biology*	1	–	1
Computing	1	–	–

*Subjects are exam courses.

The fact that some single-sex schools made French, geography, history, physics, chemistry or biology compulsory means take up figures for those subjects would be substantially increased if compulsory subjects were included with the optional figures. In physics, chemistry and French this would serve to increase the sex bias evident in the figures, since incidence of these subjects as compulsory follows a sex-biased pattern.

All schools made English language and mathematics compulsory for all. The vast majority of schools made physical education or games compulsory. Most had courses variously titled with names like social education, liberal studies, personal relationships, community studies or human studies. These were non-exam courses that included all or some of health education, careers, religious education, social studies. The two schools making child care compulsory included this as part of these general courses.

Subject take up 1973 and 1980–1

We can compare our findings with the position in 1973 when the HMI survey (GB.DES, 1975) of secondary schools in England was conducted, and before the Sex Discrimination Act was passed. HMI collected details of subject take up at fourth/fifth year level for nine of the more academic subjects in 447 schools (subjects we have classified as 'commercial', 'technical' and 'home' – where the most extreme sex bias occurs – were omitted).

A comparison of the survey schools in our samples with those in the HMI survey is found in Table 4.4.

Table 4.4 A comparison of schools in HMI and EOC samples

	HMI (1973)			EOC (1981)		
	Mixed	Boys'	Girls'	Mixed	Boys'	Girls'
Secondary modern	106	29	27	8	2	1
Grammar	21	19	27	2	2	4
Comprehensive	169	18	16	80	1	2
Other	6	4	5	0	0	0
Total	302	70	75	92	5	7
				(2 missing)		

While the HMI survey includes English schools only, ours includes some from Scotland and Wales. Given that there are problems in comparing figures for single-sex schools when we have low numbers, subject take up of the nine academic subjects is given in Table 4.5.

It seems that there has been little change in subject take up since the passing of the Act. There is no great difference in the amount of sex bias between the samples for mixed schools, with boys dominating in physics and to a lesser extent in chemistry, girls in biology and languages. There is a suggestion of a modestly increased take up by girls of chemistry, but a heightening of sex differentiation in French. For single-sex schools the apparent differences should be treated with caution due to the low numbers in our sample, but they suggest some improvement of take up by girls of physics and chemistry. Apparent in all schools is a decline in the popularity of art and music and to a lesser extent in mixed schools of German.

What the take up figures do not reveal, however, is one respect in

Table 4.5 Percentage of pupils taking a subject when offered it

Subject	Pupils' sex	Single-sex schools HMI	Single-sex schools EOC	Mixed schools HMI	Mixed schools EOC
Physics	Boys	60	57	52	55
	Girls	23	37	15	16
Chemistry	Boys	36	50	35	36
	Girls	27	41	22	26
Biology	Boys	39	48	30	29
	Girls	49	62	53	53
French	Boys	37	36	28	23
	Girls	49	54	43	43
German	Boys	21	31	11	8
	Girls	18	25	21	15
Geography	Boys	55	67	54	57
	Girls	53	54	46	43
History	Boys	45	36	40	41
	Girls	46	57	48	45
Art	Boys	36	24	38	29
	Girls	39	30	37	29
Music	Boys	11	3	13	3
	Girls	16	7	16	6

which there have been changes since 1973. This is in the numbers of pupils offered the various subjects. Thus in the HMI survey (GB.DES, 1975) 91 per cent of boys in mixed schools were offered physics and only 75 per cent of girls; 96 per cent of girls in mixed schools were offered biology and only 91 per cent of boys. In the nine subjects concerned, none of the mixed schools in our sample offered a subject to one sex only. This type of exclusion happened only very rarely in the technical, home and commercial areas as an explicit matter (what happens less explicitly in terms of guidance suggestions is indicated in our chapter on option booklets).

It is thus possible to conclude that the Act has undoubtedly led to improvements in provision, but that this as not yet affected the take up of subjects by pupils. The outcome, disconcertingly, remains much the same.

Examinations – entries and passes

The pattern of subject provision and pupil choice we have examined so far is reflected in the examination subjects pupils attempt and pass, as we have already noted. We can look at these figures in more detail here. Table 4.6 shows the numbers of school leavers in England entering and passing CSE and O-level examinations in 1979–1980, as well as those who did not attempt examinations.

Table 4.6 GCE O-level and CSE passes and attempts by school leavers 1979–80 in England only

All figures are in thousands

	Did not attempt CSE/O-level Boys	Did not attempt CSE/O-level Girls	Attempted CSE/O-level Boys	Attempted CSE/O-level Girls	Obtained CSE grade 2–5 or O grade D/E Boys	Obtained CSE grade 2–5 or O grade D/E Girls	Obtained CSE grade 1 or O grade A–C Boys	Obtained CSE grade 1 or O grade A–C Girls
Single subject groups								
Arts								
Religious knowledge	343·04	299·70	40·89	67·10	21·49	33·17	13·65	28·00
French	289·81	221·04	94·12	145·76	44·88	74·97	40·19	63·28
Other modern languages	348·70	311·76	35·23	55·04	15·58	25·29	16·01	26·01
Classics	367·47	348·40	16·46	18·40	3·02	3·35	12·06	14·12
English	73·44	50·58	310·49	316·22	208·46	197·29	121·24	154·07
History	248·01	221·53	135·92	145·27	69·56	75·11	52·70	56·38
Music, drama, visual arts	269·57	242·07	114·36	124·73	72·31	70·07	39·66	54·97
Other arts	375·53	356·53	8·40	10·27	6·17	7·37	1·44	2·34
Science								
Mathematics	82·26	74·11	301·67	292·69	176·29	184·52	112·03	85·18
Physics	197·93	318·59	186·00	48·21	100·61	21·53	74·56	23·13
Chemistry	272·16	299·33	111·77	67·47	51·03	33·07	51·62	29·17
Biology, botany, zoology	277·12	169·81	106·81	196·99	52·56	114·81	46·13	67·84
Other science	157·95	315·51	225·98	51·29	170·82	35·92	69·73	11·30

Social science							
Economics	352·00	341·67	31·93	25·13	13·32	11·37	15·22	10·72
Geography	202·42	226·47	181·51	140·33	99·44	77·54	68·47	51·02
Vocational subjects	344·18	165·46	39·75	201·34	28·68	163·76	8·35	63·52
General studies	368·44	352·91	15·49	13·89	4·41	4·13	9·27	8·25
Other social science	342·09	304·86	41·84	61·94	31·36	44·41	6·58	14·80
Any subject	47·38	36·36	336·55	330·44	141·66	127·02	189·61	199·95
Combinations of basic subjects							
English and mathematics	96·01	80·73	287·92	286·07	106·41	96·74	87·99	77·22
Mathematics and science	97·17	129·87	286·76	236·93	107·17	68·75	91·85	59·68
Science and modern languages	277·15	224·27	106·78	142·53	14·66	20·93	37·99	47·65
English, mathematics and science	107·76	133·00	276·17	233·80	98·82	66·52	76·02	57·35
English, mathematics and modern languages	276·84	210·03	107·09	156·77	14·04	24·70	39·05	49·36
English, mathematics, science and modern languages	279·72	228·81	104·21	137·99	13·42	19·15	35·40	40·08

Note: Excluding O-level passes awarded on A-level papers.
Source: GB.DES, 1980b, Table C8.

The figures show unpopular as well as the most popular subjects. On the whole, the arts and social sciences are not popular examination subjects with pupils of either sex. Well over half the school-leavers had not attempted examinations in these subjects, with the exceptions of English, geography to a lesser extent, and, for girls, vocational subjects.

Differentiation between boys and girls is particularly evident in the arts, in French and other modern languages, which nearly twice as many girls as boys attempt, to a marked extent in entries for religious knowledge, and to a lesser extent in entries to all arts subjects. In the social sciences, five times as many girls as boys attempt vocational subjects, though more boys than girls attempt most other subjects in this group, except other social sciences.

In the sciences, the proportion of pupils not entering for an examination is generally lower than in arts and social sciences, but the differentiation between boys and girls is more marked. Most pupils attempt mathematics, boys and girls roughly equally. Girls conspicuously avoid physics, chemistry and other sciences (mostly technical crafts). Three or four times as many boys as girls attempt these subjects. Boys also avoid chemistry, and in addition biology. Nearly twice as many girls as boys attempt the latter.

The DES statistics also show that there have been slight changes over the years. Table 4.7 shows the percentage increase in numbers passing various subjects for each sex between 1975 and 1980.

It will be seen from Table 4.7 that the numbers of boys passing French has not increased as rapidly as the numbers of girls passing the subject, so sex bias has increased in that subject. In biology at CSE level the number of boys has increased slightly compared to girls, but the reverse is true of O-level. Girls are catching up with boys in physics and chemistry but not in other science/technical subjects at O-level. Boys are catching up with girls in commercial subjects. There has clearly been a large increase in the numbers of girls taking technical drawing and woodwork/metalwork at CSE level, but it should be noted that numbers involved here are quite small when compared to the boys. In fact the metalwork/woodwork increase represents an increase of 511 girls to 1,830, compared to figures of 86,126 and 111,763 for boys. Figures for technical drawing are 838 to 3,157 girls and 66,400 to 84,180 boys.

The tabulations we produced from the DES school-leaver survey enable us to do more than simply look at numbers entering examinations in each subject: we have been able to examine first the subjects that individual pupils are able to avoid (as opposed to the percentages of all pupils taking or avoiding subjects), and, second, the numbers entering for particular combinations of subjects. Tables 4.6 and 4.8 show the numbers of pupils leaving school in 1979–80 without having

Table 4.7 Examination passes CSE and O-level 1975 and 1980

Subject	CSE Percentage increase Boys	Girls	O-level Percentage increase Boys	Girls
French	5·9	14·5	37·6	56·3
Physics	52·8	65·9	43·1	122·9
Chemistry	–	–	25·9	40·0
Biology	16·5	11·2	61·0	65·4
Technical drawing	26·8	276·7	–	–
Metalwork/Woodwork	29·8	258·1	–	–
Domestic subjects	101·6	42·0	–	–
Commercial subjects	61·6	48·2	–	–
Other science/Technical	–	–	20·4	17·9

entered an examination in certain subjects. In the sciences it confirms both the avoidance of science by girls, and their tendency to concentrate on biological sciences.

Relatively few pupils leave school without having attempted some kind of science examination. Even so, the avoidance of science by girls

Table 4.8 Examination entries in science and technical subjects 1979–80

	Boys	Girls
No science/technical		
CSE	17,530	45,120
O-level	1,540	2,820
CSE + O-level	4,570	24,380
Total	23,640	72,320
At least one science/technical		
CSE	105,450	64,110
O-level	12,810	11,770
CSE + O-level	125,640	120,670
Total	243,900	196,550
At least one physical science/technical		
CSE	101,800	29,040
O-level	11,880	6,870
CSE + O-level	121,700	58,390
Total	235,380	94,300
Biology only		
CSE	21,190	80,190
O-level	2,470	7,710
CSE + O-level	8,510	86,660
Total	32,170	174,560

is visible if we consider the widest definition of science including biology and 'other sciences' (which spans general science and a number of technical subjects): only 23,640 boys, but 72,320 (three times the number) of girls avoided all these. In terms of subjects studied, rather than avoided, the preponderance of boys in science in general is not great: 243,900 boys attempted at least one science examination on our widest definition, compared with 196,550 girls. But boys attempting at least one physical science outnumbered girls by over two to one. Conversely, pupils studying a biological science were in the ratio 6 girls : 1 boy.

Many schools make some sort of science compulsory for all at the 13+ stage (see Chapter 6) and it is of interest to see what girls do when faced with this. Our DES statistics suggest that, when seeking an 'easy option' among the sciences, girls go for biology rather than general science.

Tables 4.9, 4.10 and 4.11 show entries in biology and general science for pupils who have not entered for physics, chemistry or any other physical sciences. In each table the proportion of girls to boys with biology entries is far greater than the proportion with general science entries.

In combinations of science with other subjects, the figures show that the differentiation in the curriculum followed by girls and boys is heightened. Tables 4.12, 4.13, 4.14 and 4.15 show figures for examination entries for combinations of sciences, technical and vocational

Table 4.9 Biology and general science examination entries: pupils with no entries in other physical sciences at CSE level

	Boys	Girls
Biology only		
CSE	7,240	74,560
O-level	38,940	65,080
CSE + O-level	2,160	14,760
Total	48,340	154,400
General science only		
CSE	7,440	15,650
O-level	3,170	1,370
CSE + O-level	70	170
Total	10,680	17,190
General science and biology		
CSE	510	2,250
O-level	760	580
*CSE + O-level	190	1,090
Total	1,460	3,920

* Including 20 girls taking biology and general science at both CSE and O-level.

Table 4.10 Biology and general science examination entries: pupils with no entries in other physical sciences at O-level

	Boys	*Girls*
Biology only		
CSE	31,520	91,590
O-level	7,440	39,060
CSE + O-level	3,970	18,010
Total	42,930	148,660
General science only		
CSE	27,300	17,110
O-level	1,060	730
CSE + O-level	160	180
Total	28,520	18,020
General science and biology		
CSE	1,550	2,330
O-level	350	380
*CSE + O-level	460	1,120
Total	2,360	3,830

* Including 20 girls taking general science and biology at both CSE and O-level.

subjects. More boys than girls combine their sciences with technical subjects and more girls than boys combine sciences and vocational subjects. Thus, Table 4.12 reflects the familiar avoidance of physics by girls. Over 240,000 girls left school in 1979–80 without entering physics at either CSE or O-level, nearly twice the number of boys who

Table 4.11 Biology and general science examination entries: pupils with no entries in other physical sciences at CSE and O-level

	Boys	*Girls*
Biology only		
CSE	6,120	73,390
O-level	4,290	33,550
CSE + O-level	940	13,320
Total	11,350	120,260
General science only		
CSE	7,120	15,590
O-level	910	680
CSE + O-level	50	170
Total	8,080	16,440
General science and biology		
CSE	480	2,200
O-level	280	340
*CSE + O-level	130	990
Total	890	3,530

* Including 20 girls taking biology and general science at both CSE and O-level.

Table 4.12 Examination entries in physics and other subjects

	Boys	Girls
No physics		
CSE	84,540	105,680
O-level	4,920	10,780
CSE + O-level	45,880	126,160
Total	135,340	242,620
Physics and one technical subject		
CSE	12,920	380
O-level	2,690	120
CSE + O-level	28,550	2,120
Total	44,160	2,620
Physics and any two technical subjects		
CSE	13,960	20
O-level	1,340	–
CSE + O-level	28,620	210
Total	43,920	230
Physics and three technical subjects		
CSE	3,970	–
O-level	140	–
CSE + O-level	6,820	10
Total	10,930	10
Physics and one vocational subject		
CSE	5,050	1,570
O-level	500	850
CSE + O-level	9,220	7,750
Total	14,770	10,170
Physics and two vocational subjects		
CSE	210	750
O-level	–	50
CSE + O-level	550	1,890
Total	760	2,690
Physics and three vocational subjects		
CSE	10	80
O-level	–	–
CSE + O-level	50	230
Total	60	310

Table 4.13 Examination entries in chemistry and other subjects

	Boys	Girls
No chemistry		
CSE	109,180	103,120
O-level	7,590	9,940
CSE + O-level	83,830	115,670
Total	200,600	228,730
Chemistry and one technical subject		
CSE	5,270	480
O-level	1,800	130
CSE + O-level	16,890	1,860
Total	23,960	2,470
Chemistry and two technical subjects		
CSE	4,200	10
O-level	780	20
CSE + O-level	12,880	150
Total	17,860	180
Chemistry and three technical subjects		
CSE	820	–
O-level	70	–
CSE + O-level	1,920	–
Total	2,810	–
Chemistry and one vocational subject		
CSE	2,210	3,170
O-level	240	1,350
CSE + O-level	4,510	13,540
Total	6,960	18,060
Chemistry and two vocational subjects		
CSE	30	1,000
O-level	–	70
CSE + O-level	270	3,530
Total	300	4,600
Chemistry and three vocational subjects		
CSE	–	150
O-level	–	–
CSE + O-level	20	410
Total	20	560

Option choice

Table 4.14 Examination entries in physics, chemistry and other subjects

	Boys	Girls
No physics or chemistry		
CSE	79,250	100,180
O-level	3,890	8,520
CSE + O-level	36,010	104,350
Total	119,150	213,050
Physics and chemistry and technical subjects		
CSE	3,390	60
O-level	1,580	70
CSE + O-level	13,400	620
Total	18,370	750
Physics and chemistry and two technical subjects		
CSE	2,690	–
O-level	690	–
CSE + O-level	10,370	80
Total	13,750	80
Physics and chemistry and three technical subjects		
CSE	460	–
O-level	60	–
CSE + O-level	1,520	–
Total	2,040	–
Physics and chemistry and one vocational subject		
CSE	1,060	250
O-level	200	420
CSE + O-level	3,140	2,630
Total	4,400	3,300
Physics and chemistry and two vocational subjects		
CSE	10	90
O-level	–	10
CSE + O-level	130	430
Total	140	530
Physics and chemistry and three vocational subjects		
CSE	–	10
O-level	–	–
CSE + O-level	10	20
Total	10	30

Table 4.15 Examination entries in biology and other subjects

	Boys	Girls
No biology		
CSE	102,620	65,780
O-level	8,150	5,010
CSE + O-level	86,370	47,850
Total	197,140	118,640
Biology and one technical subject		
CSE	7,530	3,720
O-level	1,560	460
CSE + O-level	15,470	8,230
Total	24,560	12,410
Biology and two technical subjects		
CSE	5,230	130
O-level	460	30
CSE + O-level	10,300	500
Total	15,990	660
Biology and three technical subjects		
CSE	1,200	–
O-level	30	–
CSE + O-level	2,040	40
Total	3,270	40
Biology and one vocational subject		
CSE	3,180	20,980
O-level	30	3,280
CSE + O-level	5,480	46,040
Total	8,690	70,300
Biology and two vocational subjects		
CSE	150	10,290
O-level	–	340
CSE + O-level	420	16,420
Total	570	27,050
Biology and three vocational subjects		
CSE	10	1,780
O-level	–	10
CSE + O-level	50	2,950
Total	60	4,740

did so. But in combination with technical subjects, the proportion of boys to girls increases with the increase in technical subjects studied. Boys who studied physics with one technical subject numbered 44,160, compared with only 2,620 girls; nearly 11,000 boys combined physics with three technical subjects; but only 10 girls did so.

In a combination of physics and one 'vocational' subject, boys barely predominate; with more than one 'vocational' subject girls are in the majority: the numbers are small, simply because fewer girls take physics. Overall, the numbers of boys and girls combining physics with one or more vocational subject are not dissimilar.

Combinations of chemistry and technical and vocational subjects show a similar pattern (see Table 4.13). Although chemistry is traditionally neither a boys' nor girls' subject, in combination with one or more technical subjects almost 20 times more boys than girls study it. In combination with vocational subjects, about three times as many girls as boys study it. The disparities increase with an increase of technical or vocational subjects. Pupils studying both physics and chemistry also combine these differentially with technical or vocational subjects according to sex (see Table 4.14). The differences are most marked for combinations of the two sciences with technical subjects, which were taken by 34,000 boys but only 850 girls. Combinations with vocational subjects were rarer for boys, but more common for girls, so that the numbers studying them were approaching equality – 4,550 boys and 3,860 girls, with more girls than boys taking two or more vocational subjects.

When it comes to biology with technical and vocational subjects, the pattern changes (see Table 4.15). More boys than girls avoid biology altogether, but of those that study it, more combine it with technical subjects. Nearly 44,000 boys entered examinations combining these subjects with biology, compared with 12,410 girls. But the combination of biology and vocational subjects is overwhelmingly taken by girls: over 102,000 compared with less than 10,000 boys.

In modern languages, regarded as a traditionally girls' rather than boys' subject, the figures in Table 4.16 confirm this view, and show that it pertains more the more languages are involved. Nearly twice as many girls as boys attempted an examination in one language, nearly four times as many attempted two languages and almost six times as many (although few in absolute terms) attempted three languages.

Table 4.16 Examination entries in modern languages

	Boys	Girls
No modern languages		
CSE	113,510	90,800
O-level	6,980	4,300
CSE + O-level	89,390	64,290
Total	209,880	159,390
One modern language		
CSE	9,260	17,590
O-level	5,900	6,810
CSE + O-level	37,680	67,080
Total	52,840	91,480
Two modern languages		
CSE	160	750
O-level	1,420	3,380
CSE + O-level	3,120	13,460
Total	4,700	17,590
Three modern languages		
CSE	–	–
O-level	40	90
CSE + O-level	10	210
Total	50	300

Careers aspirations and achievements

We examined the career aspirations and achievements of pupils in our case study schools. For each case study school we aimed to collect, usually from local careers office records, the following information for 50 recent school-leavers of each sex: optional subjects studied; career or further education aspiration; job or further education pursued after leaving; hobbies and interests.

We were not always able to collect this information, because some records did not contain some details and, in one or two cases, careers offices did not allow us to examine records. In the end we gathered information on over 1,000 pupils.

With the information collected we are able to examine, first, the extent to which boys and girls aspire to different kinds of career, the jobs they actually get, and their spare-time interests. It is evident from our analysis that each sex has very different aspirations from the other. In mixed schools the most desired job by far for boys is some form of apprenticeship, whereas for girls a secretarial or office job is most often wanted (see Appendix 3). There are boys wanting employment in catering, and several consider shop work and clerical work as well as work in banks; police work is frequently nominated by both sexes. Apart from this, though, aspirations are separate. No statistics were available about aspirations in boys' schools, but those in a girls' school are interesting to compare with those of girls in mixed schools. The year group in the girls' school had received a grammar school education; higher education of some sort was aspired to by a high proportion of these girls and it is evident that this is even more the case where girls are studying mathematics, physics or chemistry in their A-levels (figures for mixed school pupils are almost all for fifth formers rather than sixth formers). While girls in the single-sex school are sometimes willing to consider higher education courses in traditionally boys' areas they more often consider traditional areas such as education or the humanities.

Aspirations are a good guide to what actually happens (see Appendix 3). Girls do get office jobs very frequently and boys enter apprenticeships; the girls' school does in fact send many girls on to humanities courses and only one or two on to physical science and mathematical courses; medical and paramedical courses are quite popular. Where the boys' grammar school is concerned, the majority go on to higher education as in the girls' school; more do engineering and accountancy, although there is a relatively high interest in humanities courses.

Appendix 3 shows that some leisure activities are exclusively pursued by either sex, whereas others are shared. Football, fishing, cars, motorbikes, model making and cricket are popular with boys: cooking, dancing, knitting, sewing and being with children are more popular with girls. Although boys quite often want catering careers, it would seem they are rarely interested in cooking at home. Music (usually meaning listening to records), swimming and badminton are activities popular with both sexes as are youth clubs and the general area of sport. There is a high number of boys expressing an interest in animals, since one school in a rural area had many boys who were interested in farming; girls' interest in animals tended to be more directed toward pets, although note the number of girls interested in dogs and horses. In the girls' school more are willing to enter non-traditional areas in subjects and jobs than girls in mixed schools, but in their spare-time interests there are few differences.

Subject take up and careers

In our case study schools we were able to examine the relationship not only between subjects studied and careers achieved, but also the career aspirations of boys and girls. Although there were some problems of low numbers, we were also able to consider the extent to which schools which promoted equal opportunities produced pupils with non-traditional careers aspirations and career destinations.

We can group the case study schools according to whether they are trying particularly hard to promote equal opportunities. A method for scoring the extent to which schools attempt to promote a policy of equality is described in Chapter 5, where we go into more detail on the association of such attempts with variation in subject take up.

While for the most part girls and boys pursue activities according to the traditional patterns (as we saw earlier), there are also some individuals who do not follow the pattern. Does the incidence of non-traditional activity vary according to whether schools are trying hard to promote equal opportunities? Are pupils who pursue a non-traditional school subject more likely to achieve non-traditional jobs? Do those who want non-traditional jobs get them? In order to answer these questions it is necessary to categorize subjects, aspirations, jobs and hobbies into those considered traditional for a sex, or neutral, and those considered non-traditional. The classifications we used are shown in Appendix 4.

We then compared pupils from three English mixed schools trying to promote equal opportunities and from five that had features which showed them to be examples of poor practice, to see whether there are any significant differences between them in terms of non-traditional take up, aspiration or destination. For boys there is a significant difference in subject take up figures.

Boys	Three good-practice schools		Five bad-practice schools	
Non-traditional subjects	20	(16%)	18	(7.6%)
Traditional subjects	105	(84%)	219	(92.4%)

Note: p less than 0·025.

For aspirations, jobs achieved and hobbies, however, there was no significant difference between the samples.

For girls there were insufficient numbers with non-traditional aspirations, jobs or hobbies for tests of significance to be valid (less than five expected frequency in some cells). There was no significant difference for subject take up.

Each of the four areas (subjects, aspirations, jobs or courses, and hobbies) was then compared with the other three, separately for each sex. It was hoped that it would be possible to see whether non-traditional choice in one area was significantly associated with such choice in another area. However, in almost all cases the numbers were too low for tests of significance to be valid. The only table where a test is valid is that for females where subject choice is cross-tabulated against aspiration. It should be noted that by this stage pupils from all types of school were grouped together.

Girls	Traditional aspirations		Non-traditional aspirations	
Non-traditional subjects	61	(78%)	17	(22%)
Traditional subjects	237	(97%)	7	(3%)

Note: p less than 0·005.

The figures above show that girls taking non-traditional subjects are more likely than others to have non-traditional aspirations.

Even though numbers are low, it is worth reporting figures, so that we may see whether those wanting non-traditional jobs/courses get them (see Table 4.17).

Table 4.17 Numbers in traditional and non-traditional jobs/courses

Girls	Traditional jobs/courses	Non-traditional jobs/courses
Non-traditional aspiration	7	2
Traditional aspiration	302	6
Boys		
Non-traditional aspiration	14	13
Traditional aspiration	301	8

The relatively high number of boys wanting and getting non-traditional jobs is largely due to those wanting catering jobs/courses.

Subject take up and further and higher education

Although most pupils who leave school go into or seek employment, an important minority go on to further full-time education. The DES school-leaver survey collects detailed information on further and higher education courses pursued by school-leavers and enables us to relate these to subjects studied at school. We have tabulated these courses according to the proportions of girls and boys studying them, and grouped them into ten groups as shown in Table 4.18.

It is clear from Table 4.18 that there is sex differentiation between these courses. For one thing, a higher proportion of girls than boys go on to some form of further education, with more boys than girls entering employment. Nearly 100,000 girls (27 per cent of girl leavers)

Table 4.18 Destinations of school-leavers, 1979–80

	Destinations	Boys (thousands)	Girls (thousands)	Per cent girls
1.	Surveying non-degree	0·19	0·00	0
	Architecture non-degree	0·08	0·00	0
	Total	0·27	0·00	0
2.	Mechanical or aero-engineering degree	1·29	0·04	3
	Other engineering or technical non-degree	2·94	0·10	3
	Electrical engineering degree	1·50	0·07	4
	Civil engineering degree	0·97	0·07	7
	Other engineering degree	1·65	0·21	11
	Other technology degree	0·88	0·13	13
	Physics degree	1·62	0·27	14
	Total	10·85	0·89	
3.	Architecture degree	0·41	0·10	20
	Not known – likely science degree	0·39	0·10	20
	Economics degree	1·96	0·60	23
	Other pure science	0·17	0·05	23
	Chemistry degree	1·49	0·61	29
	Agricultural/forestry/veterinary non-degree course	0·56	0·22	29
	Other accountancy	0·59	0·28	33
	Other OND/ONC	1·57	0.80	34
	Other science degree	2·75	1·72	36
	Total	11·86	5·59	
4.	HND/HNC	1·61	1·07	40
	Other social science or administrative or business degree	3·06	2·14	41
	Law degree	1·67	1·20	42
	Agriculture or forestry or veterinary degree	0·42	0·30	42
	Biology degree	1·90	1·42	43
	History degree	1·37	1·15	45
	Not known degree	0·44	0·41	48
	Medicine or dentistry or health degree	1·91	1·81	49
	Geography degree	1·15	1·23	52
	GCE O-level	5·49	6·38	54
	City and Guilds	0·77	0·91	54
	GCE A-level	7·81	9·92	56
	BEC/TEC	2·10	2·65	56

Option choice

Table 4.18 Destinations of school-leavers, 1979–80 –*contd.*

	Music/drama/visual arts. non-degree	2·29	3·15	58
	Music or drama or visual arts degree	0·67	0·96	59
	Total	32·66	35·06	
5.	Not known – likely arts/social science degree	0·24	0·38	61
	Other arts degree (not language)	1·24	2·00	62
	Dip HE course	0·11	0·18	62
	Unknown type of course	2·22	4·02	65
	English degree	0·90	1·90	68
	Other languages (including English)	0·07	0·16	70
	Other arts subject	0·76	1·75	70
	Other course	0·67	1·72	72
	Other, librarianship	0·03	0·08	73
	Other language degree	1·18	3·33	74
	Education degree (not B.Ed.)	0·05	0·18	75
	Other social or administrative or business	1·43	4·32	75
	Other catering	1·83	5·48	75
	Other professional or vocational	1·51	5·02	77
	Total	12·22	30·52	
6.	Teacher training (including B.Ed.)	0·36	2·21	86
7.	Other medicine or dentistry or health course	0·11	1·43	93
	Other nursing (not degree)	0·08	6·18	99
	Total	0·19	7·61	
8.	Other secretarial	0·04	18·37	100
9.	Employment and temporary employment	282·23	235·38	45
10.	Not known	33·23	31·54	49
	Total (all leavers)	383·93	366·80	49

went to destination groups 1–8, compared with 69,000 boys (18 per cent of boy leavers). Within these groups, there is further differentiation. Engineering and scientific courses attract more boys than girls, though degree courses in economics and accountancy are also predominantly boys' destinations. Secretarial, paramedical and education courses attract far more girls than boys, as do arts and language courses.

We can now relate our analysis of examination entries – as a measure of subject choice – with destinations of pupils into further and higher education courses. We grouped the destinations in the DES school-leaver survey under three headings. The destinations in categories 1 to 3 were taken up in practice by boys more than girls, in all cases the proportion of boys being more than 60 per cent. At the other end of the scale were courses where the membership was 60 per cent or more girls (categories 5, 6, 7, 8). A neutral category covered courses where a more equal balance occurs (see Table 4.19).

Table 4.19 Classification of destination groups

Destination group	Mainly boys Boys	Mainly boys Girls	Neutral Boys	Neutral Girls	Mainly girls Boys	Mainly girls Girls
1	0·27	0·00				
2	10·85	0·89				
3	11·86	5·59				
Total	22·98	6·38				
	(78%)	(22%)				
4			32·66	35·06		
9			282·23	235·38		
10			33·23	31·54		
Total			348·12	301·98		
			(60%)	(40%)		
5					12·23	30·52
6					0·36	2·21
7					0·19	7·61
8					0·04	18·37
Total					12·81	58·71
					(18%)	(82%)

Table 4.20 shows how various types of subject combination are related to subsequent destinations, as described by the three categories. The general picture is, predictably, that girls taking physical sciences and technical subjects at school are more likely than other girls subsequently to take up the 'mainly boys'' courses which are predominantly scientific and technical. However, even when girls have studied science or technical subjects at school they are less likely than boys – even boys who have not studied such subjects – to take up scientific or technical courses. For example, in Table 4.20 (a), 11·2 per cent of boys who did not study physics at CSE or O-level went on to a 'mainly boys'' course after learning; 16·5 per cent of boys who did attempt physics and one or more technical subject did so. However, only 1·4 per cent of girls with no physics went on to this kind of course and only 2·8 per cent of those girls who attempted physics and one or more technical subject did so. Similar relationships are found for other science subjects.

Option choice

Table 4.20 School subjects and destinations of school-leavers

School subjects	Mainly boys	Neutral	Mainly girls	Number (= 100%)
(a) Boys No physics	11·2	27·7	61·2	9,650
Physics and one or more technical subject	16·5	38·8	44·7	10,200
Girls No physics	1·4	18·2	80·3	54,840
Physics and one or more technical subject	2·8	38·4	58·9	730
(b) Boys No physics or chemistry	11·6	25·3	63·2	7,430
Physics, chemistry and one or more technical subject	17·1	41·2	41·6	4,390
Girls No physics or chemistry	1·3	16·6	82·1	45,360
Physics, chemistry and one or more technical subject	0	26·7	73·4	150
(c) Boys No chemistry	12·6	33	54·4	15,520
Chemistry and one or more technical subject	16·4	38·6	44·9	5,640
Girls No chemistry	1·4	18·7	79·9	46,750
Chemistry and one or more technical subject	4·4	27·9	67·7	680
(d) Boys No chemistry	12·6	33	54·4	15,520
Chemistry and one or more vocational subject	7·1	34·5	58·4	1,130
Girls No chemistry	1·4	18·7	79·9	46,750
Chemistry and one or more vocational subject	2·6	21·5	75·8	7,250
(e) Boys No biology	13·9	34·7	51	14,920
Biology and one or more vocational subject	4	33·8	62·3	1,510
Girls No biology	1·3	18·1	80·6	19,270
Biology and one or more vocational subject	1·6	16·3	82·1	28,560
(f) Boys No science or technical subjects except biology	2·9	37·2	59·8	2,390
One or more science or technical subjects	13·6	37·4	49	23,310
Girls No science or technical subjects except biology	1	17·1	81·8	37,510
One or more science or technical subjects	2·2	25·5	72·3	25,340

Note: All figures are percentages of the total in each row. The numbers in the right-hand column are actual numbers of pupils. Thus in (a) 11·2 of the 9,650 boys who entered for no physics exams went on to destinations taken mainly by boys.

Table 4.20 (e) shows that the pattern tends to hold also in reverse, in that the minority of boys taking biology and one or more vocational subject go on to 'mainly girls'' destinations more than other boys, but less than girls taking this combination of subjects. Thus we may say that subject choice at 13 + can mitigate the effect of sex on post-school destination but by no means eliminates it.

Conclusions

We have described how girls and boys differ in the subjects they choose at 13+. Evidence from our postal survey, DES statistics and careers office records confirm that boys more than girls take up the physical sciences and technical subjects, while girls take up biological and vocational subjects. When faced with a choice of sciences, girls are more likely to choose biology than general science when looking for an 'easy option'. Home economics and technical drawing are the craft subjects most attracting non-traditional choice.

Things have changed little since the Sex Discrimination Act. Compared with figures from the HMI survey conducted in 1973 (GB.DES, 1975) our results show little change in sex differentiation in nine major academic subjects. Apart from French, where sex differences have increased, and biology where there is no change, the differences have decreased in physics, chemistry and craft subjects. The main change is that there is less compulsory restriction of subjects to one sex than there used to be.

Our analysis of DES statistics shows that when pupils leave school, secretarial, para-medical and teaching courses attract girls more than boys, while engineering and scientific courses attract more boys. Careers office records show that boys more than girls aspire to, and achieve, apprenticeships, and girls more than boys aspire to, and achieve, secretarial positions. Spare-time interests of girls and boys are also very different. Subject take up and destination varies from school to school, and particularly between single-sex and mixed schools.

Our analysis also shows that taking a non-traditional subject increases the likelihood of a leaver subsequently taking up a non-traditional course, but the factor of sex far outweighs that of subject choice in predicting destination. Girls taking sciences at school go on to scientific courses more than other girls, but less frequently than boys – even those boys who have not attempted science subjects! There were difficulties in conducting this kind of analysis on careers office records, since numbers were low, but there are indications that girls studying non-traditional subjects aspire to non-traditional careers. Figures for pupils who aspire to non-traditional areas show the relatively low incidence of non-traditional choice. We look at whether what schools do to promote equal opportunities has any effect on subject and job choice in later chapters.

CHAPTER 5

School policy

One of our chief aims was to assess the extent to which schools are conforming to both the letter and spirit of the Sex Discrimination Act. As we discussed in Chapter 3, this involves looking both at whether the law is actually being broken, and also at the extent to which schools pursue positive policies for equality of opportunity between the sexes. We begin this assessment in this chapter. But before the schools are discussed we can get some indication of commitment to equal opportunities policy at local authority level from the letters we received from Chief Education Officers in response to our request for help in choosing good practice schools.

Local authority commitment

Of the 79 responses to our requests to 104 Chief Education Officers in England and Wales to nominate good practice schools, 29 made some other comments which are useful in indicating the strength of interest in equal opportunities as a policy in the authority, though they cannot be regarded as wholly representative, since the CEOs were not asked to make a detailed response on their policy.

The overall picture, however, was that nearly all commenting CEOs indicated a positive policy in their authority. Eighteen CEOs stated that generally schools tried to provide equal access to all subjects. Examples of such statements are:

> To my knowledge, no secondary school has made major policy decisions regarding equal opportunities but, overall, there is a proper liberal attitude. For example, in very many of our secondary schools the traditional boys' and girls' subjects in Design and Craft are not distinguished by sex...

> In this County there is a wide recognition of the need to present equal opportunities to boys and girls and the extent to which schools

have changed their curricula and organization with this in mind is considerable. A great deal has thus already been achieved on the initiative of the schools themselves and without any guidance from the Authority. When things are moving forward well under their own steam it is usually wiser not to intervene.

I am confident that our secondary schools are taking a broader view of these matters and have become much more aware in recent years of the need to be even-handed in curricular options and so on.

All the schools in... are advised to ensure that within existing resources equal curriculum options are available to all pupils.

We have a declared policy of providing the opportunities you speak of in all our schools, and indeed follow up such cases where this is not the case.

Six CEOs referred to particular efforts being made within their authority. One of the six noted that 'most' schools offered a common curriculum in the first two years and suggested that some were more successful than others in persuading girls to opt for physical sciences: 'This seems to be related more to the personality of the teacher than to special curriculum arrangements.' One of the six reported parental opposition to the policy:

This Authority has made a number of attempts to break down the barriers in relation to equal opportunities but has experienced some reluctance on the part of the pupils connected with parental attitudes and opposition to anything which is not traditional and peer group influence which tends to demand that a youngster proposing to take advantage of the opportunities offered needs to be a strong personable character in order to take the necessary decisions and carry them through.

The same authority reported several female teachers of technical subjects working in its schools. Another of the six reported a number of conferences, meetings and courses on the subject but that constraints on resources and parental pressures often worked against the policy.

Eleven CEOs noted that it was difficult to single out particular schools as being good practice. Most of these made this statement while emphasizing that most or all schools were acting in accordance with the law.

Two responses were less favourable. One CEO suggested that making cord or denim garments in needlework, as suggested in an EOC commentary (GB.EOC, 1979), was impractical due to special machinery being necessary for such material. Finally, one CEO did not even approve of the way in which the research was designed:

A further point is that we prefer projects in which the researchers' conclusions are not pre-determined. The structure of the project you describe is not reassuring in this respect.

School policy

Formal discussion

Our survey gives us a good indication of the level of formal concern with equal opportunities policy across the country. Schools were asked whether the issue of equal opportunities had ever been discussed as an agenda item (see Table 5.1). The picture that emerges is interesting, for it seems that the issue has cropped up more within schools than in

Table 5.1   Question 2h   Has the issue of equal opportunities between the sexes ever been discussed as an agenda matter?

In governors' meetings?

	Yes	No	Total
Nominated	24	63	87
	(28%)	(72%)	(100%)
Cluster	24	58	82
	(29%)	(71%)	(100%)
Total	48	121	169
	(28%)	(72%)	(100%)

Missing = 30

In parent–teacher meetings?

	Yes	No	Total
Nominated	28	63	91
	(31%)	(69%)	(100%)
Cluster	15	70	85
	(18%)	(82%)	(100%)
Total	43	133	176
	(24%)	(76%)	(100%)

Missing = 23

In committee meetings of school staff?

	Yes	No	Total
Nominated	56	40	96
	(58%)	(42%)	(100%)
Cluster	50	42	92
	(54%)	(46%)	(100%)
Total	106	82	188
	(56%)	(44%)	(100%)

Missing = 11

meetings where outsiders are present. In governors' meetings, the issue had been discussed in just over a quarter of responding schools; in parent-teacher meetings in just under a quarter. But over half the schools had discussed it at staff meetings.

Special responsibility

The picture is not so bright if we look at the allocation of responsibility for equal opportunities policy in schools. Relatively few schools appear to have taken executive action. Nearly 90 per cent have no one with a special interest or responsibility for promoting equality (see Table 5.2).

Table 5.2 Question 2g   Is there a member of staff or group of teachers with a special interest or responsibility for promoting equal opportunities for boys and girls within the school?

	Yes	No	Total
Nominated	18	80	98
	(18%)	(82%)	(100%)
Cluster	9	90	99
	(9%)	(91%)	(100%)
Total	27	170	197
	(13.5%)	(86.5%)	(100%)

Missing = 2

The level of staff responsible for this varies greatly, though in most schools responding to our request for details it was either a senior member of staff or a working party. Similarly, the tasks they undertake also vary. Examining sex differences in subject take up and reviewing the curriculum were the most frequent tasks.

Table 5.3   Members of staff responsible for promoting equality

Who in the school is concerned?	Nominated sample (number of schools)	Cluster sample (number of schools)
Deputy head	1	0
Management team	0	2
Senior teachers	0	3
Head, timetabler, director of studies	1	0
Director of studies	1	0
Deputy, senior teacher	2	0
Careers teacher	0	1
Senior master	1	0

Table 5.3 Members of staff responsible for promoting equality – contd.

Who in the school is concerned?	Nominated sample (number of schools)	Cluster sample (number of schools)
'Single women and divorcees'	1	0
All teachers (no one specifically)	2	4
Working party	3	0
Curriculum committee	1	0
Science teacher	1	0
'General' teachers	1	0
What do they do in the school?		
Analyse sex differences in the take up of subjects	8	2
'Nothing specific'	0	2
Review curriculum materials	3	1
Careers advice given irrespective of sex	0	1
Try to get other teachers on my side (especially mathematics teachers)	1	0
Analyse sex differences in performance in science and mathematics	1	0
Keep an eye on option choice	1	0
Representing the interests of the girls in staff meetings	1	0
Inform higher management of the situation	1	0
Analyse sex differences in destinations in FE and HE	1	0
Run in-service courses	1	0
Examine library books for sex bias	1	0
Keep parents and pupils aware of the issue	2	0
Trying to get more girls to do physics	1	0

Policy statements

So far as statements of policy are concerned, the Commission's view of what implementing the Sex Discrimination Act involves is clear:

> The Commission feels that every secondary school should include in its information for parents an explicit statement that every subject taught in the school is available to pupils of both sexes and that it is not necessary for a pupil to make a special request to attend a course which might be considered non-traditional. (GB.EOC, 1979)

Prospectuses were examined with this in mind from the 75 cluster sample schools and 76 nominated schools which returned them in response to our questionnaire. Of these only three prospectuses (two nominated, one cluster) contained statements that referred to the schools' general commitment to providing equal opportunity. The most explicit of these was a nominated school where a section entitled 'The education of boys and girls' went into some detail about the reasons why boys and girls should consider opting for non-traditional subjects and careers. The statement ended with:

> We believe that it will be beneficial to boys and girls to break down these barriers thus giving all our pupils not only the widest possible choice of subject qualifications for their careers, but also a broad background of interests and skills for the full development of leisure activities.

Another stated that 'Girls and boys are encouraged to study all subjects in the curriculum and at no point is choice affected by the sex of a pupil.' The third school wrote that 'There is similarly no discrimination by sex – boys and girls follow exactly the same curriculum and have a free choice of subjects in the Middle school.'

However, a number of the prospectuses showed other positive equal opportunities features. Seventeen schools (ten nominated, seven cluster) pointed out that a rotational craft system, where pupils of both sexes must study subjects not traditional for their sex, operated within the school. In addition one girls' school, from the nominated sample, stated that some technical subjects were offered as part of its philosophy of preparing girls for widening opportunities in jobs. The following are examples of the mixed school statements.

> The courses provided by the Craft department are designed for both girls and boys.

> In the practical subjects all pupils sample every practical subject – boys doing needlework and domestic science and girls metalwork and woodwork – so that they can appreciate that there are no jobs which can be labelled for boys or for girls, and allows them to appreciate the different problems which are involved.

> Students study in mixed-sex groups with girls developing craft skills and boys studying fabrics and food.

> Boys and girls in the first year will do both Technical Subjects and Home Economics as the Equal Opportunities Act prohibits one sex being given subjects which are denied to the other.

It should be noted that in two of the nominated sample schools where such a statement occurred there was evidence of sex stereotyping elsewhere in the prospectus.

In four schools (three nominated, one cluster) pictures in the prospectuses showed boys and girls pursuing activities not traditional for their sex, such as girls in woodwork or boys in cooking. One nominated school used 'Ms' as a title for female teachers. Two nominated girls' schools pointed out the value of science and mathematics for girls and noted that girls could achieve very high results in these subjects. On the other hand, several schools had prospectuses exhibiting 'bad practice' in respect of equal opportunities. Four schools (three nominated, one cluster) gave subject departments in the craft/home area names that *signified one sex only*. These included: 'Boys' practical department', 'Girls' technical studies', 'Boys' technical subjects', 'Boys' craft', 'Girls' craft'. One of these (a nominated one), while noting that a rotational craft system operated, showed elsewhere that needlework for boys in practice stopped after the first year. The needlework room was described as 'Crowded sometimes to overflowing with girls, and first year boys too, busy with their sewing and embroidery.'

One nominated school used the term 'girls' and 'housewifery' in describing the work of the home economics department. A cluster sample school stated that boys and girls were to study separate craft subjects; another that, although rotation occurred in the first two years, pupils were allocated on the grounds of sex to craft in the third year. Another said that a course in food and fabrics was available to girls and one in food only to boys. Another cluster school described 'a flat for teaching girls housecraft' in the school. A nominated school wrote of child development that 'This subject appeals to girls ...' A cluster school restricted a course involving domestic and consumer matters to girls only.

Several schools showed evidence that pastoral and disciplinary matters were dealt with separately for each sex by a teacher of the same sex. Thus one nominated school appointed a senior mistress to deal with girls' discipline and a senior master for boys' discipline. Three nominated and two cluster schools did this.

Three nominated and one cluster school showed boys and girls in pictures on sex-stereotyped lines only (e.g. boys only in metalwork; girls only in typing).

One nominated school stated that corporal punishment was for boys only; a cluster school stated that girls could only be struck on the hands while boys might be struck on the bottom.

One nominated school emphasized that boys must not wear earrings and a cluster school said the same, as well as saying that boys' hair must be short. One cluster school stated that 'Hair should be properly groomed, kept away from the eyes, and for boys the styles should be manly rather than effeminate.'

Other policy documents

A number of schools enclosed with their questionnaire returns documents of various types that related to their policy. Nominated schools did this more than cluster schools and on this measure show greater commitment to equal opportunities. There were several reports of working parties on sexism in individual schools sent to us by nominated schools, but none by cluster schools.

One nominated school sent a copy of an information sheet for staff applying for jobs in the school which contained the statement that all subjects were open to both sexes. Another wrote that the head had recently attended a conference on equal opportunities in schools. One presented evidence about the imbalanced intake of pupils (far more boys than girls) affecting equal opportunities. The main point was that girls were even further discouraged from taking subjects not usually done by their sex, since the ratio of boys to girls was even greater than in an equally-balanced school. It was stated by this school that:

> Since all classes contain more boys than girls, the formers more boisterous approach to life inevitably becomes the accepted norm and psychologically this must reinforce the traditional sexist situation that the Sex Discrimination Act sought to eradicate.

Nine nominated schools produced documents that indicated efforts being made to implement a policy on equal opportunities on an official, school-wide basis. Two of these were case study schools and will be discussed later. One was a document entitled 'Sexism in School' produced by a group of concerned mathematics teachers. This discussed the problem in the school as a whole and made several recommendations, including that attempts should be made to redress the imbalance of staffing, and that staff, particularly male staff, should be more careful in the attitudes they express.

> Discussions between male staff about the attributes of the pin-up on page 3 of the *Sun* in the staffroom should not be tolerated.

As an immediate result of the report, which was discussed at a full staff meeting, women staff were henceforth entitled 'Ms' and tutor set lists were compiled in alphabetical order. Another working party report reviewed the problem nationally before going into detail about the school. Figures for subject take up and career destination were presented and each subject area was discussed individually and recommendations made that related to each. The conclusion noted that while the school as a whole 'is well aware of the problems' there were some members of staff who were indifferent or cynical about the issue.

Another nominated school sent a report written by a teacher with a special interest in the subject who was clearly trying hard to get the policy more accepted in the school. Having reviewed the problem and made suggestions for its alleviation, she argued that a working party on the subject should be set up. Another nominated school sent documents that showed the responsibilities of some individual members of staff in efforts to review curriculum materials. A staff handout entitled 'Sexism' was sent, this arguing the usual case and making recommendations for practice as well as providing a booklist. Another sent a sheet that had been given to staff showing the sex biased nature of option takeup.

Another nominated school summarized a staff forum on 'Sex roles and school'. It went into detail about the national picture and a programme for action included many recommendations for how teachers should treat pupils as well as for school organization.

Three cluster schools wrote to say that since they were single-sex schools it was difficult to see how the subject had anything to do with them. One of these noted that sex roles as a topic of discussion sometimes occurred in the syllabus. One head wrote enthusiastically in support of the project and noted that his own daughter was now a production engineer who had studied technical subjects at the school. One wrote an argumentative letter; a paragraph serves as an example:

> My philosophy is simply – as with most of the situations with which our culture is faced – to open up the issues. We do not pretend therefore to solve the problems of inequality of opportunity. They are solved neither by providing equality of opportunity, nor by beating a drum about it. If girls are convinced that they will not enjoy or succeed in the sciences, or if boys are convinced that housecraft is a 'girls subject' then neither approach produces any significant change in what they choose to do.

Comments on equal opportunities policy

Many schools responded to our questionnaires with comments of a general nature about equal opportunities in the schools. These are useful in gauging whether the respondent was generally sympathetic to the policy or otherwise. In one case, it was noted that 'single women and divorcees form an unofficial pressure group'.

In 28 cases, nominated schools wrote to the effect that all subjects were open to all pupils irrespective of sex. The following are examples of this.

> All pupils are free to choose whatever subjects they wish providing there are viable numbers to support the group. All first-year pupils experience every practical subject in the school. All pupils up to the

second year must take Technical Drawing and to the third year take French. All pupils are forced into taking as part of their choice at 14 at least two subjects related to the Humanities, two Science subjects and one practical subject. Boys occasionally choose Domestic Science and girls Woodwork and Motor Vehicle Engineering.

We do not make a major issue of this. All options are open to both sexes and we ensure that pupils realize this. All school clubs/societies are mixed sex as are all school residential courses – the exception is rugby, soccer, etc. The Design department courses are effective in encouraging some girls to tackle craft and some boys Home Economics – they are however a small number but that is due to interest.

Equal opportunities are assumed by all staff in the planning and operation of the curriculum. Boys and girls have equal access to all subjects within the curriculum and there are no exclusive areas.

All pupils (in the school) are treated the same and the question of determining allocation to groups on the grounds of sex has never arisen.

There is no attempt to promote this objective beyond ensuring that options for senior pupils (for example) are equally available. We do not *then* indicate that girls or boys *should* pursue courses hitherto regarded as the prerogative of one or the other of the two sexes... This change of involvement is allowed to emerge naturally.

We try to give equal opportunities in everything.

One northern school wrote that encouraging such a policy openly would provoke opposition in the local area. One recently-opened school had found it easier to promote the policy where there was no tradition to break with in the school. Another observed that its creation from two single-sex schools had provided wider curricular opportunities for pupils than previously.

One school felt its imbalanced intake (too many of one sex) meant that equal opportunities was made difficult. Two schools observed that they did not exercise positive discrimination, since a need was not felt. Two perhaps saw a conflict between promoting such a policy and catering for 'individual needs':

Whole curriculum is based on individual needs as far as possible... The aims and objectives behind the curriculum were designed to serve people as people.

We treat boys and girls as *people* and do not emphasize the differences by making it a matter of discussions!

Five schools wrote that they felt the policy was important to promote.

Fourteen nominated schools went further in their analysis of the situation than the large group reported above. They observed that all subjects were open for all pupils, but noted that in spite of this there was still a sex-biased pattern of option choice. For example:

No distinction made at all.

In spite of all our efforts there is still polarization into 'girls'' and 'boys'' subjects, especially at 6th form level – especially worrying with physical sciences ... and languages.

All courses are open to either sex but the option choice system still brings out the following.
Physics – the majority are boys
Heavy crafts ⎫
TD   ⎬ rarely any girls
Home economics – rarely any boys

Thirteen of these schools commented on what they thought caused this sex-biased choice pattern, mentioning a wide variety of factors, from 'traditional attitudes' or 'values' or 'sexist prejudice' emanating from parents, pupils or teachers, to pressures external to the school working on pupils.

One school replied to the question about allocating pupils to subjects on the grounds of their sex with 'No. Anyway it's illegal.' Another separated the sexes for some subjects but said that special requests 'would be considered'.

Fifteen of the cluster schools wrote to the effect that all subjects were open to both sexes. The following are examples.

In the lower school the curriculum is the same for all pupils irrespective of sex. In the area of craft all boys and girls do cookery, needlework, art, woodwork, metalwork and technical drawing. In the upper school all courses are open to boys and girls.

Whilst there is no specifically formulated policy to promote equal opportunities there is a concerted attempt, for example, to make all aspects of the curriculum available to both boys and girls, subject to the usual limitations within a secondary school.

The whole approach in this school is completely non-sexist. At no time is there selection for group teaching based on sex. We therefore have mixed groups in Home Economics, Metalwork, Needlework, Art and Woodcraft. Child Care has however always remained an interest of girls only. By choice and not design.

One of these noted that Dance CSE was for girls only, though, and another two of them noted that emphasis on the policy was not strong. A further school noted that while the subject had been discussed in meetings there was 'little emphasis really'.

Seven cluster schools made comments that the policy of equal opportunities was present in the minds of staff. Some examples follow.

> The provision of equal opportunities for boys and girls is an ever present consideration.
>
> We try to be as fair as possible.
>
> The underlying philosophy of the school is such that staff are constantly 'aware' of possible sex discrimination although it is not necessarily discussed overtly.

One school felt that resources problems would arise if 'suddenly any option were taken up by the whole age group'. One school felt 'most strongly' that lack of resources inhibited equal opportunities. Another observed that it did not exercise positive discrimination. Eight schools said that they tried to promote the policy, but that sex bias still occurred in option choices. One found that imbalance in numbers of each sex inhibited the policy, another that a new curricular organization about to be made would encourage equal opportunities. Two of these felt that textbooks were sexist, another that its northern location meant that pupils absorbed strong traditional attitudes at home. One of them observed that pupils' friends as well as parents influenced choice, but that teachers tried not to do so. One noted that local prejudices were equally strong, particularly with regard to craft subjects. One found that pupils did not 'rib' each other over non-traditional choice. Three cluster schools repeated the theme of one of the schools in the nominated sample, to the effect that treating pupils as individuals was a primary aim.

> The question of equal opportunities rarely arises, as at this age we continue to treat our pupils all as children and find little reason to look upon them as boys or girls. [11–14 school]
>
> The question has never arisen as all pupils are treated as pupils.
>
> Opportunities are offered to children as individuals, since we stress the importance of individual development. Within the school, therefore, girls and boys enjoy equal opportunities.

One cluster school reported no staff with special interest in the policy: 'No – too busy teaching.' Another reported that it was not felt to be an important topic. One school wrote that

> We have more important matters to consider. I have no wish to be further engaged/questioned on what I do not regard as a priority in state educational provision which is constantly being whittled away by an unsympathetic/inhuman governmental policy. Please exclude this matter.

One cluster school wrote that

> The exercise of completing this questionnaire has prompted us to consider more closely hidden curriculum of school e.g. assembly pupils, girls before boys? Thank you!

Two nominated schools reported that they attempted to maintain a balance between the sexes in staff appointments. One noted that heads of department were often prejudiced and this was supported by another school which, although it reported the head and deputies being sympathetic to equal opportunities noted that 'middle management [heads of department] are more unpleasant about the situation'. One school with a female head stated that seeing equal numbers of women and men on the staff, and women in positions of authority, helped in promoting equality.

One cluster sample school reported that numbers of staff were balanced between the sexes and that their principal was a woman. Another emphasized that promotion was made on the grounds of ability, not sex.

Single-sex schools

In the cluster sample were 12 boys' schools and ten girls' schools; in the nominated sample were four girls' schools. These schools were sent slightly different questionnaires from mixed schools, and despite a clear note with the questionnaires, some returned the questionnaires imagining them to be sent by mistake. There was a higher level of interest in the policy in girls' schools than boys'. Only one boys' school had discussed equal opportunities in governors' meetings, one in parent–teacher meetings and two in staff committee meetings. None had a member of staff with responsibility for or interest in the issue. Four girls' schools had discussed the topic in governors' meetings, two in parent–teacher meetings and five in staff committee meetings; one reported a member of staff with responsibility for or interest in the issue.

A number of schools commented on equal opportunities issues. For example, one nominated girls' school reported that many traditionally male subjects were taught in the school and that girls helped maintain the school coach. Another aimed to offer technical drawing and design and technology and its sixth form was integrating with the local boys' school. Another felt that raising girls' expectations and broadening their aspirations was an important part of its work.

One girls' school reported having links with other institutions for the teaching of subjects it did not provide. Another found such links impossible due to the distance of other schools. This school reported having a link with an engineering scheme and having had some girls go on to study the subject at university. The school said mathematics and science were popular subjects in the school and that girls had the same subjects offered them as boys, except design and technology.

Equal opportunities practices

Schools were asked in our questionnaire about a number of aspects regarded by the Equal Opportunities Commission as good or bad practices (see Table 5.4). For good practice the picture is mixed. Most schools reported that they operated a rotational craft timetable, the percentage reaching 97 per cent for nominated schools, but very few schools offered courses in women's studies, or compensatory mathematics, science or technical courses for girls or compensatory craft courses for boys. In the tables which follow throughout this

Table 5.4

Question 2f Do the following organizational features occur in your school?

Rotation craft timetable (14–18 schools excluded)

	Yes	No	Total
Nominated	85	3	88
	(97%)	(3%)	(100%)
Cluster	72	14	86
	(84%)	(16%)	(100%)
Total	157	17	174
	(90·5%)	(9·5%)	(100%)

Missing = 2

Course in women's studies

	Yes	No	Total
Nominated	4	91	95
	(4%)	(96%)	(100%)
Cluster	1	92	93
	(1%)	(99%)	(100%)
Total	5	183	188
	(2·6%)	(97·4%)	(100%)

Missing = 11

Table 5.4—contd.

Compensatory science course for girls

	Yes	No	Total
Nominated	1	95	96
	(1%)	(99%)	(100%)
Cluster	1	94	95
	(1%)	(99%)	(100%)
Total	2	189	191
	(1%)	(99%)	(100%)

Missing = 8

Compensatory mathematics course for girls

	Yes	No	Total
Nominated	1	95	96
	(1%)	(99%)	(100%)
Cluster	1	94	95
	(1%)	(99%)	(100%)
Total	2	189	191
	(1%)	(99%)	(100%)

Missing = 8

Compensatory technical course for girls

	Yes	No	Total
Nominated	2	94	96
	(2%)	(98%)	(100%)
Cluster	2	93	95
	(2%)	(98%)	(100%)
Total	4	187	191
	(2%)	(98%)	(100%)

Missing = 8

Compensatory craft course for boys

	Yes	No	Total
Nominated	2	94	96
	(2%)	(98%)	(100%)
Cluster	4	91	95
	(4%)	(96%)	(100%)
Total	6	185	191
	(3%)	(97%)	(100%)

Missing = 8

chapter significant differences between nominated and cluster samples are shown only when they are at the 5 per cent level or less ($p < .05$), i.e. there is a less than 5 per cent probability that the differences arise from chance.

When it came to what the Commission would regard as bad practice, the picture is also mixed, but with one area where the incidence of what would seem an illegal practice is widespread.

A significant number (13 per cent) of schools allocate pupils to subjects on the basis of sex, mainly in the crafts (see Table 5.5). About a third of schools also attempt to balance the number of pupils by sex when allocating them to bands or streams. Pupils are taught in separate sex groups for games and physical education in a majority of schools and for sex education in about 10 per cent of schools, but only a small minority segregate by sex in playground areas.

Table 5.5 Allocation of pupils to subjects on basis of sex

Question 2d Are there any subjects taken by pupils at age 16 or younger where allocation to the subjects is wholly determined by sex?

	None	Craft subjects	Craft and other subjects	Other subjects	Total
Nominated	85	12	1	0	98
	(87%)	(12%)	(1%)		(100%)
Cluster	86	9	2	2	99
	(87%)	(9%)	(2%)	(2%)	(100%)
Total	171	21	3	2	197
	(87%)	(11%)	(1%)	(1%)	(100%)

Missing = 2

Question 2e Are measures taken to ensure that there is a balance in the numbers of each sex when allocating pupils to streams or bands?

	Yes	No	No streams, bands or sets	Total
Nominated	33	51	11	95
	(35%)	(54%)	(12%)	(101%)
Cluster	35	53	7	95
	(37%)	(56%)	(7%)	(100%)
Total	68	104	18	190
	(36%)	(55%)	(9%)	(100%)

Missing = 9

Question 2c Subjects for which pupils at age 16 or younger are taught separately according to sex

Physical education	Yes	No	Sometimes	Total
Nominated	65	13	20	98
	(66%)	(13%)	(20%)	(99%)
Cluster	68	15	14	97
	(70%)	(15·5%)	(14%)	(99·5%)
Total	133	28	34	195
	(68%)	(14%)	(17%)	(99%)

Missing = 4

Option choice

Table 5.5 Allocation of pupils to subjects on basis of sex—*contd.*

Sex education	Yes	No	Sometimes	Total
Nominated	6 (6%)	89 (91%)	3 (3%)	98 (100%)
Cluster	15 (11%)	80 (84%)	0 (2%)	95 (100%)
Total	21	169	3	193

Missing = 6

Games	Yes	No	Sometimes	Total
Nominated	60 (61%)	12 (12%)	26 (26%)	98 (99%)
Cluster	58 (61%)	22 (23%)	15 (16%)	95 (100%)
Total	118 (61%)	34 (17·5%)	41 (21%)	193 (99·5%)

Missing = 6

Note: When 'Yes' and 'Sometimes' are combined, p is less than 0·05 per cent.

Separate playground area for girls

	Yes	No	Total
Nominated	3 (3%)	93 (97%)	96 (100%)
Cluster	7 (7%)	88 (93%)	95 (100%)
Total	10 (5%)	181 (95%)	191 (100%)

Missing = 7   No playgrounds = 1

Separate playground area for boys

	Yes	No	Total
Nominated	2 (2%)	94 (98%)	96 (100%)
Cluster	7 (7%)	88 (93%)	95 (100%)
Total	9 (4·5%)	182 (95·5%)	191 (100%)

Missing = 7   No playgrounds = 1

Class registers list boys and girls in separate groups

	Yes	No	Total
Nominated	90 (95%)	5 (5%)	95 (100%)
Cluster	88 (93%)	9 (7%)	97 (100%)
Total	178 (94%)	14 (6%)	192 (100%)

Missing = 4   Some do, some do not = 3

In most schools pupils were listed by sex on class registers. One school commented that they had found logistical problems in having mixed playgrounds and another that younger girls had asked for separate playgrounds – a request which was 'naturally' granted.

Several schools from each sample noted that separate registers were a necessity for returns to exam boards or local authorities, and one claimed that it was easier for internal administration. Only a few schools appeared to get round these difficulties.

The few schools that said they had compensatory courses provided no further information about these courses. Schools providing a women's studies course wrote that such material was included as part of a broader social science course; many answering 'No' to this question may well have also had this arrangement.

A few schools commented on school uniform. One nominated school reported that uniform would be unisex soon. Another noted that, except for skirts, the uniform was the same for both sexes. One cluster school reported regretfully that parents and the LEA had forced the school to reintroduce uniform. Although there were trousers for girls in the uniform, which the head felt were more practical, the

Table 5.6 Courses taught to pupils at age 16 or below in local technical colleges or further or higher education institutions

Nominated sample (98 schools)

Number of courses per school	Courses where boys usually predominate	Courses where girls usually predominate	Courses where there is usually a balance of the sexes
0	71	87	86
1	11	9	10
2	12	2	2
3	0	–	–
4	2	–	–
5	1	–	–
6	1	–	–
Total courses	54	13	14

Cluster sample (98 schools)

Number of courses per school	Courses where boys usually predominate	Courses where girls usually predominate	Courses where there is usually a balance of the sexes
0	73	80	86
1	13	12	10
2	7	3	1
3	2	3	0
4	2	0	0
5	1	0	0
Total courses	46	27	12

majority of parents wanted their girls to wear skirts.

Schools were asked about link courses with further education institutions. Their responses show that courses traditionally taken by boys are offered more frequently by the colleges (see Table 5.6): in others, note was made of girls studying subjects unusual for their sex.

Courses classified as being where boys predominate:

> Painting and decorating, Building, Construction, Motor vehicle engineering, Technical drawing, Woodwork, Electronics, Engineering, Computer studies (where boys only specified), Home maintenance, Agriculture, Plumbing, Horticulture, Technical studies.

Courses classified as being where girls predominate:

> Child care, Nursing, Typing, Office practice, Commerce, Shorthand, Home management, Parentcraft.

Courses classified as being where a balance usually occurs:

> Bakery and cake decoration, Computer studies, Community care, Sociology, Local industries, General craft/interest for less able, Printing, Industrial photography, Retail trade, Travel and tourism, Business studies.

It is possible to make comparisons with HMI figures from their survey conducted in 1973 on features other than subject take up. The 1973 survey stated that 'Relatively few schools offer craft subjects on a rotating pattern in the first two years' (GB.DES, 1975, p. 7). And the EOC booklet states that 'There are at present only a few schools where both sexes have the opportunity of studying both home economics and crafts such as woodwork or metalwork.' (GB.EOC, 1979, p. 12). This situation was certainly not the case in our survey where 90 per cent of mixed schools claimed to have a rotational craft timetable. Judging from case study visits as well this is a feature of school organization that has changed since the Sex Discrimination Act and partly as a result of its requirements.

The 1973 HMI survey stated that 'Many schools ... divide the sexes, giving different subjects to each ... by the fourth form stage' (GB.DES, 1975, p. 7). Only 13 per cent of mixed schools in our sample reported that they allocated pupils to one or more subjects according to their sex below the age of 16. Incidence of exclusion of one sex from a subject at options stage – either explicitly or implicitly – is probably not much higher than this figure, as is shown in our analysis of options booklets.

A further finding of the 1973 HMI survey was that 27 per cent of schools operated a 'pre-emptive' system at options stage. The example given (GB.DES, 1975, p. 7) was a school where pupils were not allowed to opt for certain craft subjects unless they had studied them previously, but boys in earlier years had pursued different craft subjects to girls. Our figure of 13 per cent for allocation of pupils to subjects on the grounds of sex suggests that the incidence of pre-emption in our sample must be lower. However, such a pattern may operate in a school without being made explicit.

The 1973 HMI report (GB.DES, 1975) found that boys only were offered agriculture, building, engineering design and surveying in the schools (where such courses were taught in a school). Incidence of such explicit exclusion in our sample is very low (see options booklet analysis, Chapter 6).

As in the 1973 report, further education colleges provide far more subjects in areas traditionally taken by boys than they do for girls.

Single-sex schools

In boys' schools, the curriculum contained more subjects compulsory after option choice than mixed schools, two of them making physics compulsory, five a foreign language and two chemistry. None had a women's studies course. In girls' schools more subjects were compulsory than in mixed schools, with six making a foreign language compulsory and one making biology compulsory. Unlike boys' schools, none made physics or chemistry compulsory. None had a women's studies course.

A number of single-sex schools offered joint teaching programmes with other schools for pupils aged below 16 in courses traditionally the preserve of the opposite sex (see Table 5.8), but more further education link courses were in subjects traditionally seen as male than other subjects (see Table 5.7).

Table 5.7 Link courses with local further education colleges

Number of further education courses	Courses where boys usually predominate		Courses where girls usually predominate		Courses where balance is usual	
	Boys' schools	Girls' schools	Boys' schools	Girls' schools	Boys' schools	Girls' schools
0	10	10	12	12	12	12
1	1	2	0	0	0	2
2	1	2	0	2	0	0
Total courses	3	6	0	4	0	2

Option choice

Table 5.8 Joint teaching programmes with schools of opposite sex

Number of joint teaching programmes	Courses where boys usually predominate		Courses where girls usually predominate		Courses where balance usual	
	Boys' schools	Girls' schools	Boys' schools	Girls' schools	Boys' schools	Girls' schools
0	10	9	9	9	10	10
1	2	4	2	4	2	0
2	0	0	1	1	0	4
3	0	0	0	0	0	0
4	0	1	0	0	0	0
Total courses	2	8	4	6	2	8

School background and policy

We examined our questionnaire responses to see if there was any association between variations in features of school organization that might promote equality of opportunity and some background characteristics of the LEA. Cross-tabulations were produced for mixed schools of both cluster and nominated samples. Of the 49 tables generated, four contained insufficient numbers for tests of significance to be valid. Of the rest, the five below shown in Table 5.9 showed association between the variables of a significance at the 0·05 level.

Table 5.9 School organization and background characteristics

Are pupils allocated to any subjects on the grounds of their sex?

	Yes	No	Total
No selective schools in the LEA	86 (94%)	6 (6%)	92 (100%)
Some selective schools in the LEA	85 (81%)	20 (19%)	105 (100%)
Total	171 (87·5%)	26 (12·5%)	197 (100%)

Missing = 2   p = 0·0173

Does a rotational craft system operate?

	Yes	No	Total
No selective schools in the LEA	78 (98%)	2 (2%)	80 (100%)
Selective schools in the LEA	79 (84%)	15 (16%)	94 (100%)
Total	157 (91%)	17 (9%)	174 (100%)

Missing = 2   p = 0·0065

Is there a member or group of staff with interest in or responsibility for the policy?

	Yes	No	Total
Urban	17	59	76
	(22%)	(78%)	(100%)
Rural	10	111	121
	(8%)	(92%)	(100%)
Total	27	170	197
	(15%)	(85%)	(100%)

Missing = 2   p less than 0·01

Is the policy discussed in staff meetings?

	Yes	No	Total
Level of financial provision			
low	76	71	147
	(52%)	(48%)	(100%)
high	30	11	41
	(73%)	(27%)	(100%)
Total	106	82	188
	(62·5%)	(37·5%)	(100%)

Missing = 11   p = 0·023

Member or group of staff with responsibility or interest in the policy?

	Yes	No	Total
Labour control	14	39	53
	(26%)	(74%)	(100%)
Other control	12	120	132
	(9%)	(91%)	(100%)
Total	26	159	185
	(17·5%)	82·5%)	(100%)

Missing = 14   p = 0·0046

They suggest that schools in LEAs with no selective schools, compared with schools in selective LEAs, are more likely to allocate pupils to certain subjects on the grounds of sex (an indicator of bad practice) and are also more likely to have a rotational craft system (an indicator of good practice). Urban districts rather than rural are likely to have a member of staff or group of teachers with responsibility/interest in the policy, as are schools in Labour controlled LEAs rather than schools in LEAs under other political control. A higher level of financial provision in the LEAs is associated with staff discussing the matter in committee meetings. Apart from this, variation in the background variables is not significantly associated with variation in the several indicators of good practice.

76 *Option choice*

Combined indicators of good practice

We produced scores for each school of features which indicate the extent to which they seek to promote equal opportunities as a policy. Two scores were obtained called, for the sake of brevity, 'Good School' and 'Bad School'. These were made up as in Table 5.10.

Table 5.10 Good and bad schools' policy

Good school	Score
No subjects taken by pupils at age 16 or younger where allocation is wholly determined by sex	1
Measures are not taken to ensure a balance of the sexes in streams or bands	1
A rotational craft system operates	1
A course in women's studies operates	1
A member of staff or group of teachers have special interest/responsibility for promoting the policy	1
The policy has been discussed in meetings of:	
Governors	1
Parent–teacher associations	1
Staff	1
Pupils are informed in option booklets that all subjects are open to both sexes	1
Total possible score	9
Bad school	
Pupils at age 16 or younger are allocated to certain subjects on the grounds of their sex	1
Measures are taken to balance the sexes in streams or bands	1
No staff with interest/responsibility in the policy	1
Subject not discussed by:	
Governors	1
Parent–teacher associations	1
Staff meetings	1
Pupils informed in options booklet that technical subjects are for boys, home economics for girls	1
Total possible score	7

When these scores were computed the following distribution of scores for mixed schools was obtained.

School policy

Good school score	Number of schools	Bad school score	Number of schools
0	2	0	9
1	11	1	28
2	41	2	30
3	60	3	49
4	40	4	53
5	26	5	26
6	13	6	4
7	6	7	0
8	0	–	–
9	0	–	–

Total number of schools 199

A high or a low score (4 or above, 3 or below) for both 'Good school' and 'Bad school' was cross-tabulated against a number of variables to see whether there were any significant differences in the backgrounds of these schools. These variables were as follows.

1. Whether from nominated or cluster sample.
2. Whether secondary modern or comprehensive.
3. Age range of school.
4. Size of school roll.
5. Catchment area (item from questionnaire).
6. Urban/rural.
7. Type of political control in LEA.
8. Extent to which selective system operated in LEA.
9. Level of financial provision.
10. Northern, southern or middle location.

None of the cross-tabulations were significant below the 0·05 level except those in Table 5.11.

Table 5.11 Significant cross-tabulations

		Good school Low score	Good school High score	Total
Level of financial provision	(high)	59 (69%)	26 (31%)	85 (100%)
	(low)	95 (83%)	19 (17%)	114 (100%)

Missing = 0 $p = 0·0315$

78 Option choice

Thus we may say that schools with several good practice features are more likely to be found in areas of high rather than low financial provision. Apart from this, none of the background variables are associated with good or bad practice – even the nomination of schools by Chief Education Officers as being good practice schools is not associated with good practice indicators collected on the questionnaire and combined as above.

Relationship of policy to subject take up

Having obtained the figures reported in Chapter 4 on the take up of optional subjects it is possible to see whether there is any association between the extent to which schools stress equal opportunities as a policy and sex bias in subject take up. The sample was broken down according to three factors, whether schools were in the nominated or cluster sample, and a weak and strong version of the 'Good school'/'Bad school' distinction.

First, subjects usually taken more by one sex than the other were examined to see whether take up by the non-traditional sex was significantly different between schools in the nominated or cluster sample. Take up by boys of the following subjects was looked at:

Biology, Human biology, Shorthand, Typing, Commerce, Typing and office practice, Office practice, Accounts, Needlecraft, Child care, Home economics (cookery), Home economics (general), French, German, Spanish, Latin, History, Religious education, Music, Social studies, Sociology, Other English (not remedial).

The take up by girls of the following subjects was examined:

Physics, Chemistry, Physical science, General science, Environmental science, Rural studies/science, Commerce, Technical drawing, Woodwork, Metalwork, Building, Motor vehicle engineering, Engineering, Electronics, Technology, Additional mathematics, Statistics, Computer studies, Geography, Design, Physical education, Geology.

The results show that schools nominated as examples of good practice do not consistently show greater non-traditional subject take up by pupils. Indeed the results are slightly contradictory, in that cluster schools show greater non-traditional take up in some subjects. In nominated schools there is a higher take up by girls for technical drawing, computer studies, design and physical education than in cluster schools ($p < 0.005$). Numbers in building, engineering, electronics and technology are too low for valid tests of significance to be applied. But in the rest of the subjects tested there is no significant difference in take up. On the other hand, girls in cluster schools take rural studies, additional mathematics, geography and geology more than they do in nominated schools (p <0·005) in all cases).

Boys in nominated schools take typing, commerce, German, Latin, classical studies, history and sociology more than in cluster schools. (p <0·005). There were too low numbers in needlecraft for tests to be valid. In all other subjects tested there was no significant difference. But in cluster schools, boys take biology, typing and office practice, home economics (general), French and other English (not remedial) more than they do in nominated schools (p <0·005).

This suggests that the association of nominated/cluster with subject take up varies according to which subject is being examined. There is evidence that the nominated 'good practice' schools are slightly more successful in encouraging girls to take some technical subjects, but it is not possible to say that the nominated 'good practice' schools are more successful than the others in reducing sex bias over the range of subjects.

Next, we compared take up in these subjects between schools that scored moderately on our indicators of good or bad practice. Comparing schools where the 'Good schools' score is more than three with those where 'Bad schools' is more than three reveals that girls in 'Good Schools' take commerce, design, geology (p <0·005) and physical science (p <0·01) more than in 'Bad schools'. Girls in 'Bad schools' are more likely to take general science, technical drawing, woodwork, geography and physical education (p <0·005). Figures for building, engineering, electronics and technology were too low for tests to be valid. All other subjects tested revealed no significant difference.

On the same comparison, boys in 'Good schools' take commerce, French, French studies, social studies (p <0·005) more than they do in 'Bad schools'. Boys in 'Bad schools' take history (p <0·005) more. Figures for shorthand, needlecraft were too low for analysis. All other subject comparisons were not significant, below 0·025.

These comparisons suggest a similar conclusion to that for the nominated/cluster comparisons. There is an indication that the 'Good schools' have more girls studying physical science and most boys studying languages, but again, take up is very variable and neither type of school is consistent over the whole range of subjects in reducing sex bias.

Comparing schools, where 'Good school' is more than five, with those where 'Bad school' is more than four, reveals that girls in 'Good schools' are more likely to take chemistry, physical science, technical drawing (p <0·005) and woodwork (p <0·025). Girls in 'Bad schools' are more likely to take general science (p <0·005). Figures for building, engineering, electronics, technology, design and technology, additional mathematics, geology are too low. All other subjects tested show no significant difference.

On the same comparison boys in 'Good schools' take social studies and sociology more (p <0·005). In 'Bad schools' they take biology, commerce, home economics (cookery), history (p <0·005) and human biology (p <0·025) more. Figures for shorthand, typing and office practice, accounts, needlecraft, classical studies, and other English (not remedial) are too low. All other tests are not significant below 0·025. Here again the trends are contradictory, although the take up by girls is a little more consistent (less sex bias in 'Good schools') than for boys. On the whole these three comparative breakdowns do not suggest a consistent relationship between subject take up and the independent variables involved.

The take up of craft subjects in schools where not rotational craft system operated was then compared with those schools that do have such a system. It should be remembered that schools in non-selective LEAs and nominated schools are more likely to have such a system than other types of school. While we have shown little consistent relationship between nomination as a 'good practice' school and subject take up we have not looked into the relationship between selectiveness and subject take up.

Take up by boys of needlecraft, child care, home economics (cookery) and home economics (general) was examined. Figures for needlecraft are too low for a statistical test to be valid, but it is worth noting that nine boys in schools with a rotational system took the subject, whereas no boy in schools without such a system took the subject. Figures for the other subjects are shown in Table 5.12, with significance levels.

Table 5.12 Take up of various subjects by boys

Child care	Taking	Not taking	
Rotational craft system	22	4177	
No system	1	401	p >0·05
Home economics (cookery)			
Rotational craft system	494	7088	
No system	90	1652	p <0·05
Home economics (general)			
Rotational craft system	65	2585	
No system	0	104	p >0·05

Thus there is a significantly higher take up by boys of home economics (cookery) in schools with a rotational craft system. Figures for the other subjects, while not being statistically significant, suggest that the same trend could emerge if higher numbers were available.

Take up by girls of technical drawing, woodwork, metalwork, motor vehicle engineering, engineering, technology and design and technology were examined (see Table 5.13). Take up in technical drawing and woodwork is significantly higher in schools where a rotational system operates.

Table 5.13 Take up of various subjects by girls

Technical drawing	Taking	Not taking	
Rotational craft system	149	7041	$p < 0.025$
No system	19	1565	
Woodwork			
Rotational craft system	81	6570	$p < 0.005$
No system	2	1195	

Tests for the other subjects produced no significant differences, with numbers for engineering and electronics being too low for tests to be valid.

These results suggest that schools with a rotational craft system are more successful than those without one in achieving take up by the non-traditional sex of some of the craft subjects.

Finally, schools that wrote in their option booklets encouragement or discouragement to the less-usual sex to take certain subjects, were separately analysed. The form that such encouragement took was often a statement emphasizing, say, the value of technical subjects for girls, or a mention of 'both boys and girls' studying a subject usually associated with one sex. Discouragement took the form of implied exclusion of one sex as in 'boys studying metalwork', or, very occasionally, a clear statement saying that a subject was only open to one sex (for more detail on this see the later analysis of option booklets, Chapter 6). Technical subjects were analysed in a slightly different way from the rest because of low numbers. Schools encouraging or discouraging girls to take up any one technical subject were counted in the samples and then numbers studying each technical subject were counted.

Take up by boys of child care and needlework was too low for a test to be valid. For home economics (cookery) there was no significant difference. For home economics (general), while numbers were low, there was a significant difference.

	Taking	Not taking	
Home economics (general)			
Encouraged	14	418	$p < 0.05$
Discouraged	0	133	

Numbers for all technical subjects were too low, except in the case of technical drawing where no significant difference between the two samples for girls' take up was found.

Conclusions

To what extent, then, are schools implementing the letter and spirit of the Act? Chief Education Officers' letters may be regarded as encouraging by the Commission, in that all the letters with comments sought to persuade us that the topic was being taken seriously and accepted as a legitimate concern. In these letters begins the theme that is repeated in later data that parental opposition to the policy is a serious problem.

Written comments on school questionnaires are somewhat similar to Chief Education Officers' comments, in that they often show a desire to persuade us that the policy is taken seriously in the schools.

Again, the Commission may take heart from the fact that these schools are, on the whole, trying to please. The few that express doubt about the policy often do so by arguing that an approach that values individuality in pupils is not in accord with imposing rules about behaviour. Only two schools stated quite categorically that the matter was not felt to be an important one (though the cases of some single-sex schools which wondered what was the relevance of our enquiry for them, should be remembered). Written comments refer to a number of extra-school pressures working to preserve sexist attitudes; these included parents, the job market, the primary school, the peer group. Teachers' views were mentioned twice, and this is noted as a problem in other data occasionally, notably the working party reports that some schools enclosed.

Given that the Commission would like to see all schools stating in their prospectuses a commitment to equal opportunities, it might be viewed as disappointing that only three make this statement. However, there are many more schools that are strongly committed to the policy nevertheless (according to other evidence), so it may be that a number of schools simply do not feel the prospectus to be the relevant place for such points. In fact option booklets are a great deal more likely to contain statements about the policy (see Chapter 7). As with option booklets, however, the content of prospectuses in some schools reflects a history of sex discrimination. The high frequency of statements explaining that a rotational craft system operates reflects the fact that many of the schools will have only recently adopted this arrangement and still need to persuade parents of its value.

The HMI commentary (GB.EOC, 1979) suggests that governors and parent–teacher associations should be kept informed of progress in equal opportunities. A large minority of schools had discussed the subject in such meetings, and over half claimed to have discussed the subject in staff committee meetings. Another recommendation of the commentary is that working parties of teachers might be set up to look into aspects of the schools' provision relevant to equal opportunities, and that a member of staff might be given special responsibility for the policy. Only 13.5 per cent of schools had done this.

Details of school organization reveal that a high proportion of schools teach physical education and games in mixed groups. Most schools teach sex education in mixed groups. The few schools that volunteered the information that some craft subjects were taught in single-sex groups (as distinct from where each sex studies different craft subjects) most frequently did this for home economics. Such a practice allows a different curriculum to be presented to each sex in a subject, but when it occurs at option stage it tends to make the subject more attractive to the non-traditional sex.

Ninety per cent of mixed schools claim to operate a rotational craft system at some stage before option choice. This is a markedly different situation from 1973, when the national HMI survey (GB.DES, 1975) was conducted) and case study visits suggest that these systems occurred as a result of the requirements of the Sex Discrimination Act. However, in many schools this does not operate for all the years before option choice, with either a mini-options scheme, or occasionally allocation according to sex occurring after a year or two. Twelve per cent of mixed schools allocated pupils to craft subjects according to sex at some stage before 16, and this figure is increased to 13 per cent if other subjects (e.g. agriculture, forestry) are included.

The practice of balancing the numbers of each sex in streams or ability bands is unlawful under the Act, yet 36 per cent of schools claim to do so.

The few schools claiming to offer a women's studies course included this as part of a broader course and it is likely that more schools who otherwise answered 'No' did this. Very few had separate playground areas and very few ran any of the compensatory courses suggested as good practice in the HMI commentary (GB.DES, 1975). Most schools kept class registers separately according to sex of pupil and some stated that this was convenient for internal administration or necessary for statistics required by outside bodies. (One case study school had abandoned separate registers as part of its equal opportunities policy.)

There seem to be few significant associations between equal opportunities, policy and other characteristics of schools. Schools in non-selective LEAs when compared with those in wholly or partially selective LEAs were more likely both to allocate pupils on the grounds of sex and to have a rotational craft system. Schools in urban and Labour authorities are more likely to have a member or group of staff with interest or responsibility in the policy. A higher level of financial provision is associated with staff discussing the subject in committee meetings. Schools with a high score on good practice were more frequent in areas of higher financial provision. Being nominated by Chief Education Officers as examples of good practice was not associated with a high good practice score! Whether schools were from the nominated or cluster sample, or whether they scored high or low on good practice indicators were factors not consistently related to significant differences in subject take up. There is some indication that schools with a rotational craft system are more likely to have higher non-traditional take up rates in craft subjects than schools where a rotational system does not operate.

A comparison of figures from the 1973 HMI survey (GB.DES, 1975) with our own (see Chapter 4) suggests that the take up of nine of the more academic subjects has not, in mixed schools, become any less sex biased by 1981. However, since 1973, there have been changes in the craft area to make subjects more accessible to pupils of either sex and it is more rare for mixed schools to exclude pupils from subjects on the grounds of their sex.

The factor that seems to make a major difference to subject take up is single sex schools (see Chapter 4) although our sample of single-sex schools is low and may be confounded by the fact that these schools are also selective schools. Girls' schools were more likely to be interested in promoting the policy than boys' schools, and it is significant that no boys' schools were nominated by Chief Education Officers as good practice schools. Some girls' schools offered traditionally male subjects but the provision of craft subjects in single-sex schools was usually sex biased.

Generally, then, it would seem that there have been changes since 1973 to make the subjects in mixed schools open to both sexes, and this has entailed the major change of introducing a rotational craft timetable in most mixed schools. Home economics for boys and technical drawing for girls are the most popular non-traditional choices in the craft area. There is an indication that efforts made by schools to encourage non-traditional take up in these two subjects pays off. There has been little change over the years in sex biasing of the major academic subjects. While there are a number of schools with a particular interest in promoting the policy of equal opportunities, it is not clear that their efforts make a difference to subject take up.

The overall picture shows that there are some encouraging signs that schools are taking increasing notice of equal opportunities. There are a few examples of schools where the policy is taken most seriously.

On the other hand, there remain a minority of schools that still exclude pupils from subjects on the grounds of sex. Nor have we discovered any evidence that what schools do to promote the policy is consistently associated with differences in sex bias in subject take up (though it must not be imagined that this is the only valid test of the success of a policy).

The scores of 'Good school' and 'Bad school' show that 10 per cent of schools have a third or more of the features on the questionnaire that the Commission would like to see occurring. Fifteen per cent have five or more out of the seven features that the Commission would not like to see occuring. The majority of schools fall in the middle ground with some good practice and some bad practice features. This distribution of the scores supports the general impression from all the data we have collected: a small number of schools are trying hard to encourage equal opportunities; a small number still contain features that break the law; the vast majority (perhaps the middle 75 per cent) seem content with the knowledge that they are conforming with the law and that beyond this events will be allowed to take their (natural?) course.

CHAPTER 6

Option systems

It is sometimes stated in literature on sex differences in education that the way in which subjects are presented to pupils at the start of option choice tends to encourage sex-biased choices. The EOC commentary (GB.EOC, 1979) repeats this opinion: 'While many schools offer an apparent choice, the grouping of subjects ... can discourage pupils from selecting a subject which is non-traditional' (p. 12). This chapter takes the general form firstly of applying some tests of sex bias to all the 130 option schemes we have analysed, and then gives critical analysis of some individual examples of options schemes.

Tests of option schemes

Most schools employ an option choice system for the last two years of compulsory schooling. Typically, pupils select, in addition to compulsory subjects like English, mathematics and physical education, between four and six option subjects, often from pre-grouped 'option blocks'. There may or may not be rules governing the kinds of subject which must be chosen, e.g. at least one science, modern language, etc.

In order to establish the extent to which option schemes encourage or discourage a sex-biased choice we made a list of 30 standard questions to ask of each scheme. To take the first test as an example, which asks 'Is it possible to make a subject choice which includes no science or technical subjects?' it will be appreciated that this is of concern, since girls more than boys avoid these subjects.

Naturally, there are factors which determine subject choice that are not covered by such a system of tests. The sort of advice teachers give to individuals will often mean that certain subject choices, while theoretically possible in the scheme, are in practice precluded. Thus, a lower ability child may be told that physics or chemistry as separate subjects are not available to them, or a boy may be told that he would be wise to think again about his choice of needlework. Nevertheless, the formal options scheme provides the structure around which hidden influences must operate.

It was important to decide which subjects to count under the various headings of 'science', 'technical' and so on. Appendix 45 shows how subjects were categorized for the purposes of the tests. Schools varied in their practices of what they counted under such headings. Thus, one school considered that child development was a science subject. For our tests, this was considered a vocational subject. To check for researcher bias, the tests were first coded by one researcher, then 53 of the 130 schools were recorded by another person. In only ten tests (0·63 per cent of 1,590 recoded tests) the two coders disagreed.

Test results

The first five tests examine the extent to which science and technical subjects, particularly physical science, are compulsory. Clearly, schools which made a science subject compulsory (*Test 2*) would be counteracting the tendency of many girls to avoid all science subjects. A school making a physical science compulsory (*Test 5*) would be counteracting the tendency of girls to opt for biology (*Test 3*) or

Table 6.1 **Compulsory or optional science and technical subjects**

	No	Yes	Some yes, some no	Advised to do a science or technical subject
Test 1				
Can pupils do no science or technical subjects?	71 55%	29 22%	5 4%	25 19%
Test 2				
Can pupils do no science?	61 47%	40 31%	5 4%	24 18·5%
Test 3				
Can no science or technology be taken if biology is taken?	11 8·5%	112 86%	7 5%	–
Test 4				No general science offered
Can no science or technology be taken if general science is taken?	6 5%	80 61.5%	11 8.5%	33 25%
Test 5				
Is one of the physical sciences compulsory?	124 95%	3 2%	3 2%	

general science (*Test 4*) where they are forced to take a science subject. The results are presented in Table 6.1.

The results show that about half the schools made science compulsory for all pupils, but that most schools allowed this to be biology or general science. Nearly a third allowed no science. Of the three schools that made a physical science compulsory for all, two were boys' grammar schools where all boys took physics as well as chemistry. The other one was a mixed comprehensive where all pupils studied single or double science, subjects that included elements of all three sciences.

Test 6 and *Test 7* looked at vocational and technical subjects. A school making a technical subject or a vocational subject compulsory would be counteracting the tendency for girls to avoid the one and boys the other. However only one school made one of these subjects compulsory for all. This was a mixed comprehensive which, as well as making a physical science compulsory for all, insisted that a subject called 'design' be taken. This title covered art, ceramics, drama, fashion and fabrics, housecraft, metalwork, music and woodwork. However, the work was designed around a series of projects which students opted for within the subject; this would have allowed boys to avoid traditionally girls' areas and girls to avoid traditionally boys' areas. The results for these two tests are in Table 6.2.

Table 6.2 Vocational and technical subjects

	No	Yes	Yes for some	None offered
Test 6				
Is one or more vocational subject compulsory?	124	1	1	4
	95%	1%	1%	3%
Test 7				
Is one or more technical subject compulsory?	121	1	2	6
	93%	1%	1.5%	5%

Test 8 and *Test 9* asked whether it is possible for pupils to take only subjects that are traditionally taken by girls (*Test 8*) or boys (*Test 9*), excluding subjects which are part of a common core. In quite a substantial number of schools this was possible, though far more so for girls than for boys (see Table 6.3).

It should be noted, though, that if computer studies is included in our definition of technical subjects and commerce excluded from vocational subjects, the results of *Test 8* and *Test 9* would be more alike.

We next looked at whether the choice of a physical science tends to make it difficult for a pupil to study a subject traditionally studied mostly by girls, such as a modern language or a vocational subject.

Table 6.3 Taking non-traditional subjects

	No	Yes	Yes for some	Yes, but advised against it	No vocational/ technical subjects offered
Test 8 Apart from a common core, is it possible to do only modern languages, vocational subjects and biology?	53 41%	53 41%	6 5%	15 11.5%	3 2%
Test 9 Apart from a common core is it possible to do only physical science and technical subjects	92 71%	16 12%	6 5%	11 8.5%	5 4%

Various levels of strength of the test were achieved by increasing the number of language, vocational or science subjects required, in order for the answer to be 'Yes'. The answers show that most schools allow combinations of the physical sciences with traditionally girls' subjects and so are not encouraging a sex-biased choice (see Table 6.4).

But it seems to be difficult in some schools to pursue two languages as well as the physical sciences, reflecting a pressure towards specialization for more academic pupils. This emphasizes the split between boy scientists and girl linguists and makes it harder for cross over to occur.

Test 12 and *Test 14* examined whether it is easier for pupils to combine traditionally boys' technical subjects with the physical sciences than it was for them to combine modern languages or vocational subjects with the physical sciences (see Table 6.5). The results show that there is not a great deal of difference when technical subjects are substituted for vocational subjects in these tests, so a traditionally boys' combination is no easier than the non-traditional combinations. Again we conclude from this that option schemes are not strongly encouraging sex bias, though it is worth recalling that it is harder to study two languages and two physical sciences, than it is to study two languages and either two vocational subjects or two technical subjects.

If it is possible to combine two technical but not two vocational subjects with physics and chemistry (*Test 16* and *Test 17*) then it is reasonable to say that a traditionally boys' choice is favoured, and girls

Table 6.4 Combination of physical sciences and 'girls' subjects'

	No	Yes	Yes for some	No modern languages offered
Test 10 A modern language, physics and chemistry?	3 2%	108 83%	18 14%	1 1%

				Advice goes against this	No second language offered
Test 11 Two modern languages, physics and chemistry?	14 11%	78 60%	19 15%	1 1%	18 14%

				No vocational subjects offered
Test 13 Physics, chemistry and a vocational subject?	1 1%	107 82%	15 11.5%	7 5%
Test 15 Two vocational subjects and either physics or chemistry?	3 2%	107 82%	13 10%	7 5%

Table 6.5 Combinations of physical sciences and 'boys' subjects'

	No	Yes	Yes for some	No technical subjects offered
Test 12 Physics, chemistry and a technical subject?	1 1%	108 83%	13 10%	8 6%
Test 14 Two technical subjects and either physics or chemistry?	5 4%	106 81.5%	11 8.5%	8 6%

who want to take vocational subjects with physical sciences are discouraged. On these tests, too, the majority of schools are not encouraging sex-biased choice: only three of the 117 schools that offered this range of subjects were favouring boys. Two more schools offered the technical subjects combination to all pupils, but the other combination only to some. Five schools allowed the vocational subjects' combination but not the one involving technical subjects.

Test 18 and *Test 19* are similar to *Test 16* and *Test 17*, except that a modern language is substituted for one of the technical (*Test 18*) or vocational (*Test 19*) subjects. Two schools were unequal in their response to the tests, with one allowing the technical but not vocational subject combination, and the other school allowing precisely the opposite. The vast majority offered both types of combination to pupils, or offered neither. Thus, in most schools it cannot be said that a pupil taking a vocational subject and a modern language (likely to be a girl) is as able through the option system to choose physical sciences as a pupil taking a technical subject and a language (likely to be a boy) with physical sciences.

Test 20 asks whether technical and vocational subjects are arranged in such a way as to make them mutually exclusive. In no schools is this the case for all pupils. But in four schools it is the case for some pupils: these are schools which advise upper ability pupils to take only one subject in the technical or vocational area.

	No	Yes	Yes for some pupils	One or other type of subject not offered
Test 20 It is possible to take one technical subject and one vocational subject?	0 0%	114 88%	4 4%	12 9%

Test 21 and *Test 22* ask whether it is possible to take three technical subjects but not two technical subjects with a vocational subject. Apart from 12 schools that did not offer one or other of this type of subject, no schools did this. Again, then, option schemes are not encouraging sex bias.

Test 21 with *Test 23* asks whether pupils are offered three technical subjects (*Test 21*) or three vocational subjects (*Test 23*). Of the 130 schools 74 made either combination available to all pupils and a further 26 either made neither combination possible or were single-sex schools that offered no technical or no vocational subjects. Twenty-one schools did not make three technical subjects, but did make three vocational subjects available to all or some pupils. Nine favoured three technical subjects, but did not offer three vocational subjects. Thus, on balance it would seem that a large minority of schools are more inclined to allow pupils to concentrate heavily on vocational than technical subjects.

We then examined whether it was possible to take three vocational subjects but not two vocational with one technical subject (*Test 23* and *Test 24*). Such a situation would discourage girls concentrating on vocational subjects from crossing over the traditional subject boundaries. No schools did this, although 11 schools could not be tested because they did not offer any or some of these subjects.

Test 25 and *Test 27* are a stronger version of *Test 21* and *Test 23*, in that a science subject is also included. Thus, they ask whether pupils are offered three technical subjects and a science and also whether they offer three vocational subjects and a science. Nineteen made three vocational but not three technical subjects and a science available to all or some pupils. Nine were the other way round. Again, then, it seems that more schools allow pupils to concentrate on vocational than on technical subjects.

We tested whether it was possible to take three technical subjects and a science subject (*Test 25*) but not two technical subjects, a vocational subject and a science subject (*Test 26*). Apart from twelve that could not be tested due to their not offering some of the subjects, no schools did this, thus showing no evidence of encouragement of sex bias.

Test 29 asks whether it is possible to take two modern languages, a technical subject, physics and chemistry. *Test 30* substitutes a vocational subject for the technical one. We saw earlier that a large minority of schools made it impossible to take two physical science subjects with two languages and we find with these tests that 29 did not offer any or some of the subjects and 23 offered neither combination. Seventy-one offered both combinations to pupils (though in 13 schools it only applied to higher ability pupils). Four offered the technical but not the vocational subject combination, and two offered the reverse. One further school gave advice that went against the combination involving a technical subject but not the one involving a vocational subject. On this evidence, then, there is little unequal treatment between the sexes.

The samples were checked to see if there were any differences in test results between the nominated sample and the cluster sample. There were 65 schools in each sample, with ten cluster sample single-sex schools (five boys' schools and five girls' schools) and two nominated girls' schools. The only differences were in *Tests 8, 23* and *27*. In each of these tests it was less easy to take the specified combination in cluster sample schools (p <0·005 in all cases). Each of these tests concerns vocational subjects, so it may be that cluster sample schools offered fewer of these.

These tests, taken as a whole, do not provide evidence of sex bias in the majority of option schemes, though they do show that some schemes contain features that encourage a biased choice. In single-sex schools, the schemes are biased where they do not offer technical or vocational subjects. Many schools make it hard to take two physical sciences as well as two languages. It could be argued, however, that this constitutes a discouragement to take too many academic subjects. Nevertheless, it does tend to push the more academic pupil into very early specialization. It is also true that it is often harder to concentrate on technical than vocational subjects. However, this is partly a factor of what we have counted as a technical subject (we excluded computer studies) or a vocational subject (we included commerce).

Tests 1 to *9* show that schools are very variable in the extent to which they make science subjects compulsory. The Commission, it will be remembered, regards this as an important aspect of good practice, and such a move is a key one in attempts to lessen sex bias. Significantly, very few schools make a physical science compulsory. Generally what can be said is that most schools do not, through their options schemes, appear to be making it difficult for pupils to cross over the barriers between the sexes, but then neither do they make it difficult for traditional choices to be made.

Option schemes and subject take up

The tests we have reported so far are concerned with formal structural biases in option schemes. We now go one step further in examining these schemes by looking at the relationship between the schemes and the take up by pupils of different subjects. In other words we attempt to relate 'process' to 'output' – to see to what extent variations in subject take up are associated with option scheme structures.

We look first at *Test 2*, which asks whether a science is compulsory in a school. The results are shown in Table 6.6. The figures under 'Boys'/'Girls' refer to the percentage of pupils of each sex who took a subject when it was offered in 1980–1. The figures under 'Schools' refer to the number of schools offering each subject.

If it is hoped that making a science compulsory leads to more girls studying physical sciences, the results are disappointing – even slightly counter-productive. In schools where a science is compulsory the take up of physics and chemistry is not much affected, except that more boys take physics. There is no increase in the take up of the physical sciences by girls, yet there are differences (statistically significant

Option choice

Table 6.6 Compulsory and not compulsory science

Test 2	Percentage taking Boys	Girls	Schools
Physics			
A science not compulsory	50	14·5	17
A science compulsory	55	14·0	28
Chemistry			
A science not compulsory	34	26·0	17
A science compulsory	35	25·0	28
Biology			
A science not compulsory	26	45·5	17
A science compulsory	30	54·5	28
Human biology			
A science not compulsory	8	27·0	10
A science compulsory	6	25·0	12
General science			
A science not compulsory	24	16·0	10
A science compulsory	24	25·0	14

below the 0·005 level) in girls' take up of biology and general science, both of which they take more often in schools where a science is compulsory. The only aspect of non-traditional take up is the significantly higher take up of biology by boys in schools where one science is compulsory ($p < 0.005$).

In schemes identified by *Test 8*, in which it is possible for pupils to make a choice that consists only of traditionally girls' subjects (excluding a common core), we might expect that subject take up figures would be more sex-biased than in schemes where this is not possible (see Table 6.7). We tested this by comparing take up of sciences, languages and technical drawing in the two kinds of school. Our results for *Test 8* show that girls do not opt more for traditionally girls' subjects in schools where this is made easy for them by the option scheme. Indeed, precisely the opposite occurs in the case of biology and human biology, although for home economics figures for girls are significantly higher ($p < 0.005$) in schools where traditional choice is made easy for them. For French and German there are no statistically significant differences for girls' take up. However, in the case of physics, chemistry and technical drawing statistically significant differences were found for the take up of these subjects by girls (technical drawing and chemistry $p < 0.005$; physics $p < 0.025$). So we can say that in schools where traditional choice is made difficult girls are more likely to cross traditional subject barriers. However, it must be noted that take up of these subjects by boys is also higher in these schools, so other factors may be at work.

Table 6.7 Traditional and non-traditional subject take up

Test 8	Percentage taking Boys	Girls	Schools
Physics			
Able to do just traditional girls' subjects (yes)	51	14·0	29
Not able to do just traditional girls' subjects (no)	56	16·0	22
Chemistry			
Yes	33	23·0	29
No	39	27·0	22
Biology			
Yes	26	50·0	29
No	33	54·0	22
Human biology			
Yes	6	21·5	16
No	7	30·0	8
Home economics			
Yes	6	40·0	29
No	4	35·0	23
French			
Yes	22	43·0	29
No	23	42.0	23
German			
Yes	7	14.5	22
No	9	17·0	17
Technical drawing			
Yes	35	1·3	26
No	40	3·5	20

Test 9 looks at schools where a subject combination which includes only subjects traditionally taken by boys is possible (see Table 6.8). We might expect that in these schools more boys would take traditional male subjects. In fact, in the case of physics, chemistry and technical drawing, precisely the opposite is true. On the other hand in schools where a traditionally male choice is made difficult, boys are more likely to take biology ($p < 0.01$), home economics and French ($p < 0.005$ for both).

Overall, the picture that emerges from *Test 8* and *Test 9* is that girls opt in greater numbers for biology and general science rather than the physical sciences when one science is made compulsory. In schools where a traditional choice is made easy it is not clear that more pupils make traditional choices. There is some evidence that schools with

Option choice

Table 6.8 Take up of traditional 'boys' subjects' only

Test 9	Boys	Girls	Schools
Physics			
Schools where it is possible to take only traditional male subjects (yes)	47	18·5	11
Schools where traditional male subjects only is not possible (no)	55	15·0	42
Chemistry			
Yes	33	24·5	11
No	35	25·0	41
Biology			
Yes	25	47·0	11
No	29	52·0	42
Home economics			
Yes	3	38·0	10
No	6	38·0	43
French			
Yes	17	35·0	11
No	24	46·0	42
Technical drawing			
Yes	32	0·7	10
No	39	2·7	39

schemes which make traditional combinations difficult have more pupils taking non-traditional subjects.

We then combined the results of individual tests into a single score, measuring the extent to which the option scheme followed 'good practice'. The score was made up as follows:

+1 If a science or technology is compulsory for all (*Test 1*).
+1 If a science subject is compulsory for all (*Test 2*).
+1 If it is not possible to avoid other science subjects by taking biology (*Test 3*).
+1 If it is not possible to avoid other science subjects by taking general science (*Test 4*).
+1 If one of physics or chemistry is compulsory for all or some pupils (*Test 5*).
+1 If a vocational subject is compulsory for all or some (*Test 6*).
+1 If a technical subject is compulsory for all or some (*Test 7*).
+1 If it is not possible, or pupils are advised against, taking only traditionally girls' subjects (*Test 8*).

+1 If it is not possible, or pupils are advised against, taking only traditionally boys' subjects (*Test 9*).
−1 If a technical subject can be taken with physics and chemistry but not a vocational subject (*Test 12* and *Test 13*).
−1 If two technical subjects can be taken with a physical science subject but not two vocational subjects (*Tests 14* and *Test 15*).
−1 If two technical subjects can be taken with physics and chemistry but not two vocational subjects (*Test 16* and *Test 17*).
−1 If a technical subject can be taken with a modern language, physics and chemistry but not a vocational subject (*Test 18* and *Test 19*).
−1 If a vocational subject can be taken with a modern language, physics and chemistry but not a technical subject (*Test 18* and *Test 19*).
−1 If three technical subjects and a science can be taken but not three vocational subjects and a science (*Test 25* and *Test 27*).
−1 If a technical subject can be taken with two modern languages, physics and chemistry but not a vocational subject (*Test 29* and *Test 30*).
−1 If a vocational subject can be taken with two modern languages, physics and chemistry but not a technical subject (*Test 30* and *Test 29*).

Thus, a maximum score of 9 is possible, and a minimum score of −8 is possible. The distribution of scores was as in Table 6.9.

Table 6.9 Distribution of scores

Score	Number of schools
−2	2
−1	2
0	8
1	14
2	25
3	29
4	38
5	5
6	4
7	1
8	2
Total	130

This score was then related to subject take up. Mixed schools for whom figures were available were divided into two groups: those scoring more than +3 (24 schools) and those with less than +3 (27 schools).

In schools scoring high – that is, schools whose schemes apparently discourage traditionally sex-biased choice – girls are more likely to take physics (p <0·025), chemistry and technical drawing (p <0·005) than in lower-scoring schools (see Table 6.10). However, in these schools boys are also more likely to take these subjects, so the imbalance between the sexes is not necessarily reduced.

Boys in schools where the score is high are more likely to take biology, home economics and German (p <0·005), but this is not the case for human biology or French. Again the pattern in these subjects is the same for the opposite sex.

Table 6.10 Subject take up and high or low score

	Percentage taking Boys	Girls	Schools
Physics			
Low score	50	14·5	27
High score	60	15·5	22
Chemistry			
Low score	34	23·0	27
High score	39	27·0	21
Biology			
Low score	28	52·0	27
High score	35	58·0	22
Human biology			
Low score	6	20·0	15
High score	7	25·0	6
Home economics			
Low score	5	37·0	26
High score	7	40·0	24
French			
Low score	21	43·0	27
High score	20	38·0	24
German			
Low score	7	13·0	19
High score	11·5	19·0	15
Technical drawing			
Low score	34	0·85	25
High score	44	3·3	22

These tests have shown that the effect of option systems on take up is limited. 'Good' schemes are not strongly associated with non-traditional take up, though there are some subjects which seem to be affected to some extent. But the marked differences in subject take up between boys and girls thus cannot be explained solely by the formal rigidities of option schemes.

It is easy to envisage an options scheme that would *force* a non sex biased choice; this would simply involve placing further limitations on which subjects could be taken. Those in which sex bias occurs, such as the physical sciences, biology, languages, would be made compulsory, as would be one or more vocational subject or one or more technical subject. There are some examples in our survey where all three sciences are compulsory for all. Single-sex schools sometimes make a particular science compulsory and many girls' schools make a language compulsory. In the technical and vocational area our only example of a mixed school that made these compulsory in fact offered a choice that allowed sex bias within the area. But in the survey there are two examples of mixed schools that make a non-exam parentcraft course compulsory. In view of the many schools which make all craft subjects compulsory for all pupils in one or more of the pre-option years it could be that post-option compulsion is worth reconsideration.

Institutional influences

Option schemes are not, of course, the only factors in subject choice: they must take their place among a variety of institutional influences, any of which may play a major role in the decisions made by pupils. For example, it is important to know how subjects are presented to pupils in discussions and in publications which often accompany option choice forms. The attitude of subject teachers and the policy of the school is often not explicit in the structure, although each may have considerable influence on choice. Similarly, a pre-option career programme designed to combat job stereotypes may provide a foundation for free choice not available to pupils for whom option advice is compressed into a short period immediately before decisions are made. Again, a full rotational craft scheme may widen the base of experience of pupils, remove the need for 'taster' courses and weaken opposition to non-traditional choice. We were able to examine these influences in more detail in our case study schools.

The user's views

Our pupil interviews were designed to elicit information on the experience of pupils at option time. We asked them to identify the main influences on their choice of subjects, including the source of any inhibition to selection of a preferred choice.

Table 6.11 distinguishes human and systemic influences on option

Table 6.11 Source of inhibition to preferred option choice subjects

School	No problems Boys	No problems Girls	Option form or scheme Boys	Option form or scheme Girls	Parent or teacher Boys	Parent or teacher Girls	Number of respondents Boys	Number of respondents Girls
'Northern Comprehensive'	2	2	–	2	2	1	4	5
'Freelist Comprehensive'	4	2	1	–	1	2	6	4
'Inner City Comprehensive'	3	2	1	2	1	1	5	5
'Daleview Comprehensive'	2	1	1	1	1	1	4	5
'Smallchange Secondary'	3	2	–	1	2	2	5	5
'Midshire Upper School'	3	3	2	1	–	–	5	4
'New View Comprehensive'	4	6	1	–	1	–	5	6
'Northern Modern'	4	3	–	1	1	1	5	4
'Midland Comprehensive'	2	3	2	1	1	1	6	5
'Oldboys Grammar'	5	*	–	*	–	*	5	*
'Suburban Girls Modern'	*	1	*	3	*	1	*	5
'Seatown Girls'	*	–	*	2	*	3	*	6
'Scottish Academy'	1	–	2	2	1	–	4	4
'Scottish Secondary'	1	2	3	2	–	–	4	4
Total	34	27	13	18	11	11	58	61

Notes: 1. Excludes over- and under-subscription.
2. Some pupils noted more than one type of difficulty.
* Not applicable (single-sex schools).
– No response by this sex in this category.

choice. Although we were initially concerned to discover the influence on choice of the arrangement of subject blocks, we learned that a significant influence arose with parents or teachers refusing to allow the selection of one or more subjects (over 40 per cent nominated inhibitions). We were surprised at the high number of pupils who reported obstacles to their choice (49 per cent). Table 6.11 also shows that within these figures, 20 per cent more girls than boys had difficulty, and more girls than boys nominated the form or scheme as the source of inhibition.

Discussions with staff in charge of option schemes elicited an assurance that approximately 95 per cent of pupils are 'accommodated' and no reference was made to any greater difficulty experienced by girls. It is, however, reasonable to assume that many difficulties were not brought to the attention of administrators. Not all schools we visited offered a stated opportunity to discuss difficulties arising from the structure of the option form.

Not all complaints were concerned with equal opportunity. Many involved a desire to study more than the established number of subjects, or a wish to avoid compulsory subjects and/or increase the number of non-examination courses: an irreducible residue of complaints conflicting with academic policy in schools.

Further analysis of the type of complaint reveals that eight complaints by girls concerned a choice between traditional subjects and non-traditional sciences or crafts but only three resulted in a non-traditional choice (see Table 6.12).

Table 6.12 Eight complaints by girls

Source	Result
Option form	Physics and history instead of geology
Option form	German instead of geography
Option form	Art and typing instead of metalwork
Option form	Human biology instead of physics
Teacher preference	Physics instead of chemistry
Teacher preference	Chemistry instead of computer studies
Teacher preference	Refused craft and design technology
Parental preference	Technical drawing instead of Food and nutrition

Five significant complaints by boys all resulted in traditional choices (see Table 6.13).

Table 6.13 Five complaints by boys

Source	Result
Option form	Design and technology instead of needlework
Option form	Technical drawing instead of home economics
Option form	Metalwork/woodwork instead of home economics
Teacher preference	Refused home economics
Teacher preference	Refused home economics

Table 6.14 records the most frequently nominated positive influences on option choice. Our questions included prompts to identify the relative importance of friends, parents, subject and careers teachers; the 'self' column represents those who may have received varying quantities of advice but who believe they decided their choices for themselves.

Differences in the influences on boys and girls clearly emerge (see Table 6.15). For boys, parents were the main influence, followed by subject teachers. Only 17 per cent of boys nominated 'Self' as the main influence. For girls, parents and self were roughly equal influences. The main reason for choice for both boys and girls was career aspiration.

Table 6.15 Influences on boys and girls

	Per cent of responses	
	Boys	Girls
Influence		
Parents	46·6	34·4
Subject teacher	29·3	19·7
Self	17·2	32·8
Reason		
Career aspiration	53·4	42·6

Leaving aside career aspiration for the moment – which is in any case derivative – it is clear that considerably fewer girls than boys benefit from subject discussion with parents and subject teachers; and many more girls than boys make their decisions in isolation. These figures may indicate girls are more independent than boys, or less well catered for by the system. If the figures are viewed in conjunction with indications of an equal interest in career relevant choices we can conclude there is a need for extending or reorganizing guidance facilities to make more impact on girls.

Both Tables 6.11 and 6.14 can provide support for these assertions if

Option systems 103

Table 6.14 What was the main influence on your choice of option subjects?

School	Parents Boys Girls	Other family Boys Girls	Subject teachers Boys Girls	Friends Boys Girls	Self Boys Girls	Career lessons Boys Girls	Career aspirations Boys Girls	Career literature Boys Girls	Respondents Boys Girls
'Northern Comprehensive'	3 –	2 –	2 –	– 1	– –	1 –	4 2	– –	4 5
'Freelist Comprehensive'	– 2	1 –	2 –	– –	5 2	– 2	3 –	– –	6 4
'Inner City Comprehensive'	4 2	– 1	2 1	1 –	2 1	1 –	4 1	– –	5 4
'Daleview Comprehensive'	2 4	1 1	1 1	2 –	1 1	1 3	– 1	2 1	4 5
'Smallchange Secondary'	1 –	– –	– –	– –	1 –	– 2	– –	– –	5 5
'Midshire Upper School'	5 2	2 –	6 2	– 1	1 1	– 1	5 4	2 –	5 4
'New View Comprehensive'	2 1	1 1	1 2	1 –	5 1	5 1	1 2	– –	5 6
'Northern Modern'	5 2	– 1	1 –	– 1	1 –	1 –	2 2	– –	5 4
'Midland Comprehensive'	3 2	– –	– 2	– –	2 –	– 1	4 3	– –	6 5
'Oldboys Grammar'	1 *	* –	– *	– *	– 4	1 *	1 *	– *	5 *
'Suburban Girls' Modern'	* 2	* 1	* 4	* –	* –	* 2	* 1	* 1	* 5
'Seatown Girls'	* 1	* –	* –	* –	* 2	* –	* 3	* –	* 6
'Scottish Academy'	2 –	– –	– –	– –	2 1	– –	– 3	– –	4 4
'Scottish Secondary'	– 2	– –	2 –	– –	– –	– –	4 4	– –	4 4
Total	27 21	5 5	17 12	3 3	20 10	10 11	31 26	5 1	58 61

Key: * Not applicable (single-sex schools).
– No responses by this sex in this category.

Notes: 1. 'Liked it' responses and 'don't know' omitted.
2. Responses include subject influence and overall decision.

we examine responses in individual schools. For example, in 'Midshire Upper School' parent and subject teacher advice (Table 6.14) are clearly important in a middle school system which offers no timetabled careers lessons, but provides subject teacher descriptions to assembled pupils to assist in option choice. In Table 6.14 we see that advice was positive and difficulties arose only with the option system. Similarly, responses in 'Northern Comprehensive' – in an area acknowledged by the careers teacher to be 'the last bastion of [male] chauvinism' – confirm an impression that emphasis is placed throughout on advice for, or relevant to, boys.

Teacher influence

A common feature of option systems is the existence of some form of approval of choices by teaching staff. Each of our case study schools attempts to guide pupils (and parents) in a choice which results in the most acceptable balance of subjects for each child, whether by tailoring the subjects offered to individuals or ability groups, or in general recommendations for sensible combinations of subject. The balance is characteristically between craft/science/humanities, but it often takes the form of individual guidance towards sciences, languages or craft when a boy or girl exhibits a particular aptitude which is recognizably connected with higher education or a particular career.

The influence brought to bear on choice by subject teachers may be supplemented by option administrators who, in all our schools, referred to guidance to pupils to correct unacceptable combinations or choices. We were frequently told that an unusual choice had resulted from a rebellious desire to 'be different', or to stay with friends, or because the teacher and not the subject has exerted an attraction. In some cases guidance may be offered on the basis of information on pupil performance during the pre-option period, but for many subjects it appears to be based on subjective assessment of the pupil and his or her 'educational' needs. In this way, individual teachers and option administrators can have great influence, particularly in schools which provide no timetabled careers lessons. For example, we were told in 'Daleview Comprehensive' that a former option administrator placed barriers in the way of upper ability boys opting for home economics; he was said to be so successful that the teacher had none in her groups until the year after the administrator moved to another school.

In 'Midshire Upper School' the influence of subject teachers is recognized and an attempt has been made to balance the impact. Pupils are able to indicate a preference rating for subjects on the option form, and allocation is automatic in descending order of pupil priority; where over-subscription occurs it is the pupil priority rating and not that of the teachers which decides who will be allocated.

In principle the scheme is a laudable attempt to balance teacher influence. In operation, however, pupils transfer to 'Midshire Upper' from lower schools at option time and have little knowledge of the craft courses in the upper school. Subject teachers provide literature and visit the lower schools; they therefore have the potential for attracting or excluding either boys or girls from their subject in the manner of their presentation. In Chapter 7, it will be seen that strong views on the value of craft subjects to one or other sex are held by the craft staff; and that equally strong views held by the commerce teacher – of the value of the subject to all pupils – has resulted in attracting large numbers of boys. In addition, the preference rating may provide systemic influence towards allocation to traditional choices. A low priority is likely if a non-traditional subject is chosen and may be rewarded with exclusion because traditional career-oriented choices will attract a higher priority rating. It nevertheless remains a useful tool in reducing interference with choice and extending pupil awareness of their commitment to courses.

Linked subjects

The majority of schools we visited operate an option system in which some subjects are linked or mutually exclusive. In most cases this means one choice involves choosing a further complementary subject; for example, metalwork may be linked with technical drawing, or shorthand with typing. Sometimes the linked subject is available only to pupils in upper ability sets in a third subject, for example physics or English. Mutually exclusive subjects usually involve sciences designed to provide different emphasis in similar disciplines; for example, most forms require a choice of either biology or human biology, either physics or materials electrical science. We found these alternative choices to be without sex discriminatory elements, but linking subjects in craft disciplines appears to operate against girls.

In boys' craft subjects, a link between technical drawing and metalwork or technology means that to choose, say, metalwork involves two option choices. Often there is an explicit statement that priority will be given to metalwork option choices accompanied by technical drawing, or the reverse. It is likely that the double option required of what would have been a single non-traditional choice by girls will raise significant barriers to choice. They have either to take a second non-traditional subject and drop one of their other choices, or they will probably be excluded from their non-traditional choice by boys who have chosen both subjects, perhaps for career reasons. For boys choosing traditionally girls' subjects the same problem does not seem to arise. In none of our case study schools were subjects like home economics or needlecraft linked to other subjects.

We compared the position of girls seeking non-traditional subjects with the experience of boys in many cookery classes. If we were to apply conditions to cookery classes like those which apply to metalwork we would find entry restricted to (say) those in the upper ability biology sets. The result would be a much reduced incidence of boys choosing cookery.

'Northern Comprehensive' school provided an extreme example of linkages which offend against equal opportunity principles. Engineering drawing is formally linked with both craft and design and technology options, the latter of which is also open only to pupils in GCE physics sets. Internal tests in each subject are used to allocate pupils to sets and considerable effort is expended in ensuring prediction of examination success. A problem arises with non-traditional craft choices because the school's traditional rotational craft timetable operates in only the first year and so fails to provide an assessable past performance. Thus, girls are offered a taster course on which an assessment is based when they choose craft and design or technology. Boys choosing home economics are allocated to a single-sex CSE class.

The links between physics and technology, and between technology and engineering drawing create barriers to choice of engineering drawing by girls. The assessment period effectively extends to the linked subject, although success or failure is related to another subject. Similarly, the physics pre-condition will exclude more girls than boys from both technology and engineering drawing. The system almost certainly infringes the indirect discrimination provisions of the Sex Discrimination Act.

The inhibition of girls taking technical drawing is particularly important, since of traditionally boys' craft subjects it is the one they are said to enjoy and to be good at, during pre-option craft studies, and in those schools where it is not linked to any other subject. In other schools it is not automatically linked with other subjects and skills involved in technical drawing can be taught in a variety of contexts: there is geometrical and engineering drawing, graphical communication, geometrical and building drawing – to name only some of the courses we have encountered. We therefore conclude that there are no sound educational or structural reasons for exclusively linking technical drawing to metalwork or woodwork.

We believe the links we have encountered are symptomatic of a traditional emphasis preferred by some craft teachers. We appreciate the argument which supports a link between two separately examined subjects with a common theme. It is nevertheless clear that the link provides an unnecessary inhibition to choice by girls of technical drawing; that it is not paralleled with similar treatment of boys; and that it can result in the extension of a requirement for physics, which girls will find difficulty in fulfilling, to a subject for which the requirement was not intended. Schools can eliminate this practice either by removing the link (and thus recognizing the skills in the subjects in place of the relationship with engineering careers), or by providing a variety of technical drawing classes or courses. In both cases this would ensure adequate access to both boys and girls who wish to choose only a bench-based subject, or a combination of subjects without specific engineering connotations. Interestingly, this last point is poignantly demonstrated by 'Northern Modern'. The form in Block 2 (see Figure 6.3, page 118) includes shorthand with an upper English set condition and is linked with the typing option in Block 1; but there is an additional typing option in Block 4 not linked to shorthand or English. The arrangement accommodates the precondition for choosing shorthand without imposing it on pupils who wish to choose only typing.

Ability grouping

In each case study school we were aware of the enhanced equality of opportunity available to upper ability pupils. Characteristically, pupils in lower ability groups had fewer options within the system and were less flexible in their attitude and job opportunities. These conditions were presented as more or less natural states requiring development of syllabuses and techniques of education rather than as an equal opportunities issue. The majority of schools respond by 'setting' in most subjects, with practical craft and science options for those for whom rigorous academic syllabuses are inappropriate. In this way it is believed the full range of ability is catered for. In some schools, such as 'Scottish Academy', the whole option system is different for lower ability pupils.

In our view the special courses created for the lower ability groups result in reinforcement of stereotypical self image among pupils who have most need of encouragement to widen their view of traditional roles. In particular, we believe the creation of 'para-scientific' courses for lower ability pupils represents a missed opportunity to extend to this group the range of experience available to other pupils. In addition, the subject matter of para-science courses – for example, electronics or human and social biology – is likely to influence take up by boys and girls by directly subscribing to traditional views of male and female roles.

The majority of schools in our postal survey provide a general science option – usually for the lower ability pupils – and some provide a biological and physical science option for the lower ability group, in some cases in addition to a general science course.

Table 6.16 shows the pattern of take up in three case study schools where these three options are available (in addition to standard physics, chemistry and biology courses). In the general or integrated science options, take up is more balanced than in the others. By contrast, in 'Northern Modern' which does not have a general science option, take up follows stereotyped lines.

The differences between 'Scottish Academy' and 'Daleview Comprehensive' in take up of rural science in part reflects the attraction of integrated science in the former.

'New View Comprehensive' takes a different view of science courses, with its large compulsory core curriculum. Where most schools ensure pupils choose at least one science – for the lower ability this often means a para-science subject – this school has a curriculum with science studies as its focus. Pupils are assessed before allocation to an upper ability 40 per cent and lower ability 60 per cent group for examination purposes. The upper ability group follows a recommended programme of integrated science, including elements of physics, biology and chemistry, or – for the less able within the group – one physical science and biology. The lower ability group is offered Mode III Nuffield Science programmes among which an element of pupil choice is allowed. The programmes are:

Combined science, 33 per cent each of physics, chemistry and biology; or
Applied biology, 40 per cent each biology and chemistry, 20 per cent physics; or
Materials science, 40 per cent each physics and chemistry, 20 per cent biology.

All science programmes were developed with a philosophical view that all pupils shall study at least one physical and biological science until they are 16. The upper ability dual and integrated science programmes contained roughly equal numbers of boys and girls, but a pronounced imbalance is evident in applied biology which comprises 75 per cent girls, and materials science which comprises 75 per cent boys. In contrast, combined science is said to contain a roughly equal number of boys and girls. It is acknowledged within the department that the imbalance requires a change of emphasis and the school is thinking of increasing the biology content of materials science. This change will benefit boys more than girls unless it attracts the latter, in which case applied biology will become obsolete.

A second suggestion, which we ourselves would favour, is an extension of the philosophy applied to upper ability group. We were offered no educational explanation for the choice between subjects with a

Table 6.16 Pattern of take up in four case study schools

	Boys	Girls
'Daleview Comprehensive'		
General science	29	17
Rural science	58	48
Human and social biology	11	19
'Northern Comprehensive'		
Human biology	1	10
General science	4	3
Electrical studies	7	–
'Scottish Academy'		
Human biology	7	23
Integrated science	30	20
Rural science	16	–
'Northern Modern'		
Health education	3	33
Engineering science	23	1

biological and physical emphasis for the lower ability groups and we note the attractiveness of the combined science programme to both sexes. The school could dispense with applied biology and materials science while adopting the single science examination system thought appropriate for the upper ability group. In this way the opportunity for boys and girls to adopt traditional choices will be removed while retaining the ability to be examined in a science subject most suited to an aptitude. That one respondent suggested choice had been introduced for the lower ability groups to reduce discipline problems is an indication of the potency of this consideration when devising schemes for equal opportunity.

This system is also an attempt to overcome general avoidance of physical sciences. While we are bound to say that we feel the system can be improved, we acknowledge the success achieved in introducing all girls to some physical science, all boys to some biological science, and approximately 40 per cent of girls to a rigorous physical science programme. It is notable that a compulsory core has not resulted in disaffection or failure of girls in science and it is useful to stress to other schools that discipline problems can be avoided in programmes which introduce compulsory sciences to all pupils.

Rotational Craft Timetables (RCTs)

Rotational craft schemes are considered here as part of the option process because they are intended to influence option choice by introducing a full range of craft experience to all pupils. This purpose appears to be unfulfilled by the majority of schemes we encountered because the schemes are opposed by teaching staff, said to be inchoate, or rendered ineffective by discontinuity in teaching. Evidence of the opposition of craft staff is presented in Chapter 7; here we consider the coherence and timing of the schemes in relation to option choice.

In our case study schools we encountered a variety of schemes. Our survey returns had not prepared us for the liberal translation of the term; and the purest form of RCT – compulsory rotation through all craft subjects for all pupils during the ages 11–13 – was not the most common. In one school metalwork was absent from the programme, in some others jewellery classes are substituted; a number of schools provide single-sex classes; still more restrict the programme to one or two years; in two cases a narrowing choice scheme operated after the first year, allowing traditional patterns to emerge before option choice; in two schools boys and girls were channelled into traditional craft subjects after the first year; and we had several reports of schools removing or intending to remove textile/needlework from the compulsory core because boys 'switched off' from the subject by the second year.

We also encountered a variety of approaches to treatment of non-traditional choice at option time mainly, it seemed, because the rotational craft timetable had failed adequately to prepare all pupils for their choices. For example, one metalwork head of department insisted that the lower school RCT failed utterly to prepare girls for the workshop environment and nature of an engineering course; home economics teachers often, but not always, complained mildly that boys lacked the experience and ability of girls, in some cases citing unfamiliarity with equipment, or recipe interpretation as a difficulty. Differences of this type tended to be used to support an argument for 'taster' courses and single-sex classes in traditionally male and female craft subjects respectively.

Opposition to RCTs relied mainly on a loss of time argument – the idea that the rotational craft scheme represented a loss of time in which the pupils could be raised to a competent standard in examinable syllabuses. This was argued in 'Midshire Upper School' – where the pre-option syllabus is the responsibility of the lower school – and in the two northern schools, 'Northern Comprehensive' and 'Northern Modern'. It was implicit in all schools, insofar as craft staff often ascribed differences between the ability of boys and girls to influence in the home, which their programmes presumably were not designed to contradict or neutralize.

The loss of time to each subject is undeniable, but was not always resented. In the strongest expressions of hostility we were told that the pre-option syllabuses were irrelevant to GCE O-level courses and therefore a waste of time, resented for the pressure they placed on the post-option staff. These arguments are consistent with a generally hostile approach to non-traditional choice, but they are also recognized by teaching staff who promote equal opportunity, and we were impressed by the use of the discontinuity argument by both those who opposed and those who promoted equal opportunity.

A further problem arises from abbreviated RCT schemes. In schools with one or two year RCTs, the abbreviated programme is uniformly followed by allocation to traditionally male or female craft subjects in subsequent pre-option years. This is variously explained as resulting from preference for allocation of resources to the upper ability group or as a result of nature or nurture. It is notable that headmasters in the two northern schools with one year RCTs acknowledged opposition from their craft colleagues when the scheme had been discussed prior to implementation; the impression we gained was that the abbreviated programmes represented a major achievement. Such programmes are, therefore, a token gesture to the law, based on a compromise between the provisions of the 1975 Act and the preference of craft staff or the philosophy of education for specific life roles.

If we reject the principle of using education to condition pupils to limit their aspirations to traditional roles we must also reject RCTs, which only nominally assist in making decisions at option time. We may speculate further that abbreviated schemes, by reverting later to separation of the sexes, are encouraging a belief that compliance with the law is in some way unnatural: the subsequent years are increasingly useful to option choice, may be seen as 'normal' and experience sharply contrasts with the first year.

Narrowing choice schemes, however, can impose non-traditional choice in the way they group subjects for study in subsequent years; for example by offering a first choice between metalwork and woodwork and a second choice between needlework and cookery. They have an advantage by allowing a fuller coverage of individual syllabuses as a result of reducing the number of subjects studied during the pre-option period.

The use of 'taster' courses and single-sex classes implies that the RCT syllabus has failed to fulfil its purpose. This failure may arise from inadequate attention to the less experienced pupils in pre-option classes, an absence of pre-option technical facilities, or with discontinuity of the syllabus, for example from pre-option jewellery making to post-option engineering courses. Where the preference of lower school craft teachers is for a course containing appreciation of modern materials – such as plastics – in an artistic environment, a post-option engineering orientated metalwork course will attract primarily those pupils – usually boys – whose extra curricular experience has familiarized them with the subject. This reasoning is supported by pupil interviews with two girls who enjoyed metalwork and emphasized the influence of experience gained in assisting brothers or father with car or motorcycle maintenance; another rejected motor vehicle engineering when she found it contained theoretical work; and a fourth chose motorcycle maintenance because it would be an unusual choice for a girl.

The problem is intransigent when upper and lower schools have different teaching staff with opposing philosophies – as in 'Midshire Upper School'. In an 11/12–18 school it is possible to integrate pre- and post-option syllabuses. This does not always happen. It requires a will on the part of craft staff, many of whom are opposed to non-traditional choice. Altering the pre-option syllabus may involve difficulties associated with introducing heavy machinery and other dangers of a workshop environment, or it may be that machinery designed for adults is simply inappropriate for pupils below the age of 14. But these considerations appear to influence only some of our sample schools. If safety considerations impede such a change, the alternative may be the introduction of a design and technology option which employs workshop experience as a practical accompaniment to a design and problem-solving course.

Our case study schools have provided examples of such courses and several features recommend them to us. Firstly, the reduction in emphasis on workshop skills allows a five-year integrated course to be developed with minimum increase in safety problems; secondly, the reduction in workshop experience dispenses with the problem of inadequate specialist equipment; thirdly, teachers of design and technology options have consistently acknowledged the value and attractiveness of their subject to girls; fourthly, these teachers have consistently demonstrated a desire to attract girls to the subject; and, finally, in an era when working lives are less likely than before to demand skills associated with heavy machinery it may appear wilfully anachronistic when schools allow a few local engineering firms to dominate their approach to the curriculum.

We have concentrated on metalwork, but all pre-option subjects could be integrated with examination options. If boys are generally less experienced than girls in cookery it is because their extra-curricular activity is less cookery orientated; adequate educational practice consists in recognizing and acting on this condition before option choice: it suggests pre-option action to raise the experience base, not automatic allocation of boys to post-option CSE classes in passive recognition of the inadequacy. And this approach applies equally to needlework and woodwork.

Amendment of pre- and post-option syllabuses plays a large part in the changes which some teachers feel are a pre-requisite for implementation of equal opportunity and an increase in non-traditional choice. The case for change in post-option syllabuses is strengthened if the skills and not the subject of a course become the principal teaching point. Cookery syllabuses designed to prepare girls for housewifery and motherhood, metalwork syllabuses designed to prepare boys for engineering apprenticeships, needlework syllabuses which emphasize dressmaking and babyclothes, and technical drawing syllabuses which supplement the content of engineering syllabuses have no place in a curriculum which proposes to offer equality of opportunity to boys and girls. A change in the approach to school organization which will increase the usefulness of RCTs implies revision of the syllabus; an important consideration in that revision must be eradication of the stranglehold non-educational influences at present at work on some subjects.

Option forms

The arrangement of subjects on an option form may appear of small importance in relation to the host of influences operating at option time. Determined and able pupils can often circumvent an arrangement of subjects which precludes their choice by convincing staff to use their discretion. We have encountered cases where this has happened. There is, however, a great variety of option forms and schemes, each of which reflects the emphasis a school places on educational priorities and freedom of choice. They often prescribe impossible or suggest desirable combinations of subjects, which will influence choice; and we have collected material which suggests the influence is not always apparent to option scheme administrators or teachers. We have, therefore, examined in detail the variety of forms from our case study schools to identify the elements of a system which will offer least inhibition to non-traditional choice while fulfilling educational requirements.

No school we visited had an option form offering an entirely free choice. The majority grouped subjects in blocks from which a maximum and/or minimum number of choices were to be made, often within a framework of linked or mutually exclusive subjects. Some schools required reserve choices to assist in allocation in cases of over-subscription; a few employed a preference rating system for each subject. Career aspiration was mentioned as a factor to be considered on some forms, while three schools tailored their forms to individual pupils by offering only those subjects in which teachers had given approval. Some schools distinguished between the options available to upper and lower ability groups. One school provided an opportunity on the form for pupils to outline the difficulties created by the subject blocks; two other schools had an expressed policy of preferring non-traditional choice in cases of over-subscription.

The rationale for grouping subjects was varied. Ten schools provided blocks of subjects arranged in the main to reflect simply the proposed timetable. This usually meant that the subjects in each column bore no particular relationship to each other, as in Fig. 6.1. In three of the schools the arrangement was in part derived from a mock choice exercise which indicated demand for combinations: in others it was an extension of past experience.

One of the four remaining schools offered a single list of subjects but little choice, while three, including a girls' school, provided a choice from subjects grouped in disciplines. Pupils were asked to choose a minimum number of sciences, humanity and craft subjects, each of which appeared only once in the relevant block. In these cases the timetable subsequently was arranged to accommodate combinations chosen by pupils, either by constructing it following pupil choice or by using the discipline blocks as the framework for construction. All these schools claimed a better than 90 per cent accommodation of first choices and it appears the approach to option form construction depends on the weighting each school gives to the three main constraints: available resources, educational priorities and amount of free choice.

It appears to us that option forms arranged to reflect setting and timetabling arrangements place an unnecessary restriction on the number of possible combinations available to pupils. In particular, this requires the option form to reflect anticipated combinations of subject: combinations which are based on past expressions of pupil preference and current staff appreciation of what constitutes an educationally acceptable choice: not actual pupil choices. In addition, the arrangement of subjects may be influenced by the preference of individual teachers hostile to non-traditional choice or it may rigidly control choice because of resource problems.

Fig. 6.1 shows a form used in 'Daleview Comprehensive' school. The school is 25 per cent over-subscribed, and copes with its shortage of specialist accommodation by, for example, holding physics theory lessons in ordinary classrooms. This complicates the timetable and restricts option choice. Those subjects which are popular and believed to be educationally important are offered in sets for different ability groups and appear in several blocks. A pupil must not only decide which subjects to choose, but also the level at which he or she is acceptable. However, lower ability groups are not offered an oppor-

Fig. 6.1 Options: Choose one subject in each column by *underlining* it

T	U	V	W	X	Y	Z
F(16+)	P(GCE)	F(GCE)	C(GCE)	RS(GCE/CSE)	TC(16+)	WW(GCE)
B(GCE)	P(GCE/CSE)	F(16+)	C(CSE)	Games	MW(GCE)	MW(GCE)
B(CSE)	H(GCE)	F(CSE)	B(GCE)		NW(GCE)	NW(CSE)
RS(GCE)	H(CSE)	HSB(CSE)	B(CSE)		H(GCE)	HE(16+)
RS(CSE)	G(CSE)	RE(GCE/CSE)	A(16+)		HE(16+)	A(16+)
A(16+)	RS(CSE)	CS(GCE/CSE)	E(GCE)		WW(GCE)	G(16+)
G(CSE)	F(non exam/CSE)	Mu(GCE/CSE)	Games		A(16+)	J(GCE/CSE)
C(GCE)	A(16+)	Sc(CSE)			P(GCE/CSE)	
C(CSE)		Geol(GCE)			D(GCE)	
			Games	MW(CSE)	Games	H(CSE)
			MW(CSE)	WW(CSE)	A(16+)	G(CSE)
			WW(CSE)	HE(16+)	CV(non-exam)	
			NW(CSE)	HM(CSE)		
			HE(CSE)	CC(non-exam)		

Key:
A = Art B = Biology C = Chemistry CC = Child care CS = Computer studies CV = Civics D = Design E = Economics F = French
G = Geography Geol = Geology H = History HE = Home economics HM = Home management HSB = Human and social biology
J = German Lit = English literature Mu = Music MW = Metalwork NW = Needlework P = Physics RS = Rural science Sc = General
science TC = Technical communication (drawing) WW = Woodwork. *Compulsory*: Mathematics, English Language, English Literature,
Careers, Religious Education, Games

Notes:

1. It is expected that pupils in 3PH, 3MS, 3RN, 3TWJ, 3DW, 3CF will choose their subjects from the upper half of groups W, X, Y, Z and 3JBa, 3CN and 3JAd, from the lower half of groups W, X, Y, Z. (This is to assist in the timetabling and maximum use of all our limited facilities.)
2. It is expected that most pupils will choose *at least one* craft or Art.
3. Each subject is a two-year course and, therefore, changes will not be possible during the fourth or fifth years. NB: Proven ability and willingness for hard work are obvious requisites of examination courses.
4. No subject may be chosen twice but games *MUST* be chosen once.
5. If P or H in Group Y is chosen, games must be taken in X.
6. If J or G in Group Z is chosen, games must be taken in X.

Pupil: _____ Form: _____ Parent's Signature: _____

Option systems 115

tunity to choose a combination of biology and chemistry, nor may they choose human and social biology with science, because they are grouped together. Column 'U' clearly anticipates a division between physics and lower ability French selections, while column 'V' distinguishes between upper ability French groups, lower ability science groups, and those with a geological or musical interest.

These constraints on choice do not exhaust the examples provided by the form, but they indicate conclusively that option choices are limited and the school retains considerable control over pupil selections. The form is complicated because of this. In fact the form may be presented as we show in Fig. 6.2; the permutations resolve into six choices of 25 subjects plus games. If this form was used, restrictions to avoid over-subscription could include a maximum and/or minimum number of selections in each column and the choices might be numbered to avoid problems in cases of over-subscription. The school could build setting into the selections after they have been made; the timetable will follow. The major drawback for the school would be loss of control over pupil choice; the major gain for pupils is an opportunity to combine a greater variety of subjects and absence of influence to traditional choices.

The arrangement of subjects on the form used by this school presents fewer than average examples of traditional preconceptions. In 'Inner City Comprehensive' a school with a determined equal opportunity programme, a similarly constructed form results in, for example, a choice between biology, food and nutrition and design and technology. In 'Northern Modern' it is impossible to choose in combination chemistry/French, metalwork/needlework, physics/home economics or biology and engineering science; Figure 6.3 shows the option blocks. It is unsurprising that the craft staff in this school opposed the introduction of a Rotational Craft Timetable and are hostile to non-traditional choice.

The remaining three schools used forms containing subjects listed in discipline groups; as in Figure 6.4. It importantly avoids the implied subject hierarchy in forms which place the columns in a sequence, science/humanities/craft/other, reading from left to right. The school providing Figure 6.4 ('Midshire Upper' School) had designed the form to remove, as far as possible, the influence of staff in allocation to over-subscribed subjects: it employs preference rating, reserve choice and career aspiration elements to distinguish between pupils.

These forms are simple to understand, apply generally accepted educational principles without otherwise influencing choice (with one exception, see 'Alternative considerations', below), and are said to present no difficulties in setting or timetabling. Figure 6.4 was applied in a school with a claimed shortage of resources and competition for

Fig. 6.2 Alternative choices

1–3	1–3	1–3
Science	*Humanity*	*Craft*
Biology	French	Art
Rural science	Geography	Games
Chemistry	History	Technical communications (drawing)
Physicals	Religious education	Metalwork
Human and social biology	Music	Needlework
Computer studies	Geology	Home economics
General science	Economics	Design
	German	Child care
	Civics	Home management
		Woodwork

Notes:
1. Selections could be numbered in order of preference.
2. Under-subscription may be used to revoke courses and conserve resources.
3. We would prefer to omit human and social biology and general science.
4. Certain combinations may be prohibited, e.g. technical communication (drawing) and design.
5. The choice involves 6 of 25 subjects, plus games.

118   *Option choice*

Fig. 6.3   Choice of option blocks

Please indicate your child's choice of option subjects by putting figure 1 by your child's first choice subject and figure 2 by your child's second choice subject *in each block*.

Block 1
Motor vehicle Engineering	E
French	E
Typing	E
Geography	E
Chemistry	E
Basic Craft	NE
Geometrical and Building drawing	E

Block 2
Geometrical and Engineering drawing	E
Shorthand	E
Geography	E
Engineering science	E
Biology	E
Home maintenance	E
Sociology	E

Block 3
Metalwork	E
Needlework	E
History	E
Health education	E
Pottery	E
Commerce	E
Home maintenance	E

Block 4
Woodwork	E
Art and design	E
Home economics	E
Science	NE
Physics	E
Typing	E
Creative embroidery	E

Notes and restrictions:
E   indicates examination available.
NE indicates no examination available.

Girls choosing Shorthand in Block 2 MUST choose Typing in Block 1 but girls not choosing Shorthand can choose Typing in Block 1. Girls choosing Shorthand should be in English Sets 1 and 2.
Boys can only choose two from Motor Vehicle Engineering, Basic Craft, Geometrical and Building Drawing, Geometrical and Engineering Drawing, Metalwork, Woodwork, Home Maintenance.
Pupils cannot choose both Physics and Engineering Science.
Pupils cannot choose both Health Education and Biology.

Figure 6.4 Choice of discipline groups

COMPULSORY SUBJECTS					
ENGLISH			RELIGIOUS EDUCATION		
MATHEMATICS			P.E. / GAMES		

OPTIONAL SUBJECTS

SECTION A **P** (at least ONE subject)			SECTION B **P** (at least ONE subject – not more than THREE)			SECTION C **P** (at least ONE subject – not more than THREE)		
FRENCH			ART			BIOLOGY		
GERMAN			MUSIC			CHEMISTRY		
LATIN			DOMESTIC SCIENCE			PHYSICS		
HISTORY (20th. Century)			ROADCRAFT			RURAL SCIENCE		
HISTORY (Social and Economic)			TYPING			COMBINED SCIENCE		
GEOGRAPHY			POTTERY			ENVIRONMENTAL SCIENCE		
COMMERCE			METALWORK			GEOLOGY		
HUMANITIES			NEEDLEWORK					
			ENGINEERING DRAWING					
* Choices 1 to 7 must be listed in column marked **P**			PHYSICAL EDUCATION					
			WOODWORK					

Computer Studies will be offered to selected pupils. If you wish your son/daughter to be considered please ✓ the box below and indicate which of the optional subjects Computer Studies should replace.

1. If your son/daughter has a career in mind please state what it is.

The reverse of this form may be used by parents who wish to add information.

places necessitating frequent use of the preference systems. With the exception of the problems of the preference rating system mentioned earlier they are neutral; with the computer programmes now available it is possible to reduce the time-consuming task of setting and timetabling. Other systems suggest that most teachers either prefer to exercise more control of the curriculum than is necessary for the operation of an option system, or that they prefer to continue with the system they know best.

Alternative considerations

A minority of schools had introduced elements designed to overcome some problems created by the arrangement of subjects on their forms. 'Inner City Comprehensive' provided an opportunity for pupils to discuss difficulties such as two subjects they would like to choose in one column. This school and 'Northern Modern' operated mock choice exercises to assist in creating subject arrangements most likely to satisfy demands; the latter provided an additional period in the core curriculum so that a free choice which omitted a discipline could be appropriately 'topped up'. We have given examples of schools which discriminate in favour of non-traditional choices when a subject is over-subscribed; others consciously attempt to allow the widest possible choice in arrangements otherwise dominated by timetabling considerations; and one school (more, *de facto*) formally allowed pupils to re-select if they performed badly in a subject.

This hotchpotch of 'props' to faulty systems – some of which conflict with the practice of equal opportunity – are effective criticism; but forms may also be accompanied by restrictive practices such as special request systems, option guidance talks discouraging non-traditional choice, or a juxtaposition of subjects which influences choice. Schools with option schemes which require teacher approval of option choices are clearly vulnerable to teacher prejudice against non-traditional choice. In 'Smallchange Secondary', for example, we discovered that non-traditional craft subjects were never approved for boys although girls had been approved for metalwork and woodwork. In this school, a two-year Rotational Craft Timetable ensures pupils have some experience of all subjects, so the exclusion of boys from needlework and Food and nutrition is based on teacher preference. In some degree the approval system operated to reinforce traditional choice throughout the curriculum. These systems permit gross sexism in option systems. They are more properly described as satisfying staff choice of pupil than pupil choice of subject. We have ample evidence of steps taken by schools to pre-empt pupil choice and our case studies revealed many examples of teachers whose preference is to exclude non-traditional choice from the option form. Teacher approval systems can contradict the principle of rotational craft timetables and option schemes unless the approval system is restricted only to setting: subject approval schemes imply overt control of the curriculum as much as the legitimate control of the level of study.

Excluding two single-sex schools in which no non-traditional subjects were offered we discovered only one of twelve schools in which the take up of physical sciences by girls indicated successful practice. 'New View Comprehensive' with its core curriculum, controls all humanity and science examination subjects and has a less prescriptive recommendation system for art, craft and music. It has an above average complement of girls in various levels of physical science programmes. The sophisticated programmes on offer should not divert attention from the absence of a recognizable option system and a teacher approval scheme which controls the level and not the subjects to be studied. Syllabuses for the programmes were designed to expose all pupils to a physical and biological science examination study. This educational philosophy has resulted in all pupils studying non-traditional science subjects in some measure and an amelioration of the impact of teacher approval systems as they exist in other schools in the survey.

The system fails at the point where it introduces measures of choice; its success lies in not providing an option system. We have already noted criticisms of the lower ability science programmes, but the school also influences subject choice where it is available. Craft subjects are offered unequally to upper and lower ability groups, which provides a choice to the former of traditionally male and female craft subjects grouped separately. Design and technology subjects are linked with technical drawing – which absorbs both choices for the lower ability group; and astonishingly a paragraph of recommendation on craft subjects does not use the term design and technology, emphasizing instead the traditional woodwork and metalwork, and later referring to woodwork and engineering!

These successes and failures reflect the educational priorities in the school. Craft subjects enjoy a lower status than other disciplines and are last in the consideration of timetables (craft rooms are empty for 20 per cent of the week while pupils study other subjects). Similarly, concentration on science and humanity programmes results in craft programmes timetabled against each other on the form. It should be noted that the school operates a Rotational Craft Timetable in the first year; this provides a basis for recommendations. In our discussions with craft staff we encountered no hostility to non-traditional choice: the reverse was more apparent. But the school is relying heavily on external influences to provide incentive to crossover (parents, peer group, career aspiration, etc.); these are notoriously traditional influences.

Conclusions

This chapter has examined option systems in two ways. Firstly, it looked at the combinations of subjects that the systems permitted or prevented in 130 schools from our survey using simple tests.

Some systems appear to encourage sex bias more than others according to our tests, since there are differences between schools when overall scores are calculated. However, influential features are not strong, and the marked differences in subject take up between girls and boys cannot be explained solely by the formal rigidities of option schemes. It is true that most of them allow a sex-biased choice to be made; they do not, on the whole, positively force such a choice.

If option systems were to be used to engineer non-traditional choice it could easily be done by introducing limitations on subject choice. In many schools, such limitations already operate to an extent.

Secondly, we looked at the influences within our case study schools and their option systems, which may affect pupils' choices of subject. Our examination began with consideration of the potential for power and influence in the hands of individual teachers and option administrators. Our respondents had demonstrated a willingness to apply subjective criteria – deciding between 'sensible' and 'unacceptable' combinations. We cited an option form which had been designed to curb teacher influence and offer a freer choice to pupils. The main features of this arrangement were priority rating of the choices, a reserve choice and space for entering a career aspiration. While the features have drawbacks, they considerably reduce opportunity for staff to intrude their judgement in allocation.

Our second consideration was the linked course element of some forms. These appear to be discriminatory in principle – and perhaps in law – by applying conditions which girls more than boys might find difficult or onerous to fulfil.

Our third consideration was the creation of para-scientific courses for lower ability pupils. Many of our case study schools provide para-scientific subjects with distinct physical or biological emphases for the lower ability groups. These syllabuses aim to introduce pupils to the subject within a more practical context than is possible with major science options. The twin major considerations underlying the syllabuses are a desire to ensure all pupils follow a science course to examination level and to avoid indiscipline which arises when lower ability pupils are compelled to study courses in which they see no significance. We have presented a case for introducing integrated science syllabuses for lower ability groups. It appears to us that the indiscipline feared by science teachers is insufficient grounds for subscribing to the stereotypical self-image influencing pupils at option time. In our view the creation of separate biological and physical science options for the lower ability group facilitates and encourages stereotypical choice among pupils who have most need of assistance to widen their perspective. Using 'New View Comprehensive' school as our benchmark we concluded that a satisfactory programme would introduce all pupils to all science disciplines and culminate in individual science examinations at appropriate levels. The fourth consideration was related to the apparent failure of Rotational Craft Timetables to alter the patterns of traditional choice. Our examination showed that it is the practice rather than the theory of RCTs which has failed; they are

Option systems   123

not implemented in a manner consistent with achieving their aim. We concluded that many RCTs fail adequately to raise the experience base of boys and girls, thus perpetuating the argument for 'taster' courses; that omission of suitable metalwork facilities in a RCT disadvantages girls more than boys; and that either the RCT or examination syllabuses are in need of revision if the RCT is to fulfil realistic requirements. We suggested the principles should include at a high priority level: preparation of all pupils for all examination options; compensatory instruction for those with inadequate home-based experience (e.g. boys/cookery, needlework; girls/metalwork, woodwork); and a means of testing to ensure all pupils are adequately prepared for a rational choice at option time.

Finally, we considered the role of the option form arrangement in influencing choice at option time. We examined the major kinds of arrangements and identified those arranged to reflect timetabling considerations as most likely to restrict choice and encourage traditional choice. In the examples of schools providing subject lists grouped in disciplines we found the timetable either reflected the arrangement of disciplines or was constructed after choices had been made. We also noted that multi-disciplinary column arrangements could be confusing; we illustrated this point by reconstructing one such form as a discipline list.

We concluded that the instructions on multi-disciplinary column forms were often designed to overcome some of the drawbacks of the arrangement, while discipline list forms were inclined to add restrictions to choice. We rejected the use of teacher approval systems where forms are tailored to individuals, mainly because they involve control of subjects and therefore intrude teacher preference into the system. We also noted the one school with a compulsory science and humanity curriculum, remarking that it provided the one example of achieving EOC aims.

We concluded that the kind of form used by 'Midshire Upper School' was less likely to influence choice than forms in all other case study schools, that 'neutrality' is the only satisfactory method by which option schemes are compatible with 'good' combinations of subjects. The only alternative to a neutral form appears to be imposition of a large core curriculum or, less satisfactorily, teacher assessment in a school in which the staff are committed to equal opportunity programmes; both of which arrangements conflict with the concept of option choice.

A 'neutral' form eliminates many faults associated with multi-disciplinary option blocks. There is no need for pupils to juggle the column from which they choose a subject; or to choose solely because that choice is the least disliked in the column; no encouragement to choose stereotypically. Teachers do not need to predict preferred combinations, which must be made available; timetables are constructed after choice. If the choices are numbered in order of preference, allocation to over-subscribed classes becomes free of staff influence and teachers are made aware of pupil commitment to each subject. These advantages apply equally in schools with positive equal opportunity programmes and those where staff believe they offer neutrality at present.

We heard a variety of explanations for not following a programme of equal opportunity, many of which may be subsumed under the heading of inadequate resources. In our case study experience we have found that schools overcome all these problems when other educational policy is in danger of disruption.

As a result of our analysis, we can summarize the features of a good practice option scheme as follows.

1. Option forms to list subjects once only in no more than three groups, containing related subjects, e.g. sciences, humanities, practical subjects. Pupils would select a minimum number of subjects from each group; and a maximum figure could be set if required.
2. Pupils should identify choices in their preference order.
3. Timetables should be constructed *after* option choice. In the event of over-subscription, pupil preference would be used as the basis for allocation, not teacher preference or approval.
4. Different needs of children of different abilities should be catered to by setting.
5. There are no exclusively linked subjects.
6. Integrated/combined science options are offered rather than 'para-scientific' subjects with physical science or biology emphases.
7. A full range three-year rotational craft scheme should precede option choice.
8. Career advice before option choice (see also Chapter 7).
9. RCT topic content should be related to compensating for inadequate experiential base.
10. Pre- and post-option syllabuses should be integrated.

These features are present in our case study schools, though none has all of them. The fact that they are operated successfully in some schools shows that although this is a list of ideals it is not a list of impossibilities.

CHAPTER 7

Organization and teaching of subjects

In this chapter we examine the way in which subjects are presented to pupils, with particular regard to things that schools and teachers do that either encourage or discourage equal opportunities.

The overall picture

We can get an overall picture of the way schools formally present subjects to pupils from option booklets. We examined 127 options booklets from the postal survey to see whether they were sex-biased. These booklets are normally given to pupils in their third year so that they might be guided in their choice of options. Their usual pattern is to include some advice about how to choose subjects (e.g. do not choose a subject just because you like the teacher; preserve a balance between arts, science and practical subjects). They may contain a section describing the subjects required for certain careers. Most then describe the courses offered. It is in these *subject descriptions* that the majority of sex-biasing occurs.

Table 7.1 shows the incidence of statements implying or countering sex bias. Only 11 per cent of schools stated that *all* subjects were open to both sexes (and in two schools this statement was not backed up by the rest of the booklet). However, a large number of schools (57 per cent) made it clear that certain subjects could be studied by both sexes. Sometimes this amounted to a sentence or paragraph stating this explicitly about one or more subjects; at other times it amounted to the use of 'his or her' or 'boys and girls' when describing pupils on the course. Table 7.2 shows that technical and home economics subjects attract the greatest number of such statements (23 per cent and 28 per cent of schools respectively.)

On the other hand, 26 per cent of schools at least once in their booklets assumed or required one sex only to study a subject. Again

126 *Option choice*

Table 7.1 Sex bias and counter sex bias in the sample as a whole

	Nominated	Cluster	Total
Statement that all subjects are open to both sexes	6 (8%)	5 (9%)	11 (9%)
Statement as above yet elsewhere it is assumed/decreed that one or more subjects are taken by one sex only	1 (1%)	1 (2%)	2 (2%)
One or more statements or assumptions that subject(s) open to both sexes	41 (57%)	32 (58%)	73 (57%)
One or more statements or assumptions that subject(s) open to one sex only	18 (25%)	15 (27%)	33 (26%)
No statements implying any subjects are single sex, none stating any subject is open to both sexes	26 (36%)	19 (35%)	45 (35%)
One or more subjects stated or assumed open to both, yet one or more others stated or assumed for one sex only	12 (22%)	12 (22%)	24 (19%)
Total number of schools	72 (100%)	55 (100%)	127 (100%)

Table 7.2 Sex bias and counter sex bias in schools by subject area

	Nominated	Cluster	Total
Assumed or stated for one sex only			
Commercial	0	1	1
Technical	6 (8%)	7 (13%)	13 (10%)
Home economics[1]	12 (17%)	11 (20%)	23 (18%)
Physical education	3	0	3
Science	0	1	1
Technical and home economics	2	0	2
Implied or stated for both sexes			
Commercial	5 (7%)	2 (4%)	7 (6%)
Technical	11 (9%)	18 (33%)	29 (23%)
Home economics	20 (16%)	15 (27%)	35 (28%)
Physical education	4 (3%)	0	4 (3%)
Science[2]	3 (2%)	5	8 (6%)
Design	3	0	3

Notes: Percentages are of the total number of schools in each sample (as in Table 7.1).

1. Can involve a boys-only course.
2. Takes the form of encouraging girls into physical science or boys into biology.

this occurred largely in technical and home economics subjects (see Table 7.2).

About one third of the schools produced option booklets that neither assumed nor countered sex bias. It should be said that a number of schools achieved this by offering no or few subject descriptions.

Some confusion within schools is evident from the observation that 19 per cent of schools encouraged or assumed open choice in some subjects but displayed sex bias in others. In some cases this occurred in different courses in the same subject. For example, one home economics course might be concerned with cooking, laundry work and sewing and considered appropriate for girls only; another might involve more theoretical aspects of nutrition and be considered appropriate for boys wishing to enter the catering trade as well as girls. In one or two instances confusion occurred within a description of a single course, as where a course entitled 'cook and host(ess)' later used 'cook and hostess'.

Our evidence shows little difference between the two samples. If anything, the cluster sample has a slightly higher number of statements that subjects are open to both sexes.

Sciences

Table 7.2 has shown that in their option booklets very few schools make attempts to encourage choice that counters sex bias. Only three nominated schools and five cluster schools produced booklets which implied or stated that science subjects were for both sexes. In two schools, statements from the science department encouraged girls to take physical sciences. One of these took the form of a full-page document of encouragement and persuasion, the other gave the following statement:

TWO SPECIAL POINTS ABOUT SCIENCE
a. Girls are as good as boys at Chemistry and Physics.
b. ...

Only five statements of encouragement occurred under specific sciences. However, one school, drawing pupils from two single-sex feeder schools, offered CSE chemistry and CSE physics to boys only, O-level to both sexes, physics with chemistry to girls only. Three descriptions used 'his' or 'himself' to describe pupils.

Some subject descriptions indicate that some science subjects are less demanding. Human biology, which tends to be taken largely by girls, was described by one school as a good science for those disliking physics and chemistry; another included some child care in the course. General science tends to be for low ability pupils, and one school suggested that its general science course needed less mathematical ability than other science courses. Another offered girls separate topic choice from boys in general science.

Computer studies is not a subject as heavily biased in numbers of boys as are technical subjects. However, a few descriptions find it necessary to mention that girls should not be put off the subject (Table 7.3) and one school assumed that boys only would be studying the subject.

Table 7.3 Sex bias and counter sex bias in computer studies and statistics

		Girls encouraged	Boys assumed	Nothing either way	Total
Computer studies	N	1	1	38	40
	C	2	0	24	26
Statistics	N	0	0	7	7
	C	0	0	2	2
Total		3	1	71	75

In written comments on questionnaires several schools recorded special efforts aimed to attract girls to physical sciences. Three nominated schools reported having made particular efforts in the science area and one felt that it had had appreciable success in encouraging girls to take physical sciences. One of the three had a science teacher with special responsibility for equal opportunities who showed a tape-slide sequence on the subject to pupils. One school had found that local employers had been unwilling to accept its integrated science course and had therefore taught the three sciences separately. In order that girls should not opt for biology and neglect physics and chemistry, biology was not taught until the sixth form. There had been resistance to this at first but it had died down. However, it was noted that 'I do not think girls are as happy as the boys with these courses which I believe reflects the nature of such courses.'

In the cluster sample, one school offered a double science option (Schools Council Integrated Science Project (SCISP)) course and a single option environmental science course, both of which 'place importance on the social aspects of science as well as its principles' but few girls opted for the SCISP course. One school found it was necessary to persuade girls not to 'serve' boys in science lessons by writing things down while the boys conducted experiments. One sent a woman physicist to feeder high schools 'to remind girls that physics is not just for boys'. One school noted that girls attain less highly than boys in mathematics but are the same in science.

Several nominated schools had produced working party reports on sex bias in science. One school argued that teachers should try to persuade pupils to make non-traditional choices. Emphasizing the career restrictions of a sex-biased choice was suggested. The introduction of SCISP as an integrated high level science course would solve the sex-bias problem, noted the working party, but there were other problems in introducing such a course, namely that local employers and other educational institutions did not respect the qualification. The working party report of another school had been initiated largely by the mathematics department, and contained criticism of sexist material in mathematics syllabuses. A letter contained the information that in one school the HMI report on girls and science (GB.DES, 1980a) had been discussed by the science department in a meeting called specifically for that purpose. A single-sex girls' school's newsletter for parents emphasized the value of science qualifications for girls and gave examples of past leavers who had entered scientific careers.

Case study schools

The pattern of organization and teaching of science subjects in our case study schools in England reveals that during the pre-option period all pupils follow (in upper schools, have followed) a general science course provided in coeducational groups. In the majority of cases the programme takes the form of separate lessons in the biological and physical sciences, an integrated or general science programme, or a progression from general to individual subjects; no method is significantly related to take up of subjects at option time. In upper schools where transfer took place at age 12 or 13 the abbreviated programmes are designed to prepare pupils for option choice decisions and in one case ('New View Comprehensive') the period is used specifically to evaluate aptitude before recommending science options.

Two of the case studies provide examples of alternative organization. 'Daleview Comprehensive' introduces streaming in year 3 until which time all pupils study a common curriculum containing an introduction to physics, chemistry and biology as distinct subjects. In year 3 the upper ability 60 per cent continue this curriculum, but the lower 40 per cent choose from rural studies, human and social biology or general science. Teachers, however, confirmed our impression that the system still, in fact, offers an opportunity for the lower ability groups to follow traditional patterns: for example, human and social biology contains mainly girls and general science mainly boys. This pattern contrasts with the option choices of the upper ability group, but is continued for the lower ability group after option choice.

In contrast, the organization of science teaching in 'Inner City

Comprehensive' is designed to counteract stereotypical choices within an option system. The syllabus has been developed with a deliberate intention of appealing equally to boys and girls. In year 3 a general science course for all gives way to three compulsory and five optional sub-divisions. In the first half of the first term all pupils study units entitled: reproduction, disease, contraception. For the rest of the year pupils choose an option from units entitled: cosmetics, photography, forensic science, electronics, or fathers and mothers. Each unit is designed consciously to appeal to boys and girls, and teachers reinforce this approach with a pre-option departmental programme utilizing film strip sequences showing women in responsible positions in laboratories and scientific careers. The staff are aware of a small measure of success demonstrated in the take up of the cosmetics option by boys, but they pointed out that the programme is experimental and as yet is more successful in identifying than making an impact on stereotypical influences.

After option choice, science subjects were seen as an essential aspect of a well-balanced curriculum in all our case study schools and only in two cases were pupils with low motivation allowed to omit some form of science from their choice. Effectively, the schools made a science compulsory at option time, either by instructing pupils to choose a science – or a subject from each option block, one of which contained only science subjects – or by exerting considerable pressure during counselling.

The great majority of science teaching staff we spoke with were opposed to the introduction of a science to the core curriculum. Their main concern was the avoidance of discipline problems and they frequently referred to the need to take account of the relevance of each science to the aspirations and interests of individual pupils. These considerations played a part in course development and in attitudes to equal opportunities; they were thought to be particularly pertinent for the less-able pupil allocated to CSE or non-examination studies; GCE-level pupils were thought to be less stereotyped when they chose their subjects.

The general impact of this philosophy is that the majority of case study schools make little or no attempt to encourage non-traditional take up of the sciences. They are aware of the bias in physics and biology, but demonstrate little concern for its impact on career choices. Although all expressed no objection to a girl or boy wishing to cross over, unless ability precluded the choice, they defended inaction with a distinction between those pupils who needed a science for their career – GCE pupils – and those who did not. One extreme of this approach was voiced by a teacher who said parents and employers were extremely traditional in outlook and he did not see the point of attracting girls into science unless they expressed a particular interest.

In some schools, the distinction between pupils who 'need' and do not 'need' science is coupled with a concern for motivation and discipline; courses for the lower ability groups cater deliberately to observed preferences so that the science offerings as a whole may appear relevant to both sexes. Thus, in 'New View Comprehensive' the lower ability group is recommended a selection from materials science with a physics bias, applied biology, or a combined science; in 'Northern Modern', engineering science or health education are offered; and in 'Inner City Comprehensive' human biology and engineering science are offered.

At the higher ability level, sciences were also classified hierarchically. Teachers viewed physics, chemistry and biology, in that order and as distinct subjects, as career relevant at GCE level. Physics is regarded as suitable for studying engineering subjects and a majority of respondents think of physics as a basis for an engineering career – a 'hard' subject with a mathematical basis; while biology is seen as a 'soft' option based on observational skills appealing to girls; chemistry is seen as a useful conjunction either straddling the two or being between the extremes. The science subjects offered to lower ability pupils are seen as less career relevant and as subjects individually less important. The effect is to allow pupils to choose stereotypical subjects which reinforce traditional self-images and achieve only fewer discipline problems.

Apart from 'para-science' options, the schools offer mainly CSE alternatives from the individual sciences to lower ability pupils, with traditional patterns of take up. A number said they had made across-the-board attempts to encourage boys and girls to see the relevance of a non-traditional science, but in view of the emphasis on discipline problems with lower ability groups and a general belief that the upper ability groups chose sensibly with careers in mind, it appears that the majority of teachers do little more than offer a bare description of their subject and make vague reference to career relevance: an impression strengthened by (mainly male) teachers' difficulty in describing to us the range of career opportunities associated with any science subject.

A major example of procedural change was found in 'Inner City Comprehensive'. Although attempts to persuade lower ability girls to adopt physics were said to have failed, there had been encouraging signs of increased take up of biology by boys. Human biology equally had begun to attract boys following an initiative which developed links with sport. Girls, however, were said to choose 'soft' option subjects because they had low self image and aspirations which persisted despite the pre-option career interview.

'Inner City Comprehensive' also suggested that science could be adopted into the core curriculum without increasing discipline problems. It was suggested that a general course taken to CSE level might be accompanied by a core science option for non-specialists and a choice of a physical science for those intending to progress in a related career or higher education. The main thrust of the suggestion – that there should be a change in the syllabuses – finds favour with a number of our respondents as a means of removing the opportunity to choose stereotypically. One interviewee specifically mentioned that an attempt to encourage non-traditional take up became necessary only because the sciences were offered in distinct subjects. (We ourselves do not see the value of separating the sciences at this level.)

'New View Comprehensive' already includes combined science in the core curriculum. All pupils are offered recommended science subjects based on their performance and aptitude during the pre-option period. The upper ability 40 per cent are channelled into an integrated science programme or offered a double science with a bias towards biology; in effect, they are not offered a choice; the 60 per cent lower ability choose between materials science or applied biology or combined science, which results in traditional patterns of choice with combined science containing a small majority of boys. In the other groups there is said to be nearly equal numbers of boys and girls in each category.

A footnote to this unusual organization of the curriculum must be reference to the outcome of the changes. Although the pupils are equally exposed to an integrated programme there is a markedly traditional progression of able pupils through GCE A-level studies to careers. Boys progress to agriculture and horticulture; girls to paramedical and nursing careers. It seems that ensuring that all pupils experience a foundation in all sciences – and the integrated courses were created after discussions with local employers – is not enough in itself to alter the post-school direction of boys and girls.

In one other school we were told of an attempt to encourage take up of the sciences by the upper ability groups, which resulted in an increased take up of physical sciences by girls. In 'Freelist Comprehensive' between 1976 and 1979 able pupils were encouraged to opt for two sciences and the most able 25 per cent to opt for physics and chemistry. This had resulted in a leap from 10 per cent to 27 per cent of upper ability girls taking physical science examinations. However, a second result was a fall in the number of biology candidates and it was felt the imbalance should be remedied. The school now places less emphasis on encouragement, and girls have reverted to the biology option.

When it comes to classroom practice, our respondents felt that physics is more difficult for girls than boys, but few of them offered any alternative method of teaching or extra assistance to compensate. We were told that girls find the mathematical content difficult and that they lack the practical appreciation gained by boys during childhood years when mechanical toys help form aptitudes. The experimental nature of physics was often cited as an inhibition, because few girls feel comfortable with apparatus. One teacher felt that it was easy to forget the presence of girls when they formed only a small minority in the classroom.

Those who do make an effort to accommodate girls in lessons are most likely to offer them encouragement to persevere. The entirely male science staff in 'Daleview Comprehensive' believe that teacher association is an important influence at option time and in later interest. They pay special attention to the progress of girls – especially in physics – and had noticed an encouraging increase in the take up of the subject. 'New View Comprehensive' expressed a belief that different teaching methods and encouragement were unproven as a means of improving take up and performance by girls, and they prefer to rely on teacher expectation and standard teaching methods to raise all pupils' expectations of themselves.

In a number of schools the distinction between upper and lower ability courses was offered as an excuse for inaction. It was believed that pupils of either sex able to follow GCE courses were clear on what they would choose and progress equally well in the long run. By contrast, it was felt that non-traditional take up on the lower level courses reflected poor reasons for choice; some teachers are dismissive and mildly hostile. We heard examples of boys choosing human biology 'simply because they thought it was about women's bodies', girls choosing a physical science were there 'to be with the boys', and 'frivolous' was an often used word to describe the choice. In this there is the seed of attitude to classroom practice; and fewer girls than boys achieve, perhaps attempt, cross-over. Observations on the reaction of boys and girls to science proceeded from the assumption that boys would endure the difficulties of a physical science course because it is career relevant, while girls would not, that is, there is no career relevance for girls in a physical science. With rare exceptions these views appeared to condition the approach to minority groups in the science classroom in all our case study schools.

One example of initiative arises with a single-sex physics class in 'Northern Comprehensive' school. The head of department has devised systems of assessment at option time to predict which courses will be most suited to each pupil. His concern with predictability has led to the formation of the single-sex class because he has found it improves the relationship between girls' predicted success and examination results. It is a CSE class conducted by a female teacher and represents the only example we found in our case studies of a successful attempt to alter the classroom experience to improve take up of a subject and performance of the pupils. Boys were not considered to require encouragement in biology and no reference was made to the side effect of this move: enforced single-sex classes for boys.

Our respondent in 'New View Comprehensive' tackled the problem by ensuring that girls do not drop out of physics until the mock exams, when they discover they are capable and overcome their disability. He felt that this overcomes their initial lack of confidence and he said he had achieved a negligible drop out rate, whereas his previous school had lost many of its girls when the subject was discovered to be difficult.

'Scottish Secondary' school offers one notable example of poor practice. Few pupils study separate sciences after option choice; most follow a general science course and a large number study no science at all. The head of science would prefer to see more girls opting for physics and he has stressed the value of the subject when talking to pupils, but the option blocks – which oppose secretarial studies and physics/chemistry, and technical subjects and biology – guide pupils away from non-traditional choices. He has raised the matter with the staff committee managing the option system but has made no impact.

In 'Scottish Academy' the science staff pay particular attention to minorities in the classroom, which is translated as avoiding asking questions of minorities which they could not answer – it is an attempt to spare them embarrassment. Minorities tend to sit together and it is said that girls are better motivated at this age and are less likely to interfere with boys than boys are with girls. One method of overcoming problems of isolation for minorities, particularly boys in biology, has been to employ 'topping up' procedures where nominal attempts at balancing take place (nominal because there are insufficient boys actually to balance numbers). This is felt to be the major area of interest and the school would like to see positive encouragement of boys to take biology, particularly by improving career guidance and option advice.

Single-sex schools

'Seatown Girls' school appeared to expend all its energy on design and technology courses. All discussions of equal opportunities – and it has fought for equal provision of facilities with a corresponding boys' school – are centred on design and technology. The school is short of laboratory space, although it provides a compulsory science option; and the main plank of initiative in increasing take up is aimed at the lower ability groups who, it is hoped, will gain interest in physical science by learning of the links with their design and technology experience lower down the school.

The science department has an enviable record. Although biology absorbs nearly twice as many choices as physics and chemistry together, 50 per cent of girls are studying a physical science; a further 10 per cent are studying three sciences on a timetable designed to provide space for two.

'Suburban Girls' Modern' school had been provided with a new set of science laboratories within the last few years as a result of LEA attempts to equalize provision for single-sex schools within the borough. The science teacher had introduced chemistry and physics GCE O-level studies when she joined the school in the previous year, until which time only biology was available above CSE level. She was attempting to establish the subjects and encourage take up although she was aware that girls have less mathematical understanding than boys. She attributed this problem to family expectations, but believes it is on the wane and has had an encouraging response to her initiative both from pupils and parents. She introduces the sciences as separate subjects in the second year. Each is allotted a double period each week, which she believes to be adequate to provide sufficient laboratory experience. She did not feel girls were afraid of experiments, but is aware that in a single-sex school the expectations of girls may be higher and the models of achievement are mainly female. She has no special plans to encourage take up of the physical sciences except a general introduction of the subjects in the context of career and educational futures. Biology is seen as an undemanding alternative which nevertheless provides an opportunity for all girls to study at least one science.

'Oldboys Grammar' school effectively offers no options. Pupils are advised not to choose biology with physics and are encouraged to relate their curriculum to specific career goals. Parental influence was said heavily to weight choice in favour of the physical sciences, but this is an irrelevance when speaking of the figures for take up (65 per cent biology, 76 per cent chemistry and 84 per cent physics). General courses are not offered and guidance most commonly results in a choice of two sciences.

It is worth noting that both 'Oldboys Grammar' and 'Suburban Girls Modern' have a different experience of parental influence. The former is developing links with a girls' school without any problem; the latter has experienced opposition to links with a boys' school from parents who express fears of amalgamation.

Vocational Subjects

Tables 7.4, 7.5 and 7.6 summarize our analyses of subject descriptions in option booklets in 127 schools. They show that in most schools, these descriptions neither countered nor supported sex bias. In domestic science subjects 77 per cent of descriptions were neutral; in commercial subjects the figure was 95 per cent and in technical subjects 90 per cent.

In domestic science subjects, 12 per cent of booklets assumed or stated that the subjects were open to either sex; 10 per cent assumed or requested one sex (see Table 7.4). Sexist bias was highest in child care, where 15 per cent assumed or requested girls only; and lowest in home economics, where nine schools assumed girls only, but four requested boys. Similarly, home economics had the highest proportion (16 per cent) of statements assuming or stating that the subject was open to both sexes.

Two statements about domestic science courses used 'boys and girls' to describe pupils taking child care. Two schools included child care or parentcraft in their compulsory courses. A number of schools call their course 'parentcraft' rather than 'child care' and, although it has not been counted as such for Table 7.4, it may be that this reflects a willingness to consider boys. On the other hand, one school called its course 'mother and child', another 'mothercare'. One stated that 'mother's help' might be a career that the subject led to, another proclaimed that 'Today's girls will be tomorrow's mothers' and that the National Association for Maternal and Child Welfare offered certificates to those completing one course. Another suggested that if those taking the child care course did not marry, a certificate in the subject might lead to a variety of careers. One school in the cluster sample ran a course in 'typewriting and child care', another in 'good grooming', involving make up and manicure.

Cookery oriented courses rather than child care or needlework are in practice more successful in attracting boys into domestic science subjects at option choice. Almost certainly this is because there are career opportunities in catering for boys. Thus two of the four boys' only courses in this area were said to be designed specifically for those wishing to enter the catering trade. A third involved some house maintenance as well as cookery and was clearly a low level practical skills course. Fourteen statements said home economics courses are open to all.

Using 'boys and girls' or 'host/hostess' or using 'girls' and 'cook and hostess' are the most frequent examples of assuming both or one sex. One booklet contained a picture of a boy thinking 'I want to be a cook', another stated that its course prepared pupils to be a 'mother and wife/husband and father'.

Ten of the home economics courses had names like 'home management' or 'family care'. These involved some child care and one involved teaching pupils some make up. One of the home economics courses said to be appropriate only for girls focused largely on home activities.

Three courses, called variously 'home management', 'home studies,'

Organization and teaching of subjects 137

Table 7.4 Sex bias and counter sex bias in domestic science subjects

		Either sex assumed	Open to all	Nothing either way	Girls assumed	Boys assumed	Boys required	Girls required	Total subject description
Child care[1]	N	2	3	32	4	0	0	0	41
	C	0	3	13	3	0	0	2	21
	All	2	6	45(75%)	7	0	0	2(15%)	62(100%)
Home economics[2]	N	3	9	74	4	0	4	2	96
	C	7	5	41	1	0	0	2	56
	All	10	14(16%)	115(76%)	5	0	4	4	152(100%)
Needlework[3]	N	5	4	57	5	0	0	1	72
	C	2	1	57	7	0	0	1	68
	All	7	5(9%)	114(8%)	12	0	0	2(10%)	140(100%)
Total	N	10	16	163	13	0	4	3	209
	C	9	9	111	11	0	0	5	145
	All	19	25(12%)	274(77%)	24	0	4	8(10%)	354(100%)

Notes:
1. Includes child care, parentcraft.
2. Includes home economics, food and nutrition, cookery, catering, home management.
3. Includes needlework, embroidery, dress, fashion and fabrics, textiles and clothing.

and 'learning for living' focused on the home but involved both the do-it-yourself activities normally associated with home maintenance courses and cooking and needlework. Such a course thus contains material traditionally sex-biased but combines the biases. One of these courses allowed for choice of activity, which would clearly allow sex bias; the other two contained no suggestion of choice (though there may have been some in practice). Courses such as this might be seen as a way of getting round the problem of sex-biased material, but it is worth noting that none of these courses offered qualifications. The structure of the exam boards reflecting traditional sex bias, perhaps exercises a constraint on the development of such interdisciplinary courses at a higher level.

There were five statements saying needlework courses are open to all. Two statements occurred in one school where the courses involved were called 'textile arts' and 'textiles and clothing' and one was 'fabric design'. This name difference – from the more traditional 'needlework' or 'embroidery' – reflects movement towards an art and design approach and away from dressmaking. It is likely that less sex bias is involved in this more modern approach.

Forty descriptions stated that 'dress' or 'dressmaking' was involved in the syllabus or even called their courses by these names (20 of the 40). While the formal definition of this term might involve male garments it is likely that in the minds of pupils and in actual practice this activity involved female garments. The issue of boys' and girls' garments was apparent in four schools where all pupils had to make a female garment.

One school offered 'valeting' as well as 'grooming' and another noted that boys taking the course might need to make different garments from girls. Implications that the subject was appropriate for both or for one sex were apparent in the use of pronouns in the descriptions. The orientation of many of these needlework courses to home activities rather than work is evident from the 15 descriptions of needlework courses called 'homecraft' or 'housecraft'.

A feature of some of the descriptions in this section was an emphasis on teaching (or rather 'fostering in') pupils a sense of the 'responsibilities' or 'obligations' of adult life. As we shall see later this aim was also apparent in commercial courses (also traditionally associated with girls), but was completely absent from the technical subjects traditionally associated with boys. Four child care and five home economics descriptions contained this aim, expressed in terms such as:

A responsible attitude towards the family and community.

... To help pupils to become more mature and to become more aware of their responsibilities as parents or caring adults.

... Aims to cover the responsibilities of parents.

Granted that this aim may be very laudable, its presence in these subjects rather than traditionally male subjects reflects a view of female devotion to service that has been apparent in girls' education historically (see Galthorne–Hardy, 1979). The service ideal is a component of what might be considered a stereotype of female behaviour.

Courses in the domestic sciences have long been associated with girls and the evidence of the booklets shows that this influence persists quite strongly. However, the frequency of rotational craft systems and the legal requirement that all subjects be open to all has encouraged a few schools to consider critically sex bias in material presented in these courses. Only a small minority of schools persist in assuming or encouraging one sex in the subjects in their booklets; the majority have edited out references to sex and a small minority have made efforts to encourage boys. While it is unclear from this analysis what is happening at the level of the classroom, there is some evidence of new curriculum developments. The move of needlework towards design and textiles, courses including technical subjects as well, the inclusion of parentcraft in the core, are examples of a desire to counter sex bias.

In technical subjects, traditionally a boys' domain, 6 per cent of schools made statements saying their subjects were open to both sexes and statements like this occurred in 16 subject descriptions (4 per cent), particularly in technical drawing which is the most attractive technical subject for girls in practice (Table 7.5). Only one school in our survey specifically excluded girls from the subject, though a number assumed boys only would be interested.

As well as the use of pronouns, messages were conveyed by the use of 'draughtsperson' or 'draughtsman'. One school described its department as 'boys' technical subjects'. One booklet contained a line drawing of what may have been a girl studying metalwork; another contained a picture of a strong man bending an iron bar opposite its metalwork description – this assists in conveying the impression that the subject requires strength, a reason which is often used to explain the exclusion of girls in our conversations with teachers. A practice which one school employed was to give preference in cases of over-subscription of technical drawing to those opting also for woodwork or metalwork; this could have the effect of discouraging a girl who expresses only a moderate degree of interest in technical subjects. Again then, we see that most descriptions are neutral on the subject of sex bias but that some schools are aware of a need to mention it. No evidence of adopting courses to suit girls' interest was present.

In commercial subjects, Table 7.6 shows that most subject descriptions say or imply nothing about the sexes, and of those who do say anything, one is sex biased where 'girls' were described studying business studies, and another restricted all commercial courses to girls.

Option choice

Table 7.5 Sex bias and counter sex bias in technical subjects

		Either sex assumed	Open to all	Nothing either way	Girls assumed	Boys assumed	Boys required	Girls required	Total subject description
Technical drawing[1]	N	1	4	60	0	1	0	0	61
	C	4	6	26	0	4	0	0	40
Woodwork	N	0	0	50	0	1	0	0	51
	C	1	0	33	0	2	0	0	36
Metalwork	N	1	0	46	0	1	0	0	48
	C	2	0	32	0	1	0	0	11
Motor vehicle	N	0	2	23	0	0	0	0	25
	C	0	1	8	0	0	0	0	9
Design and technology/ technology	N	1	2	29	0	1	0	0	33
	C	1	1	15	0	1	0	0	18
Engineering/ electronics	N	0	0	24	0	0	0	0	24
	C	0	2	18	0	0	0	0	18
Miscellaneous[2]	N	0	0	18	0	1	0	0	19
	C	0	0	9	0	1	0	0	10
Technical generally	N	0	2	—	0	1	1	0	—
	C	0	5	—	0	1	1	0	—
Total	N	3	8	250(94%)	0	5	0	0	266(100%)
	C	8	10	143(84%)	0	9	0	0	170(100%)
	All	11	18	393(90%)	0	14	0	0	436(100%)

Notes:
1. Includes engineering drawing, graphical communication, design drawing.
2. Includes printing, general craft, building, aviation, home maintenance.

Table 7.6 Sex bias and counter sex bias in commercial subjects

	Either sex assumed	Open to all	Nothing either way	Girls assumed	Boys assumed	Boys required	Girls required	Total subject descriptions
N	4	6	130(93%)	0	0	0	0	140(100%)
C	0	0	88(99%)	1	0	0	0	89(100%)
All	4	6	218(95%)	1	0	0	0	229(100%)

Note: In addition, one department in the cluster sample restricted all commercial courses to girls only. One department stated that its courses were 'suitable for everyone'.

However, two descriptions told pupils not to wear rings and to keep their nails short and two booklets contained pictures of girls only in typing classes. These might be interpreted as reflections of the sex bias that exists in the make up of classes rather than expressions of a desire to encourage such sex bias.

A number of descriptions appeared aware of the restrictions on later careers if commercial subjects were taken at this stage. Six descriptions said that it was possible to go into secretarial work by taking a course after school-leaving age, although one suggested that taking such a course now would be a good thing for those not wanting further education. One other school warned pupils to think carefully about the restriction implied by opting heavily for commercial courses.

Office practice in two schools aimed to teach 'office etiquette' and 'good human relations in the office'. 'A sense of responsibility' was the aim of another office practice course as it was, surprisingly, of a typing class. A number of schools in both samples reported their rotational craft systems as being examples of how sex discrimination/differentiation was being eliminated.

In the nominated sample, one school which made both technical studies and needlework compulsory for all until option choice reported that boys often disliked needlework. The respondent considered that to make one or other optional would result in sex-biased choice and was thinking as an alternative of cutting out needlework altogether. Another nominated school explained its policy of separating the sexes for craft subjects as being due to boys disliking needlework and staff wanting more time with pupils to develop their subjects. One found that boys never wanted to take needlework; some had wanted to do home economics but could not because of 'lack of resources'; several girls had studied technical subjects. Two schools reported a special request system operating where they normally separated pupils by sex for craft subjects, though one said that such requests rarely occurred. Two wished soon to begin a rotational craft system, one saying that this would happen 'as soon as the staff involved had accepted the practice'. One reported that its rotational craft system had been in operation since before the Sex Discrimination Act. One found that girls sometimes opted for technical subjects but boys did not opt for traditionally girls' subjects.

The head of one nominated school had suspended the child development courses since its content was so strongly biased towards girls. Another was planning to make a modified child care course compulsory for all fourth/fifth years. One school observed that its road craft course succeeded in attracting girls, while a course in motor mechanics did not. The working party report enclosed by one nominated school noted that the child development course in the school had the potential to challenge sex roles, but failed to do so.

One school in its working party report noted that boys had once appeared the more confident sex in the workshop in technical subjects, but girls had now caught up with them. A report written for staff by a concerned teacher in another school noted that the introduction of a rotational craft system had been a step forward for equality, but that the practice of giving boys preference where craft subjects were over-subscribed at option time should be stopped. An academic board report from another school noted similarly the advantages of the 'craft carousel' but observed that it had made little difference to sex bias at option choice time.

In the cluster sample, one school found that initial resistance to a rotational craft system had since died down. Another school was soon to introduce a rotational craft system in the first year. One had resorted to giving girls priority for home economics since, due to staff reduction because of falling rolls, there were too few teachers of the subject. Another, where over-subscription for craft courses occurred, did not decide allocation on grounds of sex but on grounds of 'motivation, career intentions, etc.'. One found that many boys liked cookery. Another had made parentcraft a part of its compulsory core. One found that girls more than boys cross the traditional barriers in craft. One noted that many girls liked technical subjects and that most boys liked home economics, but 'resent' fashion and fabrics. In another school no boys had ever wanted to take this latter subject, and no girls engineering, although the school said they could do these subjects if they asked. Another said that lack of resources made it difficult to offer a free choice to each sex. Two cluster schools wrote that they were pleased to note that girls were taking more technical subjects; one said that last year a girl had been the most successful candidate in a building course.

A number of schools have developed courses in design or art and design which offered a useful means of teaching material derived from areas traditionally associated with one sex only. We examined option booklets for a wide range of art, design and miscellaneous arts subjects from our survey. One school ran a course in creative design which involved both art and fabrics, writing 'we hope, where it is possible, that boys and girls will work in mixed groups'. The design department of another school covered the traditional areas of art, technical craft and home economics/needlework. An integral design CSE course it ran included all these areas, pupils having some choice of activity within the course. Another CSE design course in the school involved both graphic design, printing and fabric work. A non-exam course run by the school also involved all three subject areas.

A general art course in one school seemed half way between traditional needlework and art, involving appliqué, air brush work, fabric printing, machine and hand embroidery, patchwork and 3-D work. The description hoped that 'Both boys and girls will find this an interesting option.' This can be seen as another example of how an art bias can lessen sex bias in a craft subject.

Case study schools

Rotational Craft Timetables were in operation in all our case study schools in England or their feeder schools. The timetable offers to all pupils, in coeducational classes, the full range of craft subjects available in the school, except in one school where it was felt that metalwork is too difficult for all pupils during the pre-option stage. In several cases these 'taster' courses are provided in purpose-built workshops which are open plan; and the curriculum often introduces 'intermediate' forms of traditional craft subjects: for example, jewellery-making as metalwork, or puppetry as an introduction to needlework. In other cases a simplified form of the post-option study is offered in traditional workshops.

Craft teachers appear to be passionately committed either to traditional practices or innovation; we found few examples of the complacency encountered among science staff. In some cases the staff in a school were conspiring to maintain traditional barriers, in others they were ranged against each other in a battle for ascendancy in the curriculum; in one case we encountered a lone innovator frustrated by the traditional approach of his colleagues. Some schools provide choice for the upper ability, but not lower ability groups, and we found two headmasters who had instituted a rotational craft scheme in limited form both to comply with the 1975 Act and mollify the fierce resistance to its introduction from staff. Only in two schools was there evidence of general adherence to the spirit of the Act, although others had made attempts to encourage non-traditional choices by a change of title and/or alterations to the pre-option syllabuses.

An outstanding example of modification of a rotational craft system because of opposition was encountered in 'Northern Modern'. In the first year all pupils experience an 'intermediate' form of all crafts in coeducational groups. In years 2 and 3, single-sex classes are introduced and boys and girls follow craft courses traditional for their sex. This arrangement is said to comply with the Act while compromising with the staff in the craft departments, who opposed it. One argument is that the subjects are more difficult to teach in mixed classes, another is that it causes indiscipline because boys and girls are not interested in non-traditional subjects; in general the staff see the scheme as an irrelevant imposition on themselves and the pupils.

In 'Daleview Comprehensive', an otherwise willing and progressive system is subverted following the introduction of ability groups in the third year. Pupils in the upper ability group are offered a free choice of two craft subjects taught in coeducational groups; the lower ability group follows a compulsory curriculum of single-sex classes in traditionally boys' or girls' subjects. This arrangement is said to arise because concentration of resources on the upper ability group necessitates timetabling 'girls' subjects against boys' subjects'.

Most schools offered either a choice of two subjects after the first year (for one school two years) until general option choices are made; or a continuous programme for all throughout the three-year pre-option period. In two cases we were told of a commitment to equal opportunity and the craft timetable is considered to be the major contribution to this policy during the pre-option period, with attention being paid to widening the horizons of pupils and encouraging non-traditional choice. A number of teaching staff clearly introduce new material and ideas as the opportunity arises. Most of the schools held traditional views about, and had traditional take up of, craft subjects. Considerable hostility to non-traditional take up exists in some schools, though in three schools there were staff with a positive interest in equal opportunities in craft subjects. In 'Midshire Upper School' we encountered comments such as:

> ... girls have a natural instinct to want to do cookery, and to press to do it [and] boys who opt have a strong interest, but girls have training and conditioning until it becomes an instinct. (home economics, Head of Department)

> ... girls have a natural fineness to their movements that boys don't possess, [and] at the option assembly I say to the boys, 'sorry lads, but this bit's for the girls'. (needlework)

> I don't want girls in the workshop; they become a focus of attention and that presents health hazards [and] I explain to girls that it's really an engineering course, but they turn up just the same. (metalwork, Head of Department)

We encountered many more such statements. One or two might be described as wild statements: for example, the female home economics teacher in 'Northern Comprehensive' who said she resented the loss of time to boys who opted for the subject and emphasized the 'inescapable biological fact that girls have a more natural aptitude for needlework' and 'CSE I is an adequate goal for boys'. These attitudes must make themselves evident in the presentation of the subject at option time. The extent of this influence may be demonstrated – although we hope not – by the option scheme controller in 'Northern Modern' who said that he threatened boys with compulsory needlework and girls with compulsory motor vehicle engineering options when they were late in returning their option forms – 'I suppose I shouldn't, and I don't mean anything by it; it's just a natural way of looking at things'. Metalwork is often presented as an engineering subject which is related to technical drawing, so that in one school over-subscription to technical drawing results in reservation of places for metalwork pupils; and considerable hostility to girls exists in some schools, an extreme example of which occurred when the Head of Department in 'Midshire Upper School' said 'frankly, if girls come into metalwork we're lumbered'. Similar views are expressed by all but one school in relation to needlework and boys, where staff often referred to the natural ability of girls, the awkwardness of boys with needles in their hands, and the embarrassment of boys and staff when fitting trousers.

Cookery teaching staff in our case studies were more flexible in their attitude towards non-traditional choices. Boys are accepted in the majority of cases and it is acknowledged that they are sometimes as skilful as girls. In 'Northern Comprehensive', a special request system operates for those who insist in crossing over, but most schools impose single-sex classes for boys and/or restrict boys to a CSE-level syllabus. A persistent theme is the large number of respondents who felt cookery is more relevant to careers for boys than girls, apparently because girls accept the subject as useful in the home while boys have to make a more positive career choice on their option forms.

Woodwork appears to be a second choice in most cases; or a 'soft' option, though the woodwork teachers we spoke to expressed a willingness to accept female pupils. One home economics' Head of Department said that girls were refused access to the school's woodwork department because the teacher preferred not to have them in the workshop; but our general experience is that the subject is open to girls and boys equally. As with needlework, our case studies indicate that the subject is not highly regarded and appears to be in decline.

Our case study schools experienced more non-traditional choices by boys than girls. That boys opt for cookery is now an established fact which is accommodated in even the hostile schools: it is girls who encounter most resistance and least accommodation when they have crossed over. Accommodation of boys in non-traditional subjects is condescending in some cases; single-sex tuition is accompanied by imposition of a CSE syllabus for all but a few boys in some schools. This is often defended as enabling tuition to cater to the different levels of skill and experience which each sex brings; this, together with the belief that girls and boys make different uses of the qualification, was a common explanation also for excluding boys (or inviting them to leave) when the syllabus reached a child care, flower arrangement or hygiene topic in coeducational classes. Similarly, lower level courses had sometimes been specially devised to accommodate boys and these contained 'pure' cookery syllabuses thought relevant to their different needs.

Explanations of the small number of girls who express an interest in metalwork included distaste of dirty, heavy work and fear of machinery, lack of career relevance, isolation in the workshop, and juxtaposition with traditional girls' subjects on the option sheet; one school's respondent said that the head teacher had taken active steps to reverse his successful attempt to attract girls to the technical department. Of these the most persistent explanation offered was the common association of metalwork with engineering careers. Whether or not the staff encourage this view of the subject, they offered the belief that this is the case and failed to cite a single example of attempts to amend the syllabus or provide alternative courses. Engineering was described as a job unsuited to girls and in which they are not interested; and it is also thought to be either pointless or wicked to encourage girls to think in terms of engineering.

In the two northern schools the defence is said to be a consideration for parents' and pupils' wishes, in 'Midshire Upper School' the staff claim to be providing sensitively for the needs of distinct groups of pupils, while in 'Daleview Comprehensive' the pursuit of excellence is said to dictate a concentration of resources on the upper ability groups at the expense of the other pupils; ironically, the best defence may lie in comparison of take up with the schools in our case study which promote equal opportunity.

'Inner City Comprehensive' stood alone as an example of positive attempts to introduce a craft programme which would appeal to boys and girls. In 'Midlands Comprehensive' non-traditional options were given priority when a subject is over-subscribed and requests to transfer are 'not treated with automatic sympathy' when they refer to a dislike of being in a small minority in a class. However, needlework is no longer compulsory for boys in the rotational craft system because it created disruption in the classrooms during the third year; and the craft Head of Department accepts but does not encourage non-traditional choices. Similarly, a change of title from needlework to textiles failed to encourage boys in 'Freelist Comprehensive' and the Rotational Craft Timetable has been amended to provide this subject optionally; boys have avoided the subject. 'Smallchange Secondary' has attempted to create a textiles course which would attract boys, but has demonstrated a willingness to discriminate against boys in a recent year when the subject was over-subscribed.

These schools have all adopted the spirit of equal opportunity but have failed to invest practice with conviction. They cited a variety of reasons for this, not least of which is parental opposition to boys either taking traditionally girls' subjects, or not following traditionally boys' subjects. Girls are said to respond less than boys to encouragement and are less disruptive in the classes, so it is inevitable that boys will provide most instances of disruption because of their dislike of the subject. The few girls who percolate through to lower level engineering courses, such as motor vehicle maintenance, are said usually to be attracted either by boys or a topic of the subject, such as the use of small motor cycles. But they are said to drift away when they discover the course contains theoretical work.

Nevertheless, the schools do provide examples of attempts to alter the self-image that they believe pupils bring to the school. We were told of option choice talks in which girls are encouraged to – at least – consider metalwork or woodwork; parental objections are discussed and persuasion is said to be mostly effective in achieving crossover; and the increasing number of boys choosing to study in cookery classes is generally thought to have a knock-on effect by reducing the inhibition of isolation in classrooms and so making it an acceptable choice. Only in needlework is there said to be a persistent refusal by boys to opt and often a titter of laughter when the suggestion is made that it can be useful or relevant to boys.

In 'Inner City Comprehensive' we were told that failed attempts to attract boys to needlework had convinced the staff that a two-pronged attack was necessary. They have developed publicity material for use at the option stage and are developing the syllabus to become more relevant to boys: including persuading a pattern maker to begin supplying juvenile male patterns for use in the classroom; they provided pupils for models of proportion. They also introduce equal opportunities as a topic. We were shown worksheets and examples of design by pupils who are encouraged to discuss the stereotypical images of different styles and uniforms. The school's view is that a general undervaluing of the craft subjects leads to opposition from all parents because even those who are not firmly traditional in outlook nevertheless want their children to concentrate on academic subjects. For this reason the main plank of change (yet to be accomplished) is a reworked and relevant syllabus where topics such as 'grooming' and 'housecraft' are replaced with, for example, 'food and community'. They believe titles such as 'child development' inhibit take up by boys of a subject which can be made relevant to social work and future home responsibilities. These topics are expected to reflect a changed content as well as a change of name; and the emphasis in cookery lessons is already placed on savoury items and modern meals with a reported increased interest among boys. The aim is to cater to home and career aspirations. However, as they progress towards the more strongly stereotyped subjects they have found increased resistance to change; only in textiles have they made major inroads on the stereotyped patterns of choice and boys are now said to be thinking in terms of tailoring careers, a small success they attribute to the introduction of a syllabus which emphasizes design and fashion in its social context.

These innovations represent action in subjects where many teachers expressed a need for change. Many teachers believe change would be effective but wicked. Decline of standards is the main objection. Needlework teachers especially have expressed resentment of an expected loss of 'pursuit of excellence', cookery teachers, too, defend single-sex classes for this reason; teachers of traditional male crafts perhaps feel less threatened. In 'Midshire Upper School' we were told of an 'exam factory atmosphere', and that sharing time between boys and girls would result in a loss of standards. This was also the explanation for single-sex classes in 'Northern Modern', where re-establishment of confidence following failure in a selective system is the dominant theme of the school. A change of syllabus is recognized as a possible means of attracting non-traditional choices but rejected for personal and 'professional' reasons.

Ironically, these considerations result in an increased take up of cookery by boys because institutional efforts are made to offer relevant syllabuses and single-sex classes: in order to protect standards and teaching methods, boys are offered systemic encouragement to view the subject as relevant; and they do not suffer from the inhibition of being a minority in a girls' class. Other factors may negate the value of this arrangement (negative approach of teaching staff, family and other social influences in strongly traditional areas) but it may be that this school is offering the most dramatic example of the promotion of equal opportunity.

Design and technology

A number of our schools offer technical studies with or without an option of craft subjects. The subject is presented as design-based and involves the use of a variety of materials rather than a concentration on either wood or metal. The graphic content and an emphasis on creative design and problem solving is thought to neutralize any traditional view and is considered a likely candidate to replace craft studies; teachers expressed the view that the subject is ideal for promoting equal opportunity because it dispenses with emphasis on workshop tools and techniques and appeals to boys and girls. In particular we were told that the design and graphic content develops skills already noticed in girls, while the experience and qualification is an open entry to technical careers in engineering and science. All teachers we spoke with in schools offering a form of this subject were enthusiastic about attracting girls to coeducational classes.

In three schools we discovered systemic inhibition to take up by girls. In 'Northern Comprehensive' a male teacher in an otherwise traditional department said that his attempts to encourage girls to opt for the subject had been successful but opposed by colleagues in both craft departments in collusion with the headmaster. In a previous year he had actively campaigned to encourage girls by poster advertisements and career discussions, which led to a large number of girls opting for the subject through the special request system. The headmaster instructed our respondent to write to parents with a withdrawal of the offer; he was told to explain that pressure on the timetable necessitated this move.

In 'New View Comprehensive' and 'Daleview Comprehensive' arrangement of the curriculum emphasizes the value of what are thought to be essential academic subjects. In the former this results in the technology rooms being unoccupied during 20 per cent of the week and an option system which places traditionally male and female subjects in opposition. Our respondent there would welcome coeducational classes and an opportunity to increase provision – both of which moves will, he believes, attract girls to the subject – but he is not willing to press for a change if it results in removing emphasis from science subjects, which at present dominate the curriculum. 'Daleview Comprehensive' effectively reserves both design and technical communication for the upper ability group, which results in the lower 40 per cent of pupils being offered a choice of craft subjects traditional for their sex following a year of compulsory study of those subjects. In view of the attitudes expressed by most craft teachers, it is particularly unfortunate that girls tend to be excluded from this subject which – whether or not it is successful as a leveller, as some claim – is staffed by teachers with fewer entrenched views concerning the exclusive value of the subject to either boys or girls.

Single-sex schools

In 'Oldboys Grammar' and 'Suburban Girls Modern' there are no rotational craft schemes nor any non-traditional craft. No links with other schools provide non-traditional subjects and neither school is concerned to develop the curriculum of craft subjects, partly, so it was said, because there is no demand for change. Other considerations must be that the girls' school lacks science laboratories, which it feels is of paramount importance for equalizing opportunities, and the boys' school places emphasis on academic subjects.

In both schools there is a point of note. In the girls' school girls opted for the needlework GCE-level course in much greater numbers than those choosing home economics; this novelty may be contrasted with a general decline in take up in coeducational case study schools. A possible explanation is that the school is only recently taking steps to emerge from a traditional approach to education for girls – as evidenced by the single option of biology as a GCE-level science until one year ago – and the reportedly conservative nature of the parents of pupils. In the boys' school a foundation course in art and design is aimed at providing furniture design skills in a course usually found only in colleges of further or higher education. The course employs some woodworking skills and bench practice, but there is no element of metalwork teaching and no tools or workshop suitable for practising metalwork skills. Apart from expressing a belief that girls would be a useful addition to his lessons, the Head of Department is sure that traditional girls' subjects are of little value to his pupils – in particular home economics; needlework appears in fabric design for the furniture – and the nature of the course removes it from consideration of stereotypical influences.

In contrast 'Seatown Girls' provides an example of a positive attempt to measure provision in a girls' school with that of a corresponding boys' school and use the resulting imbalance to promote equal opportunity. The head teacher resisted pressure to use new school buildings to increase provision of home economics when opportunity arose in 1978. Instead she enlisted the aid of the Chief Education Officer and proposed to introduce a craft design and technology (CDT) option. Public announcement of the aim attracted approval of parents; and parental subscription together with equipment from obsolete or amalgamated schools has resulted in a fully equipped set of workshops.

The school operates a Rotational Craft Timetable in the years preceding option choice and both CDT and home economics are over-subscribed – a popularity which is said to become manageable when, for a variety of reasons, pupils transfer to other subjects. Careers advice at option time is firmly rooted in relating choices to career aspirations and the head teacher is anxious that pupils will see links between CDT and sciences. At the time of our visit this had not been achieved and both CDT staff and the head teacher expressed concern that the subject is becoming a lower ability 'sink' because it has a reputation of being practical rather than academic. Measures to counteract this view include more publicity emphasizing the nature of the syllabus and the mental requirements of the examination, but it may be necessary to disassociate the subject from crafts by removing it from the craft block on the option sheet if parents and pupils are to alter their opinion. Until then the most effective method of increasing the proportion of upper ability pupils remains a policy of discrimination against lower ability pupils when over-subscription occurs.

The CDT courses follow the pattern we have encountered in other schools. The traditional crafts are not emphasized and a variety of materials are used in the context of problem solving and design. The girls tend to produce articles reflecting traditional influences – instances of playgroup equipment and aids for the disabled, kitchen equipment and jewellery, were cited; in other schools examples we were shown of work by boys usually had an engineering problem at their core. The school hopes soon to introduce a graphical communication course to capitalize on a recognized skill the girls display in their design drawings and the male head of department is confident that CDT and its variants represent the most successful method of attracting girls to a subject which has relevance for scientific and technical careers in which they are at present under-represented.

Other subjects

Girls are more likely to take languages than boys and the amount of bias is probably about the same as in science subjects. Yet, unlike in science subjects, no survey school felt it necessary to say anything in its option booklet about sex bias in languages. Nor did any school assume one sex rather than another would take a language subject. Only one school reported an experiment to determine whether single-sex French classes achieved better results than mixed classes. Limited success was had, but 'probably *not* a lot of difference'.

In the humanities, arts and social sciences, no option booklets contained anything implying sex bias, although national exam statistics show slight sex biases in passes. A number of schools commented on the topic of women's studies in these courses, since a question earlier in the survey questionnaire had made many think of the subject. One nominated school reported 'social role play' occurring as a part of a humanities course. Another reported a unit in the English course and in social education as including the study of sex roles. One school reported a theme on sexism in fourth year English and also that the library books had been checked and examples of sexist literature removed. Four cluster schools reported its inclusion as part of humanities or social studies courses and in one of these cases the course was a part of the core curriculum. One history course contained a unit on 'women's rights'.

In materials enclosed with survey questionnaires, seven nominated and one cluster school volunteered information that sex roles were discussed as a topic in social studies or social education courses; some of the courses were core rather than optional. A nominated school noted that its religious studies course involved an examination of prejudice generally. A working party report from a nominated school argued that a women's studies course should be started. The report of a concerned teacher in another school argued that much could be done in the cause of equality during social studies lessons. A girls' school noted that the subject arose in social studies courses as well as being a frequent choice as a topic for personal study by girls.

The working party report of another nominated school pointed out the predominance of girls in social studies and speculated that this might be due to a wholly female staff in the area, as well as the emphasis on written work in the subject. The same report urged humanities staff to review their materials for sexism; a piece that the humanities staff wrote concerned the issue of whether a 'purge' of library books should occur.

One working party report noted with approval that material on the lack of representation of women in music was taught by the music department, though lamented the fact that there were no female music teachers.

Most schools have compulsory physical education, but some offer the subject in various forms as an option. This may be called physical education, movement, outdoor pursuits, sport, dance, human movement studies. Our survey produced from option booklets 54 subject descriptions in this area from nominated schools and 32 from cluster schools. Most schools wrote that girls and boys pursued different activities in compulsory physical education. Many had separate boys' and girls' physical education departments. It is generally the case that girls have fewer activities to choose from than boys. Those schools which did not indicate a separation of the sexes in their booklets probably practised it anyway.

Of the schools describing optional physical education courses, three ran them for boys only. One emphasized that boys and girls mixed for all activities in human movement studies; in this case the course contained no soccer, rugby, netball or cricket where separation usually occurs. Handball, badminton, table tennis, gymnastics, swimming and athletics were offered in addition to theoretical sessions. One school referred to pupils taking dance as 'girls'.

Four nominated schools reported that there was a great deal of mixing of the sexes in extra-curricular activities, though one noted that some sports were exclusive to one sex. One of the four said that girls could play cricket and do circuit training; they could also play football though '*not* in mixed groups'. One had entirely mixed games except for football and judo. One reported occasional mixed games.

One cluster school reported that 'Army Cadet force not allowed to enrol girls, by order of Ministry of Defence! ! !' Two schools found that single-sex groupings in games tended to be the choice of the pupils. One said that girls occasionally play football.

Four nominated schools provided additional information on this area, though no cluster schools did. One school claimed that to have contact sports in mixed groups would be dangerous; as well as this it was felt that pupils would be unable to play mixed games out of school since the world of sport was not organized on mixed lines. Therefore it would be wrong to train mixed groups.

No option booklets contained information on sex education. One nominated school reported teaching girls separately for the topic of personal hygiene; a cluster school reported the same. One school circulated a three-page discussion document to staff on this subject, arguing generally for an approach which did not involve double standards for male and female sexual behaviour; that held the inevitability of marriage and heterosexuality in question and that went into the matter of sex roles in the home. Another school in its working party report wanted more done on the social aspects of sexual relationships and more on homosexuality.

Careers teaching

Careers teaching in most schools is a Cinderella subject staffed by teachers who receive relief of teaching duties for the guidance and organization they provide. We examined the arrangement for this important aspect of school provision in our case study schools, and supplemented this by analysis of the links made in option booklets from our survey schools between careers and school subjects. A number of survey schools also volunteered information on careers teaching in comments or by enclosing material.

Our respondents in case study schools are of a mind that their impact on choice is limited; they believe that even the upper ability pupils – among whom careers are said to be taken more seriously – remain uninfluenced by exposure to information concerning non-traditional careers.

Predominant influences are said to be peers, society, parents or – in the case of option choices – more 'frivolous' reasons. These, in turn, are over-shadowed in some areas by job availability, an extreme example of which was provided in a school where we were told that work experience places were eschewed when they required a 15-minute journey to the place of work; this example had been adduced expressly to emphasize the uselessness of attempting to encourage non-traditional career guidance in 'the last bastion of chauvinism'.

Pupil interviews reinforce our conviction that careers teaching as part of the curriculum currently has little direct impact on career choice. Only occasionally did a pupil mention careers teaching, advice or lessons as an influence on option choice although it is timetabled in four of the schools during the pre-option period. In addition, it appears to be a gratuitous incident when a film or visiting lecturer strikes a chord in the imagination of a pupil: it is rare to find instances of a pupil recalling follow up information provided by the guidance scheme. Often it is the case that a member of the family is cited as the principal influence on subject choice; and in many cases it is a subject teacher who has influenced the decision, either by communicating enthusiasm or in exercising persuasive skills during *ad hoc*, classroom or assembly talks.

Timetabling considerations are said to influence each of our respondents to choose co-ordination or liaison as their prime function rather than offer a positive careers teaching programme. In some cases this role is forced on the respondent by a lack of timetabled career lessons, in other schools the role is voluntarily adopted as being most useful, either because the emphasis in the school is on not influencing choice or because the aim is to bring outside experience into the classroom. No school we visited has a full-time careers counsellor.

The four schools in our study which offer timetabled careers education during the pre-option period provide weekly lessons in the second and third years ('Northern Comprehensive') or in the final year before examinable studies begin ('Daleview Comprehensive', 'Inner City Comprehensive' and 'Midland Comprehensive'). In all other schools there are pre-option choice talks provided in assemblies or classrooms, but these vary in commitment from organized subject teacher explanations of what is involved in the study, how the subject may be slotted into a career pattern and what is expected of a pupil who chooses the subject, to a general talk by the head teacher or members of staff during the period when option forms are being circulated.

Timetabled careers teaching is eclectic in its choice of material and we found teachers who used Schools Council and BBC publications as the focus of their courses, while supplementary teaching materials ranged over a wide spectrum of publications and editions of newspaper reports, film strips and films. In 'Daleview Comprehensive' the main emphasis of lessons is on sensible choice of option subjects and is therefore restricted to assisting pupils with assessment of their aptitudes and ability. Parents are said to show a strong interest in subject choice – increasingly as the job market deteriorates – but no attempt has been made to encourage non-traditional choices or introduce an examination of stereotypical influences, partly as a result of resistance from this source. The headmaster expressed a strong tradition of responding to the requirements of parents and concentrates the school's attention on providing the wherewithal for pupils to make 'sensible' choices without reference to extraneous forces which may influence the choice.

This theme is echoed in 'Northern Comprehensive', where the two year programme includes sex education and self-evaluation components. As in 'Daleview Comprehensive' the classes are coeducational, although single-sex classes are arranged where the content of sex education is 'patently only relevant to girls'. An example of a topic with singular relevance is the menstrual cycle; equally singularly the class had been conducted by a male teacher – a point which some may consider a neat example of confused reasoning. Our respondent firmly disapproved of encouraging pupils to opt for any subject in which no aptitude was shown and relies on the option booklet, previous experience of the subject and availability of individual teachers to answer questions for his belief that pupils are fully informed before making their choice.

'Midland Comprehensive' provides an example of intermittent concern with stereotype influence on option choice in that we were told the programme 'occasionally' includes an examination of advertisements for signs of bias in attracting either sex. In these lessons the topic includes a discussion of sex roles, but it clearly is not thought insufficiently important to form a part of the programme each year. In some part this will reflect our respondent's view that pupils at that stage are very traditional in their outlook, thus rendering the exercise of peripheral value; but our impression, later confirmed by the headmaster, is that our respondent belongs to the group of careers education staff who are – at least – uncommitted to the promotion of equal opportunity policy.

Once again 'Inner City Comprehensive' stands alone of our case study schools as the sole representative of a determined effort to combat traditional influences on subject choice. The female head of careers teaching sees her role as breaking down sex stereotypes that pupils bring to lessons and believes that the critical period is the pre-option stage. To some extent she believes the rotational craft scheme and other sampling exercises in years 1–3 have been successful in reducing the association of separate subjects with boys and girls, but subjects are still 'sold' by her as 'unisex' during the third year. Her choice of teaching material includes carefully edited standard films, pictures and text to ensure a balance of images supporting her theme. Experience has shown her that it is easier to break down subject choice prejudice than that of job choice. She has found girls are willing to accept the concept of needing qualifications similar to those offered by boys if they are to compete for careers, but traditional job choices persist even when the subject choice aspect has been fought over and won. She intends to develop some areas of guidance for the post-option period which will overlap and influence the pre-option stage insofar as her main concern is to influence what she believes to be 'massive parental pressure to encourage pupils to aspire to jobs which are disappearing'.

A number of our survey schools also reported that they made attempts to break down traditional influences on career choice. Four nominated schools and two cluster schools reported that the topic of sex roles was covered in careers education and another which was taking many steps to promote EOC policy gave some single-sex careers talks in order to broaden girls' aspirations. One cluster school reported that the careers programme stressed the importance of science qualifications. Another said the programme sometimes discussed equal opportunities though there was no strong emphasis. Three nominated schools (including one girls' school) stated that they used textbooks such as the CRAC publication *Male and Female* and the EOC publication *Breakthrough* (GB.EOC, 1980) during careers programmes; two cluster schools said the same. Another nominated school noted that the careers teacher was particularly keen to avoid sexist practices, but observed that unisex careers material was 'often to the detriment of the girls' (no further explanation offered).

A working party report from one of our survey schools argued that careers teachers should be critical of sex roles and actively challenge the assumptions of both pupils and parents. A staff forum on sex roles in another survey school recommended that careers teaching should begin before year 3, and a handout to staff on sexism in another school argued that the efforts of careers teachers were particularly important in promoting the policy. The report of a concerned teacher in another school stated that this area was 'immensely important' and advised that careers teachers should encourage pupils to think of non-traditional jobs, have speakers of non-traditional gender and include discussion of sex roles in the careers syllabus. The working party report of another survey school noted that since the Sex Discrimination Act careers materials were no longer sex-biased and that local employers were quite willing to take on a person of non-traditional sex for a job. It observed that some outside speakers had requested single-sex audiences but the school had insisted on mixed-sex groups.

One survey school had done a great deal in the area of 'compensatory counselling'. Key stages in girls' careers in school had been identified, these being the stage before third year option choice, that before the sixth form and that before higher education. Intervention was planned for these stages and 'all girl' assemblies, which involved talks to fifth form girls from female staff and female sixth formers on a variety of feminist issues, with particular emphasis on career choice, were planned.

After option choice, all our case study schools in some measure provide careers teaching in groups, either in year groups or interest groups or in formal classes. These groups are not systemically single sex except for discussion of some topics in 'Northern Comprehensive' where the syllabus contains items thought to be relevant only to girls.

The absence of systemic division of the sexes, however, appears less important to the experience of boys and girls when it is realized that most careers teaching is organized on the basis of interest or vocational groups. The majority of pupils have little flexibility after selecting their option subjects and career decisions are dominated by consideration of the possible jobs open to a candidate with a given set of qualifications. When most girls have eschewed the physical sciences, technical drawing, metalwork and related subjects, there is little point in attending film shows or talks provided by outside speakers on the subject of engineering. Similarly, boys are said to choose not to attend sessions on nursing or secretarial careers. This gravitation to unbalanced groups is reinforced in the case of talks by the army and navy, which provide male and female speakers to give separate talks to boys and girls. However, there is said to be a great deal more cross-over by boys because of their acceptance of catering and business or financial management careers.

Our case study schools sometimes defend, rarely attempt to affect, and most often simply accept traditional values in careers teaching. Where academic emphasis is paramount – for example in 'Daleview Comprehensive' and 'New View Comprehensive' – interest grouping and voluntary attendance at lectures given by outside speakers is explained as providing information to young adults to enable informed decisions to be made. Schools with an emphasis on pastoral education – for example 'Northern Modern' and, to a lesser extent, 'Northern Comprehensive' – refuse on principle to accept encouragement to non-traditional choice. In the latter our respondent emphasized his role as:

> If they want information on jobs they must come to me individually and ask, otherwise I teach *self evaluation*, conditions of work and features of employment.

In the former we were told:

> I don't attempt to influence choice of job, or raise equal opportunity issues; if a boy enjoys helping his father, or a girl enjoys helping her mother, I'm happy to advise them to choose a career based on the skills they learn doing that.

In both these schools the prevailing belief is that some of the teaching aids are unrealistic in their presentation of the world of work. In 'Northern Modern' a BBC 'Going to Work' series was criticized for showing girls in an engineering environment which is clean and pleasant 'with good relationships between the men and women'. It was said that, in visits to engineering works, the group was invariably accompanied by a male teacher because:

It is a dirty, filthy job full of men who aren't necessarily aware of how to behave in the presence of a woman visitor with children in tow.

In 'Northern Comprehensive' the respondent has on occasion found it necessary to remind speakers that they must mention career prospects for girls as well as boys and he points out to fifth year girls that their opportunities for careers are getting greater all the time. An example of his approach was provided in relation to encouragement to fourth year girls:

> I occasionally give them brief encouragement to consider the world as possibly being more suited to them in future because technology is bringing a need for high manual dexterity and hand and eye co-ordination.

The examples of a 'neutral' approach to provision of careers teaching are repeated throughout our case study schools with one exception. The general approach of schools is governed by a concentration of effort on job or career selection and all advice in syllabuses is designed to assist in a 'free choice' uninfluenced by teacher preference or bias. Where a topic in the syllabus is rejected by boys or girls – our only examples concern rejection by boys – the philosophy allows the distinction to be made on what is 'appropriate'; advice on particular careers or jobs is provided to individuals when questions are raised individually; and an occasional talk is given to attempt to awaken an interest among girls in the wide range of possible careers including non-traditional choices.

'Inner City Comprehensive' rejects this approach. The preference for traditional choices of voluntary groups is seen as a problem. Our respondent intends to introduce single-sex grouping of compulsory topics during the year following our visit, mainly in order to provide positive discrimination for girls. An outline proposal included seeking out and inviting women speakers on a variety of subjects non-traditional for their sex and in particular from 'women's engineering organizations'. The programme will, she feels, be assisted by the emerging 'new' careers – such as computing – 'which have yet to be dominated by the stereotypes associated with other careers'.

This response has developed from an acknowledgement, shared in other schools, that pupils are influenced in their choices by external considerations. Few of our schools provided examples of cross-over in career choice by girls and boys; and those few either cited the pupils with higher academic attainment or indicated failed attempts or a vague remembrance of a girl 'a few years ago' who succeeded.

'Smallchange Secondary' mentioned examples of girls expressing an interest in engineering or taking engineering link courses with the local further education college, but our respondent was unaware whether the aspiration had been achieved; one girl had entered the army as an engineer apprentice, another had entered farming; and boys had entered nursing and catering careers. 'Northern Comprehensive', on the other hand, felt that parents would object if, for example, a boy wanted to become a hairdresser because 'parents are so entrenched in their views in this area'.

'Northern Modern' may be cited as an example of the differential experience of boys and girls noted in the section on craft and vocational subject teaching:

> I don't have much experience of girls and boys choosing non-traditional careers – those I can think of are predominantly boys breaking out of the mould – going into catering or nursing.

The common thread of non-interference in pupil choice and avoidance of raising aspirations to non-traditional careers is further explained in terms of the preference of employers for either sex in specific jobs. An extreme example was provided in 'Northern Comprehensive' where we were given a list of work experience placements *provided by the careers office* for the area. In it, approximately 33 per cent of placement offers specify which sex is preferred for the job. There are 65 placements on the list which includes a large range of industrial commercial and professional organizations. A chemist offering a warehousing placement specifies a male for heavy lifting and one sales assistant placement will consider a male, while a 'Quango' insists on a female for their switchboard and a local authority wants a male for gardening duties. When we consider that 'Inner City Comprehensive' – with a positive discrimination programme being developed – also acknowledges discrimination by employers who offer work experience placements and regrets the necessity of accepting the placements on the employers' terms, it is apparent that a degree of collusion across the spectrum of careers guidance provision is reinforcing the self-images of boys and girls.

Neither 'Daleview Comprehensive' nor 'New View Comprehensive' have noticed any discrimination by employers; in 'Midshire Upper School' a distinction is drawn between the discrimination applied to lower ability pupils and those of the upper ability group; in 'Northern Modern' there is said to be one engineering firm which is only interested in boys and a department store which 'probably unconsciously' always allocates jobs in a stereotypical pattern; and in 'Smallchange Secondary' where there is no work experience programme we were told that a union representative had advised the careers officer that employers were not willing to accept girls in engineering because it was a wasted investment. 'Midland Comprehensive' school felt that engineering aspirations were more appropriate for grammar school girls because the GCE requirement was too great for the academic attainment of girls in that school. With evidence of this type it must appear that the schools are sometimes in breach of the 1975 Act; but it may be viewed sympathetically when it is acknowledged, as the respondent in 'Inner City Comprehensive' put it:

> When I began the job I started to take up the matter [preference for boys or girls] with employers, but they simply don't offer places if you do that – and then you haven't got any work experience programme.

In 'Daleview Comprehensive' and 'Midshire Upper School' the work experience programmes are said to attract few non-traditional choices and no opposition from employers; in the former this is said to be a feature of the rural environment – a number of girls choose farming for their programme, while the latter believes it results from work experience largely reserved for the lower ability groups with very traditional outlooks and fewer opportunities for flexibility. In contrast, 'New View Comprehensive' has no work experience programme but organizes a career symposium each year to bring local employers into the school as guest speakers and for preliminary career interviews. Another feature of the career programme in some of our schools is organized visits to workplaces. Some, as in 'Northern Modern', are included in career lessons while others are conducted in subject groups. In 'Midland Comprehensive' visits occur in office practice and craft lessons which, we were told, results in mainly boys visiting engineering firms and mainly girls visiting offices. Our analysis of jobs that pupils aspire to suggests that no significant re-direction of interest among boys or girls is achieved in any school; it therefore appears that pupil self-image coupled with passive career programmes results in conformity with the majority view apparently held by employers providing placements.

In Scotland, a guidance system operates for pupils, in which members of school staff are allocated the responsibility of getting to know pupils and monitoring their progress throughout their school career. The guidance team is thus concerned with post-school careers advice, though schools may also designate specific careers teachers, who will be part of the guidance team.

In both our Scottish case study schools, career guidance is organized in the second year to provide some assistance with option choices. In 'Scottish Academy' there are guidance staff for each of the four years of compulsory education and a further new member of staff has ten, one-period weeks to present careers guidance, which mainly takes the form of a video series 'Its Your Choice' containing a session which deals specifically with non-traditional careers. A booklet entitled *Careers Link* is provided during this period and a leaflet created by the careers service for the area is to be included with the option choice booklet. 'Scottish Secondary' has a head of guidance and six staff with other responsibilities; there is, however, no timetabled career guidance. During the pre-option period second year assembly talks are supplemented with class lectures by local career officers to assist pupils in making their choices.

The guidance teacher in 'Scottish Academy' maintains and is improving school library information on careers with the help of the librarian. He prefers to work with literature than to invite speakers or organize work visits and he has a display concerned with a specific career on show on a two-week cycle. An unusual feature of his organization is a job file listing the types of job available among local employers, based on information obtained by circulating a questionnaire to employers. Post-option lessons utilize a teaching aid 'Anyone Can Apply', which contains a programme on non-traditional choice similar to the topic introduced during the pre-option period. In both cases pupils are said to respond well in discussions which follow the video sequence.

Work experience for the fourth-year pupils is reserved for those leaving school at Christmas. They are arranged at the request of pupils and reflect traditional career aspirations which the careers teacher does not attempt to influence. Link courses in further education colleges are dominated by boys studying technical subjects, but it may be more significant that although girls are welcomed on to agricultural courses local farmers often refuse to employ girls – we were told that a common excuse is that they (girls) 'can't handle a tractor'. Similarly, the careers teacher is aware that some YOP courses are effectively reserved for either boys or girls.

'Scottish Secondary' provides individual career interviews for the third- and fourth-year pupils but any equal opportunity discussions arise by chance and not as a topic. The pattern of choice at voluntary career lectures and in take up of link courses is said to be very traditional with, for example, joinery, engineering and construction talks attracting only boys and link courses in hairdressing, child care and beauty attracting only girls. Our respondent feels that the local employers are 'extremely traditional' in their employment practices and that isolation in the classroom was a significant factor in deterring non-traditional subject choice.

Our visit to the careers office which serves leavers from both schools provided further (and striking) evidence of the reluctance of employers to accept non-traditional career choices. The overall picture of the careers aspirations and jobs of pupils was overwhelmingly traditional.

It was common for employers to specify in their requests to the careers office the sex of candidate sought. This happened most notably on Youth Opportunities Programmes, where a surveying office wanted only boys for certain jobs, as did a fashion cutter, a menswear department and a weighbridge operator. The proprietor of a petrol station wanted only girls as forecourt attendants. Restrictions of this kind present almost impossible dilemmas for the careers office staff. In this case they simply accepted them, conspiring with the employers to restrict job offers to one or other sex.

Single-sex schools

'Oldboys Grammar' school offers its boys no discussions of non-traditional careers and no topics concerned with equal opportunity. Guidance is firmly rooted in assisting with option choices and appropriate careers in a framework reflecting close co-operation between parents and the career service. The respondent conducts three of four lessons with pupils during the third year when the booklet *Your Choice at 13+* (CRAC, annual) is supplemented with assembly lectures. *Ad hoc* lessons may be conducted subsequently, but the emphasis is placed on pupils' own research in the careers library and discussions with individual teachers. We were told that the majority of outside speakers are male and usually represent the financial sector, local authority departments, engineering and legal professions: this is said to reflect pupil choice and attendance is voluntary.

The careers teacher is aware of no interest in non-traditional careers. An attempt to establish a link course with a local school for girls failed to attract boys although he has had occasional requests for information on catering careers. As the school offers an art foundation course for post-option craft study – and parents provide the majority of work experience places, dominated by financial and professional spheres of activity – it appears unlikely that pupils are given any encouragement to consider non-traditional careers.

In 'Seatown Girls' the third-year girls receive a ten-week block of careers teaching as part of a general course in personal relations: 'We spend a lot of time on the options scheme and that's really what the third year programme is for.' Girls are recommended to preserve a balance in their choice and are informed about the career consequences of dropping or taking up certain subjects. Science staff encourage able girls to take sciences; sometimes the careers teacher finds herself trying to ease such pressures from subject departments: 'I suppose we do encourage them to do physics quite a lot because they can do biology in the sixth form as an extra. There is a tendency for the less able girls to do biology because we find they have more success.'

In the fourth year, pupils receive career lessons in a 13-week block; and in the fifth year a period of a fortnight. The careers teacher points out the problems faced by women in the current circumstances of unemployment and assists girls in forming opinions about their career expectations. Although equal opportunities is not a topic, a video tape sequence concerned with careers in science and a section devoted to discussions about unions contains material relevant to equality between men and women.

Most visiting speakers address the sixth form and provide information about aspects of industry. Further education colleges provide speakers and a wide variety of industrial and professional occupations are represented. Among these it is said that nursing, accountancy, solicitors and the BBC are most popular; but a recent speaker from an engineering firm informed girls that Saudi Arabian contracts precluded his firm from employing women. Of similar interest is the local firm of which it was reported:

> No, he won't put girls on lathes – he's only got the chaps on what are really the good earning jobs. And the apprenticeships – he won't offer an apprenticeship to a girl.

Work experience of one week occurs on a voluntary basis after GCE examinations. The most popular areas are teaching, nursing and other ancillary medical work, but girls have been placed with the coastguard, in a mechanical workshop of the local radio station and in other mechanical workshops with local firms. We were told that the most unpopular work experience placements and jobs are any type of factory work including factory management, and our respondent expressed regret that few girls follow scientific careers; the few who do are generally associated with medical aspects.

In 'Suburban Girls Modern' school the new careers teacher is in the process of developing a course within constraints of one lesson each week in the third year and fifth year. A social studies course includes career guidance in the fourth year. The third-year lessons are reserved for option choice guidance which takes the form of assisting girls with choices fitted to aspirations, ability and preferences; in some cases it results in channelling those without a clear aptitude. There were no teaching materials available for our inspection, but the teacher has plans to present information as it had been in her previous coeducational school. In this she believes there is a wealth of material available to provide a balanced, coeducational view of job opportunities. She also believes the single-sex environment provides female models for the girls and has the impression that pupils are more aggressive and competitive than in her previous school. Although she feels that girls are in general less positive than boys about careers, she has no intention of influencing pupils in their choice of jobs and feels strongly that career lessons are for assisting with decision making rather than to be used for promoting equal opportunity. On the other hand she spoke of plans to invite a female electrician who is a previous pupil at the school to lecture in career lessons; and she will ensure that work experience placements offer a wide range of opportunities, avoiding if possible those employers who insist on traditional roles.

Links between subjects and jobs

Option booklets provide information about the linkages between subjects and jobs that schools emphasize to pupils. A count was made of the possible careers mentioned in relation to each subject in the option booklets from our survey schools to see what messages schools convey to their pupils. Results are contained in Appendix 6.

Unsurprisingly, traditionally boys' subjects are most often associated with male jobs and girls' subjects with female jobs. Physics, technical subjects and technical drawing are said to be required most often for technical and engineering jobs; lower level commercial subjects are most often required for office work; child care for social services; needlework for fashion/beauty; home economics for food; biology is only once suggested for a technical job and never for engineering. Child care, home economics, needlework and lower level commercial subjects are all repeatedly said to be useful for personal and home life; technical subjects are also frequently described like this. We have ranked subjects according to how many times on average, individual careers are mentioned in relation to them (see Table 7.7).

Table 7.7   Subjects related to careers

Subject	Careers per subject
Physics	2·11
Chemistry	2·04
Biology	1·58
Human biology	0·79
Home economics	0·64
Commercial subjects	0·49
Child care	0·45
Technical and technical drawing	0·43
Languages	0.41
Needlework	0·21

Thus the sciences, particularly physics, are seen as being most important for jobs. Home economics, a subject that attracts more boys than child care, commercial subjects or needlework, is more career related than other craft subjects. Opportunities in catering and hotel management are often stressed in relation to home economics.

If an explanation for sex bias in subject take up is sought, a persuasive case can be made from these results. For example, the main three sciences are associated with medical and para-medical careers about equally in the option booklets; both men and women do these jobs and so both should be attracted to each science if these careers are desired. However, one school stated that biology was not essential for a career in medicine; physics and chemistry are needed more by those wanting higher level medical careers and less for lower level para-medical jobs. Physics, mostly taken by boys, is associated far more often with the male jobs of engineering and technology than the other two sciences. Chemistry, where take up is only slightly biased towards boys, has some technical, scientific and engineering relevance but is also seen as important for jobs involving food (home economics is often said to go well with chemistry) and as having some relevance for work with animals and fashion/beauty (mainly hairdressing), both strongly female areas. Biology, taken more by girls than boys is nowhere described as relevant to engineering and rarely to scientific or technical careers. Its relevance for medical and para-medical areas is stressed as well as some emphasis on food, work with animals and social sciences (largely female job areas). Work in agriculture very likely attracts some boys to biology. Human biology, a lower status subject than biology and more often taken by girls, is nowhere seen as having relevance to engineering or a technical job and only once to a scientific job; medical, para-medical and social services applications are stressed.

Thus the distribution of jobs seen as relevant to subjects in option booklets might be seen as having a strong influence on subject take up, given that boys and girls aspire to sex stereotyped careers. The argument can be extended to other subjects: home economics and technical drawing are the two subjects that are more successful than other craft subjects in attracting non-traditional choice. This may readily be explained in the case of home economics because catering and hotel management opportunities appeal to boys in a way that the much more traditionally female areas associated with needlework and child care and lower level commercial subjects do not. Technical drawing, unlike other technical subjects, holds some appeal for upper ability girls who aspire to jobs in town planning, surveying, architecture, draughtsmanship or design – these are office-based and of a different nature to the apprenticeships and trades to which technical subjects are more usually advertised as leading and which are far less populated by females. Computer studies, taken by slightly more boys than girls, is noted as having relevance for both commercial and scientific careers.

There is a remarkable similarity between the national figures on sex bias in subject take up and sex bias in the association of careers with subjects in options booklets. No doubt schools could be said to be reflecting the requirements of the labour market in their careers advice. However, if the circle of influence – from sex-biased subject choice to career choice and back to subject choice – is to be broken in any way it may be that schools could make changes to options booklets.

Certain examples from our survey suggest that this is not unreasonable: German is said by some schools to be useful in a scientific career. Typing is seen as relevant to police work by one school and to scientific work by another. It is likely that a case could be made for its relevance to many other careers followed by boys. The home and hobby applications of technical subjects might be given greater stress in order to attract girls. Tailoring in needlework might be made more of; catering careers already attract many boys to home economics but the possibility of doing such work in the forces – mentioned by one school – may be a stronger lure. These suggestions take it as read that career aspirations are stereotyped; but if pupils are persuaded to opt more for non-traditional subjects they may later become more flexible in their attitudes to work.

Similarly, it is noticeable that the general value of the sciences and particularly physics as ways of thinking (of use in any job) is not stressed. In the case of geography, history, mathematics and English their general value to employers is so much assumed that specific careers to which these subjects lead are rarely mentioned in options booklets. Surely a girl applying for a job in a bank or office would stand a better chance if she had a physics qualification? The general career value of science qualifications might be stressed in order to attract the non-traditional sex.

Conclusions

This analysis of the organization and presentation of subjects, particularly science, vocational and careers education, shows that the presentation of subjects in option booklets is symptomatic of the approach of teaching staff, and reflects presuppositions of departmental staff and the purpose of a course; in turn this reflects decisions to provide some career-specific courses – mainly for lower ability pupils. Only in schools with a declared policy of positive discrimination are the presuppositions which shape option descriptions likely to communicate a sense of free access to all subjects.

The analysis therefore presents us with two types of problem requiring different solutions. Subject descriptions may be altered; they can be scrutinized to identify bias and be rigorously revised to attract, or at least not discourage, choice by both boys and girls. The presuppositions of teaching staff present a less tractable problem which, though it may be confronted and solved in the longer term through discussion and policy formulation, still affects current provision.

Our analysis of subject descriptions shows that while a small minority of schools set out to restrict, to either boys or girls, access to some options, there is a disturbing incidence of inattention to detail resulting in discontinuity of presentation: an equal opportunity preamble may be followed by sex-biased subject descriptions. This can arise with the commonest method of creating option booklets: canvassing the departments for individual contributions which are uncritically accepted for inclusion. A small number of schools overcome this elementary error by scrutinizing and rewriting contributions, often at the level of head or deputy head editorship, but a number of respondents state the availability of all subjects to all pupils in a preamble and ensure their contributors are aware of the policy when they write their descriptions. In view of the wider issues including the influence of unquestioned presuppositions we believe it desirable for schools to convene a committee or working party with responsibility for examining contributions to ensure they are consistent and contain no bias or include positive discrimination, according to school policy.

It is clear that some schools have a policy of neutrality in relation to subject descriptions; they prefer to provide descriptions – oral and written – containing a minimum of encouragement. The approach appears to be based on a desire to avoid choices influenced by transient attractions such as persuasive or likeable teachers; in these schools the concept of positive discrimination will conflict with existing policy. We believe schools will want to examine the role of neutrality, because it may inadvertently support stereotypical views pupils bring to bear on their option choices. There is a place for positive discrimination in encouraging non-traditional choice in selected subjects simply because it will assist in overcoming existing negative influences on choice.

While we agree that option booklets benefit from a declaration that all subjects are open to all pupils we consider that neutral subject descriptions fail to remind and reinforce the message; it is especially easy to forget the words when they are stressed at the beginning of a booklet, with pages of intervening subject descriptions before the reader reaches (say) craft subjects. There are two common methods of overcoming this problem; schools can either repeat the message on each page or double-page spread where it is appropriate, or it can be contained in subject descriptions as a matter of course.

Sex bias may often be accidental. Some subject descriptions will be inappropriately couched in exclusive terms simply because we all tend to write in gender specific pronouns, or familiar patterns of take up have conditioned the thinking of the writer. Similarly, those booklets which include images of pupils in subjects could be scrutinized to ensure that neither boys nor girls are provided with an impression that a subject which is open to all may be thought appropriate to either sex. A corollary of this approach is removal of the impression that either sex will be in a minority in the classroom.

This will still be insufficiently positive for those schools which agree that neutral descriptions fail to overcome the stereotypes pupils apply when making their choices. It may be considered that both pupils and parents require positive persuasion to accept the value of a subject and its relevance to their aspirations. Schools will then wish to consider stressing topics within a subject; consideration can be given to selective promotion of topics which are known to appeal to both boys and girls; where positive discrimination is thought appropriate it may be that specific topics will be emphasized to attract non-traditional choice. To those who believe persuasion is dishonest it is relevant that a number of teachers are sure parents are unaware of the actual content of subjects. We encountered two examples of publicity campaigns mounted to obtain agreement from parents to changes the school wished to implement; in both cases it was believed that parents were persuaded to allow girls to be encouraged in non-traditional subjects (physical sciences and design and technology) when their lack of understanding of the value and relevance of the topics the subjects contained was remedied.

An increasingly popular method of increasing non-traditional choice is to change the title of the subject, though most of the examples we encountered were accompanied by alterations to syllabuses; and may be categorized as positive discrimination; the practice is most commonly found in craft departments where cookery courses have become home economics or food and nutrition and needlework courses have frequently become textiles or textile design. In sciences the introduction of integrated courses can result in topic-related units and options such as forensic science, or photography. Less controversially, the connotation placed on commerce has concerned some teacher to change the title to business studies. The predominance of alterations to syllabuses when the title is changed may be taken as a measure of our assessment that option booklet presentation is symptomatic of presuppositions and not of itself capable of overcoming subject stereotypes.

The impact of unbiased descriptions and positive discrimination needs consideration. In one school an attempt to change a pattern of take up had foundered on its success. Encouragement of girls to choose a physical science had resulted in a decline in take up of biological sciences; this threatened the balance of subjects the school thought it desirable to offer, and the status of the biology department. The school reversed its policy of encouragement and girls obligingly reverted to a choice of biology. We cannot endorse the remedy but we must sympathize with the problem; through discussion a more satisfactory answer can be sought. For example, in some schools the biology option is reserved for the sixth form, in others an integrated science course ensures biological and physical sciences are studied by all; in other schools a combination of at least two science options is compulsory; in each case departmental status and a balanced curriculum are preserved.

What might be called 'The resource argument' is commonly offered as a reason for maintaining restrictive practices and opposing change. The argument has little impact in those schools which wish to introduce change and mystifies schools which have a policy of positive discrimination. It is frequently encountered in response to suggestions for change in craft departments, but we feel it fails to convince because it appears to affect only those subjects in which girls are unwelcome. We have encountered schools in which the personal preference of cookery teachers has resulted in single-sex classes and distinct syllabuses for boys and girls. In the same schools the rigours of the syllabus, inadequate facilities and course aims are all cited as compelling reasons for excluding girls from metalwork classes.

The significance of single-sex classes in effecting non-traditional choice cannot be ignored. We have recorded the ironic institutional encouragement to non-traditional choice provided by single-sex classes in schools where the craft staff actively approve career and role stereotypes. In one school more girls achieved greater success in physical sciences after a teacher introduced a single-sex CSE group conducted by a female teacher. However, in some circumstances this organization can have undesirable secondary affects. For example, we occasionally encountered agreement between craft departments that girls should be discouraged from choosing traditionally male craft subjects. The attitudes and reasoning of the male craft staff are already clear, but it is also in the interests of the cookery department to oppose non-traditional choice. Because girls are most often allocated to GCE-level classes, the provision of single-sex classes and distinct syllabuses in cookery renders those classes vulnerable to undersubscription. We encountered no schools in which this consideration in isolation is responsible for discouragement of non-traditional choice, but it suggests caution in introducing single-sex classes into an otherwise unchanged craft studies environment.

The problem of isolation in the classroom for a minority sex is well known; our respondents believed it discourages non-traditional choice and plays a part in under-achievement by girls in sciences. Pupils in case study schools nominated isolation as an influence on their choice; boys talked of embarrassment and a sense of inferiority, girls of hostility from boys and inadequate attention from teachers. It was not a common problem and it rarely continued for long – with the exception of inadequate attention from teachers – but some pupils clearly avoid subjects where isolation is expected.

Some schools have used single-sex classes to encourage take up, and others have set out to encourage non-traditional choice by only a few pupils because a small minority (say five) has an accumulative impact. Some schools will reject positive discrimination and others will decide they lack resources to provide single-sex classes. In these cases we suggest a positive effort is made to group the minority gender in one or more mixed class. This can provide shelter and support during disruptive stages and encouragement to choose in the confidence that there is no possibility of being in a minority of one. It is said to have a significant impact on the problem of a minority sex 'disappearing' in the classroom and provides an opportunity to avoid the subordinate role girls tend to adopt during science experiments.

This aspect of organization raises the issue of whether schools have considered the implications of isolating the topic of equal opportunities within the syllabus of one subject. We can rephrase the issue as: Should equal opportunities be a topic in the syllabus or an influence upon the whole curriculum? Considering the school as a whole we find that the contradictions of presentation and organization between subjects lead us to question whether treatment of equal opportunities as a single topic has any useful result; does it reduce the issue to peripheral importance? Or does it acclimatize most pupils to a view that it is an esoteric consideration, somehow not connected with the real business of education or employment?

All this is not to recommend teachers to remove the topic from a syllabus merely because school policy is opposed to a broader curricular stance. But it does argue at the very least for full consideration of the issues and the aims of any syllabus. In some schools this will mean revision of the approach to the topic, in others it will imply urgent reassessment of the extent to which presentation and organization of individual subjects varies. A broader curricular stance, which we favour, implies considering the nature and purpose of education as a whole. Our views on this were reinforced by our experience in talking to teachers about their subjects. Few could articulate the skills, the qualities or experience that their subject offered to pupils in general: we suggest that this inability reflects a general failure of teachers to consider their basic aims and objectives, which failure manifests itself also in the patterns of sex differentiation we have observed. In other words, the issues of equal opportunities raised by this study point to a need to reassess not just the differences in curriculum offered to boys and girls, but the curriculum as a whole.

The two major themes resulting from our examination of careers provision concern the limits on time and extent of provision and the conspiracy between employers, careers officials and teachers which inhibits a non-traditional choice of career. A variety of imaginative approaches emerged in case study and survey schools, but the persistent preference of boys and girls for traditional careers testifies to the inadequacy of these measures to overcome job stereotypes. More seriously, we found widespread evidence of employer preference for either sex including a range of public bodies which expressed stereotypical preference, so we conclude that the majority of careers guidance is at present unlikely to have any serious impact on patterns of pupil choice.

Of those features of organization which are within the control of individual schools, we believe the most urgent need of change lies in allocation of time to careers guidance and a careers staff. The range of duties undertaken by existing staff is inadequately compensated by relief of other teaching duties and frequently falls to an interested amateur. In some respects this is inevitable when there already exists an external careers service whose responsibilities exceed their capacity to provide constant guidance within schools: the tendency is to 'fill in' between essential visits at key stages of pupil development. Most teachers rely on a liaison role accompanied by passive exposure of pupils to literature and available visiting speakers, though many careers staff also develop materials which assist pupils in learning self-evaluation and job application skills. In some schools careers lessons are effectively a form of social studies including hygiene and life role topics. In all case study schools the most effective guidance was said to be at pre-option stage when, presumably, the majority of pupils were less inhibited by imminent career decisions.

The role of career advice is a more sensitive issue even than subject choice; the consequences of careers choice can be far more serious than subject choice decisions. But the principal question to which careers teachers should address themselves is that of deciding whether they consider it right to prepare pupils blindly to accept the restrictions on choice exercised by employers. A commonly expressed ideal of not influencing choice of job or career must appear ill-considered when this feature is taken into account. One consequence of this is a need for provision of adequately trained teachers with a full timetable allowance for career guidance.

Those schools which believe in positive discrimination already provide elements of sex role evaluation in their careers programme; by counselling and a range of films, film strips and literature to introduce pupils to alternative careers. However, it is the common experience of teachers that lectures by visiting speakers are dominated by pupils of either sex, reflecting interests based on possible careers linked to expected examination attainment. We found this aspect of organization more disturbing than the relatively uncomplicated single-sex divisions employed by some schools to introduce, for example, hygiene topics. The composition of an audience at voluntary lectures is more likely to reflect a set of decisions taken within a stereotyped framework than the specific interests of the pupils. Option choices which eschew physical sciences and traditionally male craft subjects result in rational decisions not to attend engineering lectures. At least one school in our case study visits recognizes this point and intends to ensure girls are introduced to engineering careers before option choices are made: other schools occasionally expressed intentions to introduce non-traditional speakers, but few had made strenuous efforts. To some extent this difference in commitment reflects the personal qualities of guidance teachers, but it must also reflect the inadequate time allocated to organization and conduct of careers guidance in general.

The extent to which the job market controls pupil aspirations may be gauged by the evidence we received of conspiracy between teachers, career guidance counsellors and employers. Work experience programmes were said to be dominated by employer preference for either sex in specific jobs and LEA careers staff compiled sexist lists of placements which they gave to schools. The attitude of school staff varied between production of the list to justify a neutral approach to job choice and disconsolate recognition that the placements contradicted school policy on encouragement to non-traditional choice. The principal explanation for continuing with the scheme in its biased form is its value for pupils who are below average in their academic achievements: a bad scheme is seen as better than no scheme at all.

This is not a problem that schools can satisfactorily solve: they can attempt persuasion, perhaps with the external careers service, to alter the minds of employers, following which they must accept the conditions or ignore the offer of work placements. But the practice is illegal and could be changed by pressure on local and central government institutions, though goodwill may be lost and a declared policy of equal access may be accompanied by withdrawal of placement facilities. Similar results will almost certainly arise if independent businesses are coerced into altering their policy.

We suggest schools seriously reconsider the value of work experience schemes, the organization and breadth of choice. For example, the principal forms of organization involve either attempting to match pupils with available jobs or finding jobs to match demands. If jobs are sought to match demand, they will, if available, be relevant to the interests of the pupil. But if the pupil is offered a range of possible placements it is often Hobson's choice. This raises the question whether work experience is fulfilling its role. Similarly, it is questionable whether placing a pupil within a stereotyped framework is an improvement on simply acknowledging that freedom of choice may mean that placements are not always available.

CHAPTER 8

Teacher attitudes

This chapter presents the results of a survey of teacher attitudes and it is complemented by Chapter 9 on pupil attitudes. Our sample consisted of over 850 teachers in 50 schools in England and Wales in 1981–2. Table 8.1 presents the distribution of respondents by subject and according to sex; Table 8.2 identifies scale posts of respondents. It can be seen that the whole sample has a fairly balanced contribution from men and women although within subjects the distribution is very uneven.

Four of the eight subjects which contributed 5 per cent or more of responses have a wider than 60:40 imbalance; in each case the subject is dominated by males; imbalance is most pronounced among craft staff. We had a fairly high proportion of staff on scales 3 and 4, which, as other researchers have found, are dominated by males, as are more senior posts. At the lower levels, there were twice as many women as men on scale 1.

In subsequent analyses we have adopted a 5 per cent minimum contribution as our measure for highlighting subject group responses in the whole sample: biology teachers are within this measure but physics teachers are grouped along with chemistry responses. Subjects such as social studies and mathematics are identified as they constitute a more than 5 per cent response, although they are not controversial option choice subjects.

Teacher attitude scales

Tables 8.3, 8.4 and 8.5, utilize a measure we have called 'Score T'. It represents the simple addition of the number each respondent ringed for each statement, taking into account a need to reverse the values of statements where a high number represented sympathy with equal opportunity principles. On this measure, a low score indicates a

Option choice

Table 8.1 Distribution of respondents: subject and gender

Subject	Female (%)	Male (%)	% of all responses
English	61 (54·0)	52 (46·0)	13·2
Mathematics	30 (35·3)	55 (64·7)	10·0
Physics	5 (13·5)	32 (86·5)	4·3
Chemistry	6 (17·1)	29 (82·9)	4·1
Biology	21 (47·7)	23 (52·3)	5·2
Integrated science	5 (31·3)	11 (68·8)	1·9
French	31 (59·6)	21 (40·4)	6·1
German	3 (25·0)	9 (75·0)	1·4
Geography	19 (33·3)	38 (66·7)	6·7
History	22 (34·9)	41 (65·1)	7·4
Art	10 (28·6)	25 (71·4)	4·1
Drama	2 (22·2)	7 (77·8)	1·1
Typing	11 (91·7)	1 (8·3)	1·4
Office practice	1 (100)	— —	0·1
Needlework	3 (100)	— —	0·4
Home economics	40 (100)	— —	4·7
Child care	3 (100)	— —	0·4
Metalwork	— —	8 (100)	0·9
Woodwork	— —	9 (100)	1·1
Technical studies	5 (13·5)	32 (86·5)	4·3
Computer studies	— —	2 (100)	0·2
Business studies	— —	3 (100)	0·4
Economics	2 (15·4)	11 (84·6)	1·5
Physical education	24 (47·1)	27 (52·9)	6·0
Remedial education	8 (66·7)	4 (33·3)	1·4
Careers	5 (38·5)	8 (61·5)	1·5
Latin	1 (25·0)	3 (75·0)	0·5
Social studies	23 (39·0)	36 (61·0)	6·9
Music	6 (27·3)	16 (72·7)	2·6
Other	3 (75·0)	1 (25·0)	0·2

Table 8.2 Distribution of respondents within scale post and gender

Scale Post	Males	Females	Male %	Female %	Whole sample
Head teacher	37	11	77·1	22·9	5·8
Deputy head	30	17	63·8	36·2	5·7
Senior teacher	42	9	82·4	17·6	6·1
Scale: 4	154	44	77·8	22·2	23·8
3	124	95	56·6	43·4	26·4
2	52	73	41·6	58·4	15·1
1	47	94	33·3	66·7	17·0
Totals	486	343	58·6	41·4	100

Note: 34 missing observations.

sympathetic attitude to equal opportunity, a high score, a lack of sympathy; the minimum possible score is 28 and the maximum 140: (1 or 5 × 28 statements); in the event, no respondent scored more than 117. We have presented our results according to the distribution of responses in the whole sample, in approximately 20 per cent groups. Thus, roughly 20 per cent of respondents scored between 28 and 49; 50 and 58; 59 and 65; 66 and 74; 75 and 117. Scores of 65 and below indicate a positive commitment for promoting equal opportunities, those of 66 and above increasing opposition to it.

Table 8.3 Agreement with EOC policy on good practice: Score T in nominated and cluster schools

	28–49	50–58	59–65	66–74	75–117	Base
Nominated	20·9	20·7	20·0	17·7	20·7	
	106	105	102	90	105	508
Cluster	16·3	18·9	14·9	25·9	23·9	
	58	67	53	92	85	355
Totals	19·0	19·9	18·0	21·1	22·0	
Base	164	172	155	182	190	863

Table 8.3 shows that the teachers within nominated and cluster schools display attitudes generally corresponding with the assessment of CEOs who assisted with the definitions. 'Score T' is not a subtle tool, but Table 8.3 clearly demonstrates that more teachers in nominated than cluster schools were interested in promoting equal opportunity as defined in the attitude scale.

Table 8.4 Agreement with EOC policy on good practice: Score T by sex of respondent

	28–49	50–58	59–65	66–74	75–117	Base
Females	24·3	24·3	18·1	18·6	14·7	
	86	86	64	66	52	354
Males	15·2	17·0	17·8	22·9	27·2	
	77	86	90	116	138	507
Totals	18·9	20·0	17·9	21·1	22·1	
Base	163	172	154	182	190	861

Table 8.4 indicates that gender has an impact on the responses. Fifty per cent of male responses indicated opposition to equal opportunity, 27 per cent of which are found in the most negative category, compared with 33 and 15 per cent of female responses. However, we must qualify this with reference to our examination of responses from major subject groups. As we note later, subject specialisms appear to be related to responses, especially where a statement implies change in the teacher's or a related department.

Table 8.5 records the scores of teachers by major subject groups. It shows that there is a significant difference in emphasis between subject groups. The male-dominated physical sciences and mathematics teachers, together with craft and technical teachers had fewest scores indicating very positive attitudes to equal opportunity (range 28–49); and they are the most likely to oppose it (score 75–117). Teachers of domestic and secretarial subjects and languages did not have strong positive attitudes, but this is balanced in the middle range of scores to indicate slightly less opposition and acceptance of the need for change. Biology respondents are less opposed to equal opportunities than other teachers in the sample but not strongly in favour of it. The subjects with the highest proportion of staff expressing agreement with equal opportunities were English and social studies. The latter included teachers of religious knowledge, sociology, etc., but interestingly is predominantly male. The group of English teachers is fairly evenly split between men and women.

Table 8.5   Score T by subject

Subject	28–49	50–58	59–66	67–74	75–117	Base
English	33·0	27·2	17·5	8·7	13·6	103
Mathematics	5·3	19·7	18·4	30·3	26·3	76
Social studies	34·0	18·0	12·0	20·0	16·0	50
Physical education	10·4	14·6	20·8	18·8	35·4	48
History	24·1	17·2	24·1	12·1	22·4	58
Geography	20·4	18·5	25·9	13·0	22·2	54
Physical science	7·5	12·0	25·4	17·9	37·3	67
Biology	17·5	22·5	20·0	27·5	12·5	40
Domestic and secretarial	12·7	14·6	25·5	27·3	20·0	55
Bench and technical	7·8	21·6	25·5	19·6	25·5	51
French and German	8·3	21·7	26·7	20·0	23·3	60
Others	25·2	23·4	18·0	12·6	20·7	111
Note:						
French	4·2	20·8	27·1	22·9	25·0	48
Technical	8·8	26·5	20·6	20·6	23·5	34
Chemistry	12·1	18·2	21·2	9·1	39·4	33

These results thus reveal some striking differences in teacher attitudes, not only in option subjects, but in 'core' subjects. In virtually every school, pupils follow English, mathematics and usually physical education until leaving age. The teachers of these subjects hold widely differing views on schools' responsibilities to encourage equal opportunities, with English teachers generally strongly in favour, and mathematics and to a lesser extent physical education teachers, distinctly lukewarm towards encouraging equality. The attitudes of mathematic teachers are particularly significant as they suggest that girls' reluctance to continue to study mathematics – and by association physical sciences – is unlikely to be widely recognized as a matter of concern by mathematics teachers. Similarly, the results show that in traditionally stereotyped subjects, such as physical sciences and crafts, pupils are taught by teachers with low positive commitments to equal opportunities, who are unlikely to wish to redress disparities in take up.

Basic beliefs

We examined responses to particular statements in more detail. Our starting point was the possibility that teachers a) believe there are sound psychological grounds for maintaining existing practices, or b) believe current practices treat boys and girls fairly. We therefore stated:

Statement 24 Innate psychological differences between the sexes are largely responsible for the different subject and career choices of boys and girls.

Statement 14 The educational system treats girls less favourably than boys.

Statement number	Strongly agree	Mildly agree	Unsure/ uncommitted	Mildly disagree	Strongly disagree	Base
24	8·5	28·5	16·4	16·5	30·2	849
14	11·5	27·2	15·0	24·7	21·6	846

The response was, at best, equivocal insofar as nearly 50 per cent indicated there are no natural impediments to change. But over a third thought there are differences between the sexes, and nearly half think the present system treats girls and boys fairly. Male teachers are less committed than females to strong views on *Statement 24*; though more are mildly in agreement with the statement. On *Statement 14*, more women than men feel the system treats girls less favourably (see Table 8.6).

Responses (see Table 8.7) to *Statement 24* include strong agreement by domestic and secretarial staff (21 per cent and 24·2 per cent), high levels of agreement among bench and technical staff (13 per cent and 38·9 per cent) and least agreement by biology staff (4·7 per cent and 27·9 per cent). Physical science teachers were unsure. The 618 teachers, mainly of English and history, outside these groups collectively demonstrate positive disagreement.

Option choice

Table 8.6 Responses of female and male teachers to Statements 24 and 14

Statement 24 Innate psychological differences between the sexes are largely responsible for the different subject and career choices of boys and girls.

Sex	Strongly agree	Mildly agree	Unsure/ uncommitted	Mildly disagree	Strongly disagree	Base
Female	10.8	24.7	11.6	19.3	33.5	352
Male	6.8	31.0	20.1	14.7	27.4	503

Statement 14 The educational system treats girls less favourably than boys.

Sex	Strongly agree	Mildly agree	Unsure/ uncommitted	Mildly disagree	Strongly disagree	Base
Female	13.4	30.4	13.6	22.4	20.2	352
Male	10.0	24.8	15.8	26.4	23.0	500

These responses indicate a wide spectrum of views among teachers of different disciplines, with physical education teachers agreeing most strongly, and social studies most strongly disagreeing; mathematic teachers were (characteristically?) most uncertain. Remembering from Table 8.1 that history, mathematics and social studies teachers are predominantly male, it is clear that gender is not necessarily the most significant factor influencing the response (but see Table 8.7 below).

Table 8.7 Responses to Statement 24 by subject

Statement 24 Innate psychological differences between the sexes are largely responsible for the different subject and career choices of boys and girls.

Subject	Strongly agree	Mildly agree	Unsure/ uncommitted	Mildly disagree	Strongly disagree	Base
English	5.3	22.1	14.2	21.2	37.2	113
Mathematics	8.3	29.8	26.2	10.7	25.0	84
Social studies	0.0	20.7	8.6	20.7	50.0	58
Physical education	11.8	39.2	13.7	13.7	21.6	51
History	5.0	32.8	13.4	13.4	35.3	119
Physical science	8.3	26.4	29.0	15.3	20.8	72
Biology	4.7	27.9	11.6	27.9	27.9	43
Domestic and secretarial	21.0	24.2	12.9	24.2	17.7	62
Bench and technical	13.0	38.9	18.5	9.3	20.4	54
French and German	12.5	29.7	14.1	14.1	29.7	64
Other	8.5	27.1	15.5	15.5	33.3	129

Responses (see Table 8.8) to *Statement 14* polarized like those to *Statement 24*, though physical science and mathematics staff were least in agreement with the statement and the biology response was close to the whole sample agreement.

Table 8.8 Responses to Statement 14 by subject
Statement 14 The education system treats girls less favourably than boys.

Subject	Strongly agree	Mildly agree	Unsure/ uncommitted	Mildly disagree	Strongly disagree	Base
English	22·5	32·4	19·8	16·2	9·0	111
Mathematics	3·5	28·2	12·9	29·4	25·9	85
Social studies	24·1	25·9	12·1	27·6	10·3	58
Physical education	5·9	27·5	9·8	31·4	25·5	51
History	14·2	27·5	19·2	23·3	15·8	120
Physical science	5·7	24·3	14·3	34·3	21·4	70
Biology	7·0	32·6	7·0	32·6	20·9	43
Domestic and secretarial	8·2	24·6	11·5	18·0	37·7	61
Bench and technical	5·6	18·5	13·0	25·9	37·0	54
French and German	11·1	19·0	14·3	17·5	38·1	63
Other	13·3	28·2	16·2	23·6	18·8	130

Physical education and mathematics teachers emerge as disagreeing most with the statement and thus as the least critical of the current system. Social studies teachers are most strongly critical of the system, but English teachers are a close second and least likely to agree with the statement.

Commitment to equal opportunity

We selected four statements to reflect a range of commitment to encouragement of equal opportunity.

Statement 1 Schools should set an example in reducing sex discrimination.

Statement 7 I am generally sympathetic to teachers and educationists trying to encourage equal opportunities between the sexes.

Statement 20 Teachers should encourage equal opportunities between the sexes even when there is no parental support for this policy.

Statement 16 I am particularly interested in encouraging equality between the sexes in my teaching.

Responses were as follows.

Statement number	Strongly agree	Mildly agree	Unsure/ uncommitted	Mildly disagree	Strongly disagree	Base
1	60·6	32·0	4·4	2·0	1·1	848
7	68·0	25·0	3·8	1·6	1·5	851
20	51·4	34·9	8·5	3·1	2·1	847
16	41·9	30·6	21·0	4·2	2·2	849

We anticipated considerable difference between responses to *Statement 1* and all others because teachers in case study schools had given the impression that although they favoured reduction of sex discrimination they were opposed to positive discrimination policies. But this was not the case in our attitude survey. More respondents voted more positively for encouragement to equal opportunity (*Statement 7*) than for the school to set an example in reducing sex discrimination. Moreover, teachers in general expressed a strong commitment to both the institutional role of the school in reducing discrimination and the role of the teacher and educationist in promoting equality of opportunity. Over 90 per cent of teachers agreed with *Statement 1* and *Statement 7*.

When faced with issues of implementation teachers are less sure of their opinion and less positive towards equal opportunities. Of the sample 5·2 per cent want parental approval before implementing the policy *(Statement 20)*, and a further 8·5 per cent are unsure or uncommitted. Six per cent are not particularly interested in encouraging equal opportunities in their teaching (*Statement 16*), and a massive 21 per cent are unsure or uncommitted; only 42 per cent are strongly committed to encouragement. In all cases, more female teachers than males were strongly committed to equal opportunities (see Table 8.9).

Table 8.9 Responses of female and male teachers to Statements 1, 7, 20 and 16

Statement 1 Schools should set an example in reducing sex discrimination

Sex	Strongly agree	Mildly agree	Unsure/ uncommitted	Mildly disagree	Strongly disagree	Base
Female	68·2	28·1	2·8	0·9	0·0	352
Male	55·4	34·5	5·4	3·0	1·8	502

Statement 7 I am generally sympathetic to teachers and educationists trying to encourage equal opportunities between the sexes

Sex	Strongly agree	Mildly agree	Unsure/ uncommitted	Mildly disagree	Strongly disagree	Base
Female	76·7	18·8	2·6	0·9	1·1	352
Male	62·0	29·5	4·6	2·2	1·8	505

Statement 20 Teachers should encourage equal opportunities between the sexes even when there is no parental support for this policy

Sex	Strongly agree	Mildly agree	Unsure/ uncommitted	Mildly disagree	Strongly disagree	Base
Female	59·9	30·1	5·7	2·0	2·3	352
Male	45·3	38·5	10·4	3·8	2·0	501

Statement 16 I am particularly interested in encouraging equality between the sexes in my teaching

Sex	Strongly agree	Mildly agree	Unsure/ uncommitted	Mildly disagree	Strongly disagree	Base
Female	51·1	32·3	12·3	2·3	2·0	350
Male	35·7	29·6	26·8	5·6	2·4	504

While the overall response to each of these statements is overwhelmingly positive, there are differences of emphasis according to subject (see Table 8.10). In general, teachers of English and social science agree strongly with the statements. Mathematics, physical education, physical science and bench and technical teachers show least positive agreement with them. However, there is also low support for *Statement 1* from teachers of domestic and secretarial subjects, and less enthusiasm for *Statement 16* by history and French and German teachers than for other statements.

Table 8.10 Responses to Statements 1, 7, 20 and 16 by subject

Statement 1 Schools should set an example in reducing sex discrimination.

Subject	Strongly agree	Mildly agree	Unsure/ uncommitted	Mildly disagree	Strongly disagree	Base
English	78·6	15·2	5·4	0·9	0·0	112
Mathematics	48·8	42·9	4·8	2·4	1·2	84
Social studies	73·7	26·3	0·0	0·0	0·0	57
Physical education	43·1	49·0	5·9	2·0	0·0	51
History	64·2	30·8	4·2	0·8	0·0	120
Physical science	49·3	39·4	4·2	4·2	2·8	71
Biology	63·6	29·5	4·5	2·3	0·0	44
Domestic and secretarial	47·5	44·3	6·6	1·6	0·0	61
Bench and technical	50·0	35·2	3·7	7·4	3·7	54
French and German	59·4	28·1	6·3	4·7	1·6	64

Option choice

Table 8.10 Responses to Statements 1, 7, 20 and 16 by subject—*contd.*

Statement 7 I am generally sympathetic to teachers and educationists trying to encourage equal opportunities between the sexes

Subject	Strongly agree	Mildly agree	Unsure/ uncommitted	Mildly disagree	Strongly disagree	Base
English	83·2	11·5	2·7	0·0	2·7	113
Mathematics	60·7	32·1	3·6	3·6	0·0	84
Social studies	71·2	27·1	1·7	0·0	0·0	59
Physical education	52·0	36·0	10·0	2·0	0·0	50
History	69·2	26·7	1·7	0·8	1·7	120
Physical science	54·9	28·2	8·5	5·6	2·8	71
Biology	68·2	29·5	0·0	0·0	2·3	44
Domestic and secretarial	65·6	26·2	4·9	3·3	0·0	61
Bench and technical	63·0	29·6	5·6	0·0	1·9	54
French and German	71·9	21·9	1·6	3·1	1·6	64

Statement 20 Teachers should encourage equal opportunities between the sexes even when there is no parental support for this policy.

Subject	Strongly agree	Mildly agree	Unsure/ uncommitted	Mildly disagree	Strongly disagree	Base
English	62·8	29·2	5·3	1·8	0·9	113
Mathematics	44·6	42·2	8·4	4·8	0·0	83
Social studies	55·2	39·7	3·4	1·7	0·0	58
Physical education	41·2	37·3	11·8	7·8	2·0	51
History	52·9	35·3	8·4	3·4	0·0	119
Physical science	44·3	37·1	5·7	5·7	7·0	70
Biology	53·5	34·9	9·3	0·0	2·3	43
Domestic and secretarial	48·4	30·6	11·3	4·8	4·8	62
Bench and technical	38·9	38·9	16·7	3·7	1·9	54
French and German	51·6	37·5	6·3	1·6	3·1	64

Statement 16 I am particularly interested in encouraging equality between the sexes in my teaching.

Subject	Strongly agree	Mildly agree	Unsure/ uncommitted	Mildly disagree	Strongly disagree	Base
English	51·3	30·1	15·9	0·9	1·8	113
Mathematics	33·7	33·7	25·3	4·8	2·4	83
Social studies	57·6	16·9	20·3	3·4	1·7	59
Physical education	30·0	28·0	28·0	14·0	0·0	50
History	28·3	40·0	25·0	5·0	1·7	120
Physical science	32·4	31·0	29·6	2·8	4·2	71
Biology	53·5	23·3	16·3	4·7	2·3	43
Domestic and secretarial	44·3	34·4	11·5	4·9	4·9	61
Bench and technical	42·6	31·5	24·1	1·9	0·0	54
French and German	34·4	28·1	23·4	7·8	6·3	64

The role of careers education

In *Statement 11* and *Statement 26* we find reinforcement of the contrasts apparent in the general questions.

Statement 11 It is important that careers education should encourage pupils to look critically at sex roles in society.

Statement 26 A careers teacher should make positive efforts to encourage pupils to consider taking up subjects or careers that are not normally done by their sex.

Statement	Strongly agree	Mildly agree	Unsure/ uncommitted	Mildly disagree	Strongly disagree	Base
11	44·5	30·4	14·9	5·9	4·3	852
26	26·3	37·3	17·7	12·5	6·1	847

The agreement with encouragement of pupils to look critically at sex roles in society is not matched by a desire to encourage take up of non-traditional subjects or careers. In other words teachers are willing to endorse a programme designed to widen appreciation of the issues of equal opportunity, but not to extend that endorsement to positive efforts to change things. Our case study interviews often elicited this distinction between passive provision of information and active encouragement to non-traditional choice, including a belief that equal opportunities are made available simply by providing a 'neutral' atmosphere in which pupils seek, or are given, relevant information.

There were again differences in responses from male and female teachers, with more of the latter in agreement with the statements and more strongly in agreement (see Table 8.11). Nearly half of them are either uncommitted to or disagree with *Statement 26*.

Table 8.11   Responses of female and male teachers to Statements 11 and 26

Statement 11   It is important that careers education should encourage pupils to look critically at sex roles in society.

Sex	Strongly agree	Mildly agree	Unsure/ uncommitted	Mildly disagree	Strongly disagree	Base
Female	50·8	26·6	11·3	6·5	4·8	354
Male	40·3	32·9	17·5	5·4	4·0	504

Statement 26   A careers teacher should make positive efforts to encourage pupils to consider taking up subjects or careers that are not normally done by their sex.

Sex	Strongly agree	Mildly agree	Unsure/ uncommitted	Mildly disagree	Strongly disagree	Base
Female	31·1	38·0	15·7	10·6	4·6	350
Male	22·9	36·8	19·3	13·9	7·2	503

Some subject groups provided extremes of opinion on each statement (see Table 8.12).

Table 8.12   Responses to Statements 11 and 26 by subject

Statement 11   It is important that careers education should encourage pupils to look critically at sex roles in society.

Subject	Strongly agree	Mildly agree	Unsure/ uncommitted	Mildly disagree	Strongly disagree	Base
English	65·5	22·1	8·0	1·8	2·7	113
Mathematics	32·9	29·4	23·5	9·4	4·7	85
Social studies	59·3	28·8	6·8	3·4	1·7	59
Physical education	21·6	39·2	27·5	9·8	2·0	51
History	42·5	36·7	13·3	4·2	3·3	120
Physical science	32·9	34·3	18·6	8·6	5·7	70
Biology	31·8	43·2	13·6	9·1	2·3	44
Domestic and secretarial	46·8	25·8	11·3	9·7	6·5	62
Bench and technical	35·2	27·8	22·2	9·3	5·6	54
French and German	43·8	28·1	10·9	4·7	12·5	64

Statement 26 A careers teacher should make positive efforts to encourage pupils to consider taking up subjects or careers that are not normally done by their sex.

Subject	Strongly agree	Mildly agree	Unsure/ uncommitted	Mildly disagree	Strongly disagree	Base
English	34·5	41·6	14·2	7·1	2·7	113
Mathematics	21·7	34·9	19·3	18·1	6·0	83
Social studies	42·1	29·8	19·3	7·0	1·8	57
Physical education	23·5	25·5	19·6	23·5	7·8	51
History	24·2	40·0	17·5	13·3	5·0	120
Physical science	20·0	34·3	21·4	14·3	10·0	70
Biology	18·2	54·5	13·6	9·1	4·5	44
Domestic and secretarial	24·6	36·1	13·1	19·7	6·6	61
Bench and technical	18·5	33·3	20·4	18·5	9·3	54
French and German	20·3	43·8	17·2	7·8	10·9	64

Again, English and social science teachers are most positive in agreement, mathematics, physical science, bench and technical and physical education teachers least, though fewer biology teachers than other groups agree strongly with *Statement 26*.

Physical sciences and technical subjects

One of the most obvious disparities in subject take-up by boys and girls is in physical sciences and technical crafts. We can examine teachers' attitudes by looking at *Statement 22* and *Statement 6*.

Statement 22 At least one of the physical sciences should be made compulsory for all up to the age of 16.

Statement 6 Where there is insufficient workshop space in technical subjects (e.g. metalwork, motor vehicle engineering) then boys should be given preference over girls in these subjects.

Overall responses to these statements were as follows.

Statement	Strongly agree	Mildly agree	Unsure/ uncommitted	Mildly disagree	Strongly disagree	Base
22	43·2	30·0	13·0	8·3	5·7	848
6	11·5	26·0	6·6	19·6	36·3	849

We can note in overall responses the surprising support for the notion of compulsory core physical science, yet a considerable number of teachers believe bench and technical subjects are more appropriate to the education and career needs of boys than girls.

There was little difference in the responses of male and female teachers to the idea of compulsory physical science.

Statement 22 At least one of the physical sciences should be made compulsory for all up to the age of 16.

Sex	Strongly agree	Mildly agree	Unsure/ uncommitted	Mildly disagree	Strongly disagree	Base
Female	44·9	30·6	13·1	7·4	4·0	350
Male	41·9	29·6	12·7	8·9	6·9	504

In response to *Statement 6*, there was some differentiation with over 40 per cent of male teachers agreeing that boys should be given preference in technical subjects, compared with a surprisingly large 30 per cent of female teachers:

Statement 6 Where there is insufficient workshop space in technical subjects (e.g. metalwork, motor vehicle engineering) then boys should be given preference over girls in these subjects.

Sex	Strongly agree	Mildly agree	Unsure/ uncommitted	Mildly disagree	Strongly disagreee	Base
Female	8·0	22·2	6·6	22·5	40·7	351
Male	13·7	28·4	6·5	18·1	33·3	504

Table 8.13 Responses to Statements 22 and 6 by subject

Statement 22 At least one of the physical sciences should be made compulsory for all up to the age of 16.

Subject	Strongly agree	Mildly agree	Unsure/ uncommitted	Mildly disagree	Strongly disagree	Base
English	51·8	28·6	9·8	5·4	4·5	112
Mathematics	37·6	35·3	12·9	8·2	5·9	85
Social studies	46·6	27·6	15·5	6·9	3·4	58
Physical education	34·0	40·0	10·0	12·0	4·0	50
History	45·4	26·9	15·1	8·4	4·2	119
Physical science	65·3	12·5	6·9	11·1	4·2	72
Biology	36·4	27·3	9·1	13·6	13·6	44
Domestic and secretarial	43·5	37·1	6·5	9·7	3·2	62
Bench and technical	38·9	42·6	14·8	3·7	0·0	54
French and German	38·1	22·2	17·5	12·7	9·5	63

Statement 6 Where there is insufficent workshop space in technical subjects (e.g. metalwork, motor vehicle engineering) then boys should be given preference over girls in these subjects.

Subject	Strongly agree	Mildly agree	Unsure/ uncommitted	Mildly disagree	Strongly disagree	Base
English	12·4	15·9	8·0	24·8	38·9	113
Mathematics	11·9	27·4	3·6	22·6	34·5	84
Social studies	13·6	20·3	3·4	16·9	45·8	59
Physical education	19·6	21·6	7·8	25·5	25·5	51
History	5·9	29·4	5·0	16·8	42·9	119
Physical science	4·2	35·2	8·5	21·1	31·0	71
Biology	2·3	31·8	9·1	27·3	29·5	44
Domestic and secretarial	16·4	34·4	4·9	14·8	29·5	61
Bench and technical	24·5	26·4	1·9	15·1	32·1	53
French and German	15·9	15·9	12·7	23·8	31·7	63

In terms of the subjects they teach, teachers show wide differences in their views on these isssues. Physical science teachers show themselves to be most in favour of equal opportunities when this means compulsory physical science! History, physical education and biology teachers show the least strong agreement though have high percentages of mild agreement. Teachers of bench and technical subjects are most in favour of *Statement 6*, though their opinions are roughly evenly split between agreement and disagreement (see Table 8.13).

Stereotyped subjects

In *Statements 4, 5* and *17* we sought to establish attitudes towards stereotyping subjects (*Statement 4*) and the role of teachers in this process (*Statement 5* and *Statement 17*).

Statement 4 It would be a good thing if pupils did not regard certain school subjects as 'girls' subjects' and others as 'boys' subjects'.

Statement 5 Teachers generally tend to support pupils' existing ideas about what subjects and jobs are appropriate for each sex.

Statement 17 The teaching profession tends to give pupils the impression that some subjects are more appropriate for one sex than the other sex.

Statement Number	Strongly agree	Mildly agree	Unsure/ uncommitted	Mildly disagree	Strongly disagree	Base
4	73·3	19·9	1·5	3·2	2·1	851
5	7·2	47·0	15·9	21·9	8·1	851
17	16·5	55·2	10·7	12·3	5·3	852

Statements 4, 5 and *17* and their responses are a measure of the gulf between recognition of a problem and the difficulty of implementing a policy to achieve a solution. Strong and nearly complete agreement that subjects should not be stereotyped is matched in *Statement 4* with mild majority agreement that teachers in practice support and encourage stereotyping of subjects by pupils.

There were few differences in the views of male and female teachers on these statements. Fewer male teachers than female strongly agreed with *Statement 4*, and more disagreed (though the latter figures are small): there were only slight differences in responses to *Statement 5* and *Statement 17* (see Table 8.14).

Table 8.14   Responses of female and male teachers to Statements 4, 5 and 17

Statement 4   It would be a good thing if pupils did not regard certain school subjects as 'girls' subjects' and others as 'boys' subjects'.

Sex	Strongly agree	Mildly agree	Unsure/ uncommitted	Mildly disagree	Strongly disagree	Base
Female	82·6	13·7	0·6	2·0	1·1	351
Male	66·8	24·3	2·2	4·0	2·8	506

Statement 5   Teachers generally tend to support pupils existing ideas about what subjects and jobs are appropriate for each sex.

Sex	Strongly agree	Mildly agree	Unsure/ uncommitted	Mildly disagree	Strongly disagree	Base
Female	5·9	50·1	14·2	20·7	9·1	353
Male	7·9	45·0	17·1	22·4	7·5	504

Statement 17   The teaching profession tends to give pupils the impression that some subjects are more appropriate for one sex than the other sex.

Sex	Strongly agree	Mildly agree	Unsure/ uncommitted	Mildly disagree	Strongly disagree	Base
Female	19·5	54·0	8·5	12·7	5·4	354
Male	14·7	56·0	12·1	12·1	5·2	504

Least support for *Statement 4* came from physical education, bench and technical and domestic and secretarial teachers, with 12 per cent of the latter in favour of pupils identifying 'boys' and girls' ' subjects (see

Table 8.15). An unusual agreement between bench and technical and social science teachers occurred in response to *Statement 5*, who showed most positive agreement that teachers tend to support pupils' views on stereotyping of subjects and jobs, though presumably for opposite reasons. Bench and technical teachers also agreed most strongly with *Statement 17*, again closely followed by social science

Table 8.15 Responses to Statements 4, 5 and 17 by subject

Statement 4 It would be a good thing if pupils did not regard certain school subjects as 'girls' subjects' and others as 'boys' subjects'.

Subject	Strongly agree	Mildly agree	Unsure/ uncommitted	Mildly disagree	Strongly disagree	Base
English	84·1	11·5	1·8	1·8	0·9	113
Mathematics	74·7	19·3	2·4	1·2	2·4	83
Social studies	78·0	18·6	0·0	3·4	0·0	59
Physical education	52·9	37·3	2·0	5·9	2·0	51
History	74·2	18·3	1·7	4·2	1·7	120
Physical science	68·1	26·4	0·0	2·8	2·8	72
Biology	79·5	15·9	0·0	2·3	2·3	44
Domestic and secretarial	65·0	21·7	1·7	6·7	5·0	60
Bench and technical	57·4	29·6	5·6	7·4	0·0	54
French and German	81·3	15·6	1·6	1·6	0·0	64

Statement 5 Teachers generally tend to support pupils' existing ideas about what subjects and jobs are appropriate for each sex.

Subject	Strongly agree	Mildly agree	Unsure/ uncommitted	Mildly disagree	Strongly disagree	Base
English	7·1	54·0	20·4	13·3	5·3	113
Mathematics	6·0	43·4	15·7	24·1	10·8	83
Social studies	13·8	53·4	8·6	19·0	5·2	5·8
Physical education	5·9	52·9	17·6	21·6	2·0	51
History	5·9	47·9	14·3	25·2	6·7	119
Physical science	5·6	36·0	20·8	29·2	8·3	72
Biology	4·5	40·9	18·2	25·0	11·4	44
Domestic and secretarial	3·2	46·8	12·9	22·6	14·5	62
Bench and technical	11·1	46·3	13·0	20·4	9·3	54
French and German	7·8	39·1	10·9	28·1	14·1	64

Table 8.15 Responses to Statements 4, 5 and 17 by subject—*contd.*

Statement 17   The teaching profession tends to give pupils the impression that some subjects are more appropriate for one sex than the other sex.

Subject	Strongly agree	Mildly agree	Unsure/ uncommitted	Mildly disagree	Strongly disagree	Base
English	22·1	48·7	14·2	9·7	5·3	113
Mathematics	9·4	62·4	12·9	9·4	5·9	85
Social studies	22·4	56·9	10·3	6·9	3·4	58
Physical education	15·7	58·8	9·8	11·8	3·9	51
History	12·6	56·3	9·2	18·5	3·4	119
Physical science	6·9	45·8	16·7	27·8	2·8	72
Biology	13·6	45·5	20·5	11·4	9·1	44
Domestic and secretarial	17·7	61·3	4·8	6·5	9·7	62
Bench and technical	27·8	57·4	0·0	11·1	3·7	54
French and German	15·6	51·6	7·8	17·2	7·8	64

teachers. Mathematics and physical science teachers showed least strong agreement, thus disclaiming their own views expressed on other statements.

The responses in Table 8.15 suggest that of teachers of stereotyped subjects, bench and technical staff are least likely to approve innovation aimed at encouraging pupils to widen their view of appropriate subjects. In their responses to *Statement 5* and *Statement 17* they stand in opposition to the majority of staff in our survey, more frequently indicating that in their opinion stereotyping is not a problem.

Encouragement of non-traditional choice

In the following set of statements we have again matched proposed solutions with defined problems, in this case the problem of stereotyped subjects and encouragement to choose non-traditionally.

Statement 21   Boys should be encouraged by teachers to take subjects like child-care and home economics.

Statement 23   Efforts to encourage boys to opt for domestic subjects like child care and home economics are generally misguided.

Statement 28   Schools should encourage girls to study technical and scientific subjects.

Statement 27 Efforts to encourage girls to opt for technical subjects like motor vehicle engineering and technical drawing are generally misguided.

Responses were as follows.

Statement Number	Strongly agree	Mildly agree	Unsure/ uncommitted	Mildly disagree	Strongly disagree	Base
21	40·0	35·3	13·9	5·3	5·4	846
23	6·9	12·9	24·9	25·8	29·6	846
28	53·8	35·1	7·5	2·0	1·5	845
27	4·7	14·2	21·5	31·5	28·1	847

Respondents clearly desire positive action to oppose stereotyping of subjects (*Statement 21* and *Statement 28*), but they are unsure of the validity of the action proposed (*Statement 23* and *Statement 27*). An interpretation is that they have not linked the questions, but treat them as separate items: they believe encouragement should take place whether or not it is misguided. It is notable that the whole sample is most confident when faced with the issue of girls and science or technology, though respondents remain consistently unsure of the remedy.

There are some differences according to the sex of respondents (see Table 8.16). Male teachers show less strong agreement than female to *Statement 21* and *Statement 28*, and more uncertainty to all statements. Apart from male teachers' uncertainty, responses to *Statement 23* are almost identical, while more men feel that encouraging girls to opt for technical subjects (*Statement 27*) is misguided.

Teachers of different subjects exhibited wide differences in response to some of these statements (see Table 8.17). Only a third as many physical science teachers as English teachers expressed strong agreement with *Statement 21*; 32·7 per cent of physical science and mathematics respondents were unsure/uncommitted to *Statement 23*; 31·2 per cent unsure/uncommitted to *Statement 27*. Bench and technical staff, too, had difficulty with *Statement 23*: 34 per cent were uncommitted. Contradictions are also present: 49·2 per cent of secretarial and domestic responses expressed disagreement with *Statement 23*, but 85·5 per cent expressed agreement with *Statement 21*; a similar confusion was expressed by bench and technical respondents in relation to *Statement 28* and *Statement 27*. The responses from Biology teachers are most consistent in relation to *Statement 28* and *Statement 27*.

Table 8.16 Responses of female and male teachers to Statements 21, 23, 28 and 27

Statement 21 Boys should be encouraged by teachers to take subjects like child care and home economics.

Sex	Strongly agree	Mildly agree	Unsure/ uncommitted	Mildly disagree	Strongly disagree	Base
Female	52·4	33·7	7·6	2·8	3·4	353
Male	31·1	36·7	18·4	6·8	7·0	499

Statement 21 Efforts to encourage boys to opt for domestic subjects like child care and home economics are generally misguided.

Sex	Strongly agree	Mildly agree	Unsure/ uncommitted	Mildly disagree	Strongly disagree	Base
Female	6·8	11·4	19·4	25·1	37·3	351
Male	6·8	13·8	28·9	26·5	24·0	501

Statement 28 Schools should encourage girls to study technical and scientific subjects.

Sex	Strongly agree	Mildly agree	Unsure/ uncommitted	Mildly disagree	Strongly disagree	Base
Female	61·1	31·4	4·6	1·7	1·1	350
Male	48·9	37·7	9·4	2·2	1·8	501

Statement 27 Efforts to encourage girls to opt for technical subjects like motor vehicle engineering and technical drawing are generally misguided.

Sex	Strongly agree	Mildly agree	Unsure/ uncommitted	Mildly disagree	Strongly disagree	Base
Female	3·4	9·7	20·5	33·0	33·3	351
Male	5·6	17·1	22·3	30·7	24·3	502

Table 8.17 Responses to Statements 21, 23, 28 and 27 by subject

Statement 21 Boys should be encouraged by teachers to take subjects like child care and home economics.

Subject	Strongly agree	Mildly agree	Unsure/ uncommitted	Mildly disagree	Strongly disagree	Base
English	53·1	32·7	8·0	1·8	4·4	113
Mathematics	27·4	35·7	20·2	10·7	6·0	84
Social studies	37·9	41·4	12·1	0·0	8·6	58
Physical education	33·3	41·2	5·9	13·7	5·9	51
History	36·1	37·8	21·0	3·4	1·7	119
Physical science	18·6	48·6	20·0	1·4	11·4	70
Biology	37·2	41·9	11·6	4·7	4·7	43
Domestic and secretarial	50·0	35·5	3·2	3·2	8·1	62
Bench and technical	35·8	32·1	18·9	9·4	3·8	53
French and German	43·8	28·1	12·5	12·5	3·1	64

Statement 23 Efforts to encourage boys to opt for domestic subjects like child care and home economics are generally misguided.

Subject	Strongly agree	Mildly agree	Unsure/ uncommitted	Mildly disagree	Strongly disagree	Base
English	6·3	9·0	18·0	20·7	45·9	111
Mathematics	8·3	9·5	32·1	31·0	19·0	84
Social studies	8·8	10·5	12·3	33·3	35·1	57
Physical education	2·0	21·6	35·3	15·7	25·5	51
History	6·7	11·8	24·4	31·1	26·1	119
Physical science	6·9	11·1	33·3	33·3	15·3	72
Biology	2·3	15·9	29·5	31·8	20·5	44
Domestic and secretarial	14·8	14·8	21·3	19·7	29·5	61
Bench and technical	5·7	17·0	34·0	18·9	24·5	53
French and German	6·3	17·2	23·4	20·3	32·8	64

Option choice

Table 8.17 Responses to Statements 21, 23, 28 and 27 by subject—*contd.*

Statement 28 Schools should encourage girls to study technical and scientific subjects.

Subject	Strongly agree	Mildly agree	Unsure/ uncommitted	Mildly disagree	Strongly disagree	Base
English	63·4	29·5	5·4	1·8	0·0	112
Mathematics	48·2	43·4	4·8	1·2	2·4	83
Social studies	53·6	33·9	10·7	1·8	0·0	56
Physical education	39·2	43·1	13·7	2·0	2·0	51
History	52·5	32·5	9·2	4·2	1·7	120
Physical science	54·9	35·2	4·2	2·8	2·8	71
Biology	63·6	27·3	9·1	0·0	0·0	44
Domestic and secretarial	59·7	33·9	3·2	1·6	1·6	62
Bench and technical	50·0	35·2	13·0	0·0	1·9	54
French and German	47·6	36·5	7·9	3·2	4·8	63

Statement 27 Efforts to encourage girls to opt for technical subjects like motor vehicle engineering and technical drawing are generally misguided.

Subject	Strongly agree	Mildly agree	Unsure/ uncommitted	Mildly disagree	Strongly disagree	Base
English	3·5	10·6	16·8	30·1	38·9	113
Mathematics	4·8	12·0	31·3	34·9	16·9	83
Social studies	3·6	12·5	17·9	30·4	35·7	56
Physical education	2·0	27·5	25·5	23·5	21·6	51
History	3·3	8·3	18·3	45·0	25·0	120
Physical science	5·6	9·9	31·0	35·2	18·3	71
Biology	0·0	18·2	20·5	34·1	27·3	44
Domestic and secretarial	4·8	14·5	19·4	33·9	27·4	62
Bench and technical	9·4	26·4	15·1	18·9	30·2	53
French and German	6·3	15·6	25·0	29·7	23·4	64

It is clear that a majority of teachers in all subject groups are in favour of encouraging non-traditional choice, though more emphasis is placed on encouraging girls to the academic and career widening subjects than boys to the craft subjects.

When we compare these responses to *Statements 21* and *28* with those to *Statements 11* and *26* it appears that teachers discriminate between encouragement to choose non-traditional subjects and non-traditional careers. In view of this it is perhaps time for schools to examine their approach to careers teaching: non-traditional subject choice is a laudable aim for school policy; it cannot be the whole aim until a clearly reasoned career policy has been formulated. Similarly, teachers are unsure about positive equal opportunities practices (*Statements 23* and *27*). This problem is overcome in some schools by policy workshops, or committee discussions on general and specific issues. In some case study schools these have been recognized as effective methods of encouraging teachers to express innovative ideas and clarify opinion; in others they have assisted in establishing new arrangements following formulation of policy. We believe this kind of discussion involving all staff is essential for the provision of adequate education suited to the needs of pupils and society at large.

School organization

Four of the statements in our survey were concerned with issues of school organization.

Statement 3   Girls and boys need separate playgrounds at school.

Statement 13   The same punishments should be used for both boys and girls.

Statement 19   There should be more female teachers of the technical subjects traditionally taught and studied by males, such as metalwork and woodwork.

Statement 25   There should be more male teachers of the subjects traditionally taken by females, such as home economics and child care.

Statement (number)	Strongly agree	Mildly agree	Unsure/ uncommitted	Mildly disagree	Strongly disagree	Base
3	4·5	7·8	5·7	15·1	66·9	847
13	43·0	26·6	7·0	14·9	8·5	845
19	28·6	32·3	23·6	10·2	5·3	846
25	23·4	33·5	25·7	10·6	6·9	846

The great majority of teachers do not believe in separate playgrounds, but *Statement 3* evoked a substantial number of comments on the desirability of providing both communal and separate areas. In essence all comments referred to the observed contradiction between provision of communal playgrounds and the preferred activities of boys and girls; most commonly respondents cited the space needed for boys to play football while girls were skipping or otherwise engaged.

The response to *Statement 13* showed most agreement by teachers. It is possible that teachers thought that the statement advocated an extension of corporal punishment, and the responses were less favourable to the statement as a result.

The responses to *Statements 19* and *25* indicate that teachers are familiar with the concept of encouraging change by providing non-traditional role models, but many are unsure of the value of this move.

There were some differences in the male and female teachers' responses (see Table 8.18). A slightly higher proportion of men disagreed with the idea of separate playgrounds, and fewer men were in favour of the same punishments for boys and girls and for non-traditional teachers of stereotyped subjects.

More English teachers than teachers of other subjects agreed strongly with the need for separate provision of playgrounds; more

Table 8.18 Responses of female and male teachers to Statements 3, 13, 19 and 25

Statement 3 Girls and boys need separate playgrounds at school.

Sex	Strongly agree	Mildly agree	Unsure/ uncommitted	Mildly disagree	Strongly disagree	Base
Female	6·3	9·8	6·1	16·7	61·1	347
Male	3·2	6·3	5·5	14·2	70·8	506

Statement 13 The same punishments should be used for both boys and girls.

Sex	Strongly agree	Mildly agree	Unsure/ uncommitted	Mildly disagree	Strongly disagree	Base
Female	48·6	25·0	6·0	13·9	6·5	352
Male	38·5	27·9	7·8	15·6	10·2	499

Statement 19 There should be more female teachers of the technical subjects traditionally taught and studied by males, such as metalwork and woodwork.

Sex	Strongly agree	Mildly agree	Unsure/ uncommitted	Mildly disagree	Strongly disagree	Base
Female	34·1	32·4	19·6	9·1	4·8	352
Male	25·0	32·4	26·2	10·8	5·6	500

Statement 25 There should be more male teachers of the subjects traditionally taken by females, such as home economics and child care.

Sex	Strongly agree	Mildly agree	Unsure/ uncommitted	Mildly disagree	Strongly disagree	Base
Female	29·6	34·5	18·8	9·7	7·4	351
Male	19·4	32·7	30·1	11·4	6·4	501

physical education teachers than others disagreed. When it came to punishments, English teachers were most in agreement with equal treatment, and mathematics teachers least. Interestingly bench and technical teachers were most in favour of non-traditional role models for traditionally boys' crafts, showing least uncertainty of all teachers in their responses; for traditionally girls' crafts, they exhibited less enthusiasm and more uncertainty about non-traditional role models. In both cases the teachers of the girls' crafts showed only mild agreement with the idea. (See Table 8.19.)

Table 8.19 Responses to Statements 3, 13, 19, 25 by subject

Statement 3 Girls and boys need separate playgrounds at school.

Subject	Strongly agree	Mildly agree	Unsure/ uncommitted	Mildly disagree	Strongly disagree	Base
English	9·7	5·3	8·8	13·3	62·8	113
Mathematics	3·6	8·3	9·5	15·5	63·1	84
Social studies	3·5	12·3	5·3	7·0	71·9	57
Physical education	0·0	2·0	5·9	17·6	74·5	51
History	4·2	6·7	3·4	12·6	73·1	119
Physical science	1·4	9·7	5·5	16·6	66·6	72
Biology	2·3	9·3	4·7	16·3	67·4	43
Domestic and secretarial	4·9	6·6	3·3	16·4	68·9	61
Bench and technical	3·7	3·7	9·3	24·1	59·3	54
French and German	6·3	9·4	4·7	17·2	62·5	64

Statement 13 The same punishment should be used for both boys and girls.

Subject	Strongly agree	Mildly agree	Unsure/ uncommitted	Mildly disagree	Strongly disagree	Base
English	50·5	25·2	6·3	10·8	7·2	111
Mathematics	24·7	30·6	4·7	21·2	18·8	85
Social studies	46·6	25·9	5·2	17·2	5·2	58
Physical education	33·3	27·5	5·9	19·6	13·7	51
History	41·5	26·3	7·6	14·4	10·2	118
Physical science	31·0	29·6	11·3	22·5	5·6	71
Biology	47·7	27·3	4·5	18·2	2·3	44
Domestic and secretarial	47·5	29·5	6·6	11·5	4·9	61
Bench and technical	40·7	25·9	7·4	20·4	5·6	54
French and German	46·9	23·4	7·8	12·5	9·4	64

Table 8.19 Responses to Statements 3, 13, 19, 25 by subject—*contd.*

Statement 19 There should be more female teachers of the technical subjects traditionally taught and studied by males, such as metalwork and woodwork.

Subject	Strongly agree	Mildly agree	Unsure/ uncommitted	Mildly disagree	Strongly disagree	Base
English	37·2	32·7	23·9	4·4	1·8	113
Mathematics	16·7	34·5	28·6	13·1	7·1	84
Social studies	32·8	32·8	20·7	6·9	6·9	58
Physical education	19·6	33·3	19·6	19·6	7·8	51
History	29·4	33·6	22·7	10·1	4·2	119
Physical science	20·0	30·0	37·1	7·1	5·7	70
Biology	25·6	25·6	39·5	4·7	4·7	43
Domestic and secretarial	19·7	31·1	23·0	14·8	11·5	61
Bench and technical	43·4	26·4	13·2	9·4	7·5	53
French and German	22·2	36·5	20·6	14·3	6·3	63

Statement 25 There should be more male teachers of the subjects traditionally taken by females, such as home economics and child care.

Subject	Strongly agree	Mildly agree	Unsure/ uncommitted	Mildly disagree	Strongly disagree	Base
English	31·9	34·5	25·7	5·3	2·7	113
Mathematics	14·3	33·3	33·3	10·7	8·3	84
Social studies	33·3	24·6	24·6	10·5	7·0	57
Physical education	21·6	25·5	27·5	19·6	5·9	51
History	25·2	32·8	23·5	13·4	5·0	119
Physical science	11·4	31·4	40·0	10·0	7·1	70
Biology	18·6	37·2	32·6	7·0	4·7	43
Domestic and secretarial	18·0	36·1	16·4	16·4	13·1	61
Bench and technical	27·8	27·8	24·1	11·1	9·3	54
French and German	17·2	40·6	25·0	9·4	7·8	64

All science respondents were considerably above the norm in the unsure/uncommitted category for both statements. The response from bench and technical staff appears to contradict their attitude to other statements; here they are quite enthusiastic for non-traditional change. It may be that the responses are a sign of confused reasoning or frivolousness, but we suggest when taken with the responses from domestic and secretarial teachers that they are an example of a complex distinction between the acceptability of women in technical departments and men in domestic departments. The generally held traditional attitude to sex roles by the former is less threatened by competition for their role from women, than by men competing for a woman's role. In contrast, in domestic and secretarial subjects more boys than girls choose non-traditionally and there may be a fear that men will predominate if they are attracted to the department, as evidence by the higher status of men in all departments in which they are currently employed.

Two other statements which relate directly to school organization illuminate the reasoning which teachers bring to bear on the systems they create and operate.

Statement 2 Separation of boys and girls for physical education lessons, where it occurs, is often unnecessary.

Statement 9 Some separation of the sexes for sports and games is appropriate, given physical differences between boys and girls.

Statement (number)	Strongly agree	Mildly agree	Unsure/ uncommitted	Mildly disagree	Strongly disagree	Base
2	15·2	37·1	17·2	20·2	10·3	843
9	39·2	44·8	6·4	5·4	4·1	854

Clearly our respondents feel that too much attention is paid to separating boys and girls for physical education, but they are firm in their belief that physical differences dictate separation at times. This general picture is more or less closely adhered to by teachers of either sex, though there were wider differences between groups of subject teachers (see Tables 8.20 and 8.21).

Table 8.20 Responses of female and male teachers to Statements 2 and 9

Statement 2 Separation of boys and girls for physical education lessons, where it occurs, is often unnecessary.

Sex	Strongly agree	Mildly agree	Unsure/ uncommitted	Mildly disagree	Strongly disagree	Base
Female	14·1	39·7	14·7	21·3	10·3	348
Male	16·0	35·5	19·0	19·4	10·2	501

Statement 9 Some separation of the sexes for sports and games is appropriate, given physical differences between boys and girls.

Sex	Strongly agree	Mildly agree	Unsure/ uncommitted	Mildly disagree	Strongly disagree	Base
Female	38·0	46·7	5·4	5·9	4·0	353
Male	40·0	43·6	7·1	4·9	4·3	507

Table 8.21 Responses to Statements 2 and 9 by subject

Statement 2 Separation of boys and girls for physical education lessons, where it occurs, is often unnecessary.

Subject	Strongly agree	Mildly agree	Unsure/ uncommitted	Mildly disagree	Strongly disagree	Base
English	17·3	43·6	16·4	19·1	3·6	110
Mathematics	19·3	26·5	18·1	27·7	8·4	83
Social studies	25·9	37·9	12·1	10·3	13·8	58
Physical education	13·7	45·1	3·9	27·5	9·8	51
History	17·6	33·6	19·3	16·0	13·4	119
Physical science	9·7	23·6	26·4	29·2	11·1	72
Biology	11·4	47·7	15·9	18·2	6·8	44
Domestic and secretarial	11·5	34·4	19·7	23·0	11·5	61
Bench and technical	13·2	35·8	24·5	11·3	15·1	53
French and German	11·1	28·6	22·2	23·8	14·3	63

Statement 9 Some separation of the sexes for sports and games is appropriate, given physical differences between boys and girls.

Subject	Strongly agree	Mildly agree	Unsure/ uncommitted	Mildly disagree	Strongly disagree	Base
English	30·1	46·0	11·5	8·0	4·4	113
Mathematics	41·2	47·1	4·7	4·7	2·4	85
Social studies	32·2	39·0	11·9	10·2	6·8	59
Physical education	66·7	29·4	0·0	3·9	0·0	51
History	37·5	45·0	7·5	6·7	3·3	120
Physical science	38·8	48·6	2·8	5·6	4·2	72
Biology	38·6	45·5	6·8	9·1	0·0	44
Domestic and secretarial	52·5	36·1	3·3	3·3	4·9	61
Bench and technical	37·0	51·9	7·4	1·9	1·9	54
French and German	46·9	40·6	7·8	1·6	3·1	64

Physical education teachers exhibited curious responses to this, an issue central to their practice. Few were uncertain, but most only expressed mild agreement or, less frequently, disagreement with the statements. On the need for some separation, however, physical education teachers were most emphatic in agreement, followed by teachers of domestic and secretarial subjects.

Teacher preference for stressing the importance of physical differences is reflected in the responses to these statements and we suggest that it is these preferences, and not the explanations we have been given in case study schools, which dictate segregation.

Role of parents

Few of our respondents agreed with the following statements, despite their responses to some of the statements discussed already.

Statement 10 Parents should place more stress on helping boys than girls to plan their future working lives.

Statement 18 In general, sons in a family should be given more encouragement than daughters to take up higher education.

Statement (number)	Strongly agree	Mildly agree	Unsure/ uncommitted	Mildly disagree	Strongly disagree	Base
10	3·6	4·0	2·2	8·0	82·2	855
18	1·9	4·3	2·0	8·8	83·0	855

It is the most positive whole sample response we received and firmly rejects the idea that working lives and higher education are more appropriate to boys than girls. In both cases, more female than male teachers expressed strong disagreement (see Table 8.22).

Table 8.22   Responses of female and male teachers to Statements 10 and 18

Statement 10   Parents should place more stress on helping boys than girls to plan their future working lives.

Sex	Strongly agree	Mildly agree	Unsure/ uncommitted	Mildly disagree	Strongly disagree	Base
Female	2·5	2·0	0·6	3·4	91·5	354
Male	4·3	5·3	3·4	11·0	75·9	507

Statement 18   In general, sons in a family should be given more encouragement than daughters to take up higher education.

Sex	Strongly agree	Mildly agree	Unsure/ uncommitted	Mildly disagree	Strongly disagree	Base
Female	1·7	1·1	0·0	5·4	91·8	354
Male	2·0	6·5	3·4	11·0	77·1	507

Within our subject groups there are differences of emphasis which reflect strong views of teachers of several stereotyped subjects (see Table 8.23). Teachers of domestic and secretarial subjects reject both statements most strongly; bench and technical teachers showed most, though still a small minority, agreement with both. The craft staff responses are perhaps less surprising than those of biology staff who may be influenced by the relatively low status of their science and the relevance of some topics to the traditionally female domestic role.

Table 8.23 Responses to Statements 10 and 18 by subject

Statement 10 Parents should place more stress on helping boys than girls to plan their future working lives.

Subject	Strongly agree	Mildly agree	Unsure/ uncommitted	Mildly disagree	Strongly disagree	Base
English	1·8	3·5	1·8	2·7	90·3	113
Mathematics	2·4	2·4	2·4	12·9	80·0	85
Social studies	0·0	6·8	0·0	6·8	86·4	59
Physical education	3·9	5·9	2·0	13·7	74·5	51
History	5·0	3·3	2·5	7·5	81·7	120
Physical science	1·4	5·6	6·9	9·7	76·4	72
Biology	6·8	2·3	2·3	11·4	77·3	44
Domestic and secretarial	0·0	1·6	0·0	3·2	95·2	62
Bench and technical	7·4	5·6	5·6	9·3	72·2	54
French and German	4·7	3·1	3·1	3·1	85·9	64

Statement 18 In general, sons in a family should be given more encouragement than daughters to take up higher education.

Subject	Strongly agree	Mildly agree	Unsure/ uncommitted	Mildly disagree	Strongly disagree	Base
English	3·5	4·4	0·0	0·9	91·2	113
Mathematics	1·2	5·9	1·2	9·4	82·4	85
Social studies	1·7	3·4	0·0	11·9	83·1	59
Physical education	0·0	5·9	2·0	17·6	74·5	51
History	0·8	4·2	2·5	7·5	85·0	120
Physical science	1·4	2·8	5·6	15·3	75·0	72
Biology	2·3	0·0	4·5	11·4	81·8	44
Domestic and secretarial	1·6	1·6	0·0	1·6	95·2	62
Bench and technical	3·7	14·8	5·6	9·3	66·7	54
French and German	3·1	3·1	1·6	6·3	85·9	64

Teachers and the idea of 'neutrality'

The teachers in our attitude survey were invited to comment on any of the statements or the survey in general. A number did so, and their comments illuminate some of the reasons for their responses to the statements, particularly the thinking underlying the responses of the minority of teachers who are not in favour of positive equality of opportunity policies.

Several teachers advocated a view (which we also encountered in case study schools) that the equal opportunities are irrelevant.

> Most teachers are too busy getting on with the job of teaching to bother too much about most of the issues raised here [in the attitude scale statements].

> Pupils should be given an introduction to a wide variety of practical areas so that they may choose those that they *like* or *merit* rather than on *any pre-conceived ideas.* (Our italics.)

> Overall the educational system is neutral...

In support of this view, some teachers distinguished between 'educational' values and the values implied by the scales – especially in the statements which used the word 'encouragement'.

> Pupils should not be 'encouraged' in any particular direction, they should be advised of their capabilities and career opportunities.

> The emphasis must be on the right of the individual to make a choice. It is the school's task to provide the background and information which will enable the individual to make an enlightened choice.

> I would only agree to this [encourage consideration of non-traditional subjects and careers] if the students were first determined to be suitable for a particular career.

But the 'background and information' which is to 'determine' capability and career opportunities is not neutral; the greatest number of responses identified positive goals and undesirable influences; employers and parents are interchangeably honoured or indicted as consumers or tyrants.

> I agree wholeheartedly with positive discrimination as a long-term aim in education, but I worry about short-term job prospects with our less than radical employers.

> Education has to reflect society to some extent and likely future prospects of either sex must be taken into consideration.

> I'm not so sure here [*Statement 20*] because as professionals we're trying to meet the needs of our consumers (parents).
>
> Encourage perhaps but not direct or your school could rapidly suffer from falling roles if it was too far ahead of present parental opinion.

And these views clearly translate into a course of action.

> Schools have to prepare pupils for work in society as it is. Some boys *need* restricted workshop space more [than girls] at present, desirable as it [equal access] may be in future for equality.
>
> In practice I would not like boys to be excluded from traditional male subjects which may lead them to a career in order to make room for girls. . . . Equally I would not like girls to be excluded from needlework, typewriting, etc., as these subjects may be of greater use in life to girls.

At times, these statements lead us to a belief that teachers wish the school system to be seen as the executive arm of a policy making public.

> Many of the questions [i.e. attitude scale statements] suggest that we should deliberately draw students' attention to possible sex discrimination in schools. If a school is conducted in a climate of *assumed* equality, whether regarding sex or race, there should be no occasion to make a self conscious and overt attempt to gear one's teaching towards this view. To do so might suggest that there could or should be an alternative view thus sowing seeds of discord where none originally existed.

But even in its own terms the goal of neutrality is chimerical: 'neutrality' can lead to coercion.

> As one of the organizers of the option scheme I have been able to collect figures of uptake in different subjects e.g. 25 per cent of boys opt for domestic science, (in fact this has to be actively discouraged to reduce the number as the department cannot cope with any greater number).

The context of this comment was an explanation that schools should not encourage pupils to take particular subjects because experience had shown this writer that his school's organization of providing a 'balanced idea of opportunities' rather than encouragement led to non-traditional choice. The school was included in our case studies – it operated a special request system for girls choosing technical or craft subjects and suppressed attempts by the technology teacher to encourage girls to choose his subject.

Some teachers disagreed with neutrality and took it upon themselves openly to declare their interest and influence. Others pointed to the influence of the school environment in shaping the views – and, therefore, choices – of pupils.

> Biological imperatives indicate that (a) women are less likely to be able to pursue a continuous career, and (b) that the children of those who do may, in some cases, lose thereby, *judging by the pupils I teach*. On the other hand, in a higher socio-economic bracket, they seem likely to benefit. Thus one cannot generalize on the benefits of careers for women. (Our italics.)

And the benefits of careers for men? One correspondent was quite clear on the role of the school.

> A lot of sexism is evident not in direct teaching but in general organization – i.e., boys carry, girls mark off medical lists, girls staple things, put raffle tickets in bins, fetch the head's dinner . . .

Clearly all this is irrelevant for those who agree with the correspondent who, in one sentence asked for a survey of parental attitude and roles in the home, and in the next wrote in response to the statement on football and cricket for girls (*Statement 8*).

> Isn't there still a flavour of the absurd about this? Will we advocate boxing for girls next?

Perhaps when girls in the higher socio-economic bracket ask for it, for 'neutrality' appears to differentiate or accept differentiation on the basis of class as well as sex. The lower ability pupil in case study schools is identified with the low socio-economic pupil.

> Technical and engineering trades tend to have a physical or 'labouring' aspect and so will remain more suited to boys and less attractive to girls. There are many more other careers which have been largely the domain of males which could be considered 'open' – particularly the professions, e.g. surgeons, doctors, accountants, pilots, clergymen [sic] stockbrokers, bankers, civil servants, etc.

> As childcare involves most people I think it should be part of the core curriculum, whereas it is generally left for girls of low ability.

This is sometimes reflected even in attempts to provide equal opportunities in, for example, science.

> All pupils should study a course including some physical science. For the *majority* this should be a single homogeneous course – not physics or chemistry.

> At this school all our science is of an integrated nature stressing environmental, sociological and technological implications. Physical science principles are an integral part of these courses which are considered equally applicable to boys and girls.
>
> A more successful approach is to positively timetable a curriculum so that mixed physical education, science for girls, homecraft for boys, etc., cannot be avoided.
>
> There are now 22 girls and 34 boys in the physics option in year 4. When I arrived, three years ago, there were three girls in that year. However, less able pupils, in general, would do an integrated science course. This is 60-70 per cent physical science in our school.

In case study schools we considered the influence of employers and parents. In one or two cases it fully endorsed the view expressed by some teachers that their opportunity for encouraging non-traditional choice is limited by narrow emphasis on local job stereotypes. But against this we have indicated that some schools involved local employers and parents in the creation and endorsement of science or technical programmes which offered access to girls as a matter of equality with boys. The indications were that neither parents nor employers had a clear idea of what was being taught in the lessons and that on being informed of the content of the proposed courses they raised no objections to the change. One of our respondents pinpointed the teachers' role in relation to pupils and parents.

> Teachers should encourage and support pupils in looking at areas traditionally reserved for the opposite sex. Parents need educating about *equality*.

A design and craft teacher was more explicit in identifying an aspect of that education.

> I have been involved in discussions [regarding] 'traditional' boys' and girls' subjects. This will continue as long as their [sic] are labels such as 'woodwork' and 'home economics' with the subsequent connotations derived by parents and teachers of the standards and work that should be done in these subjects.

The question thus arises of whether teachers can be sure that the constraints placed on equal opportunity by educational goals represent not only a self-imposed, but a false dichotomy of interest. The parental views to which they respond may be inaccurate views of syllabus content. Subsumed within this discussion is the assumption that teachers provide a structure which both adequately informs and monitors the views of parents. Judging from the experience of teachers in case study schools there is often little communication between parents and schools; and least between schools and the parents of lower ability pupils.

Ultimately it is of paramount importance to acknowledge that teachers are not only an active influence operating within their perception of environmental demands, but that the barrage of new demands exposes their supposed consensus approach's weakness towards accepted social engineering – the first comment in this discussion an eloquent reminder that they have an educational role defined by training and experience on to which they are asked to graft changing roles reflecting new values in society. Often the values are ill-defined or the clamour for action is characterized by a constant stream of advice, sometimes contradictory. Priorities are re-defined by what may appear at times as a small and unrepresentative group within society as a whole; parents, or employers are then cited to defend educational goals which have been formed in the absence of parental consultation and at the dictate of the job market.

We have added to the demands made of teachers: that they should take responsibility for the role they play in shaping the views of pupils and influencing choice. The additional burden of work implied by this requires support and guidance. Programmes do exist to fulfil this role insofar as it affects action to examine and influence aspects of school organization which teachers wish to change. But for many teachers the wider issues of changed curriculum, equal opportunity and reconciliation of conflicting demands will imply structured assistance. In turn we believe this demands time for in-service training so that teachers may explore the new issues; it demands advice from policy making and supervising bodies; and it argues for establishment of channels of communication which effectively disseminate ideas and initiative.

If teachers succeed in reconciling equal opportunity between the sexes and their educational goals they will have succeeded in understanding that their parental or public role does not conflict with their professional role. One correspondent identified this supposed conflict.

> The wording of the questions [statements] seems to suggest that the aim of every woman should be to be capable of doing everything a man does. This is not the same as being able to see how the sex roles present in society now operate and challenge them if and when they feel it to be necessary.

Apart from the man/woman labels we second the sentiment and the implied goal of education: pupils should be capable of examining roles and all other aspects of society and of challenging them if and when they feel it necessary. It is a skill and responsibility which we should aim to place on the shoulders of all our pupils.

CHAPTER 9

Pupil attitudes

The discussion which follows is based on responses to a questionnaire by 515 girls and 453 boys in the fourth or fifth form of their secondary school in 1981–2. The questionnaire was administered more or less compulsorily by teachers working from guidance notes and, for their convenience, often with a class of pupils during a lesson; the imbalance in numbers of boys and girls arises solely because classes vary in size and teachers found the process of selecting pupils invidious. The questionnaire was applied only in those schools in which staff had volunteered their co-operation with the teacher survey.

Pupil attitude scales

Tables 9.1, 9.2 and 9.3 tell us which subjects the respondents had chosen, their short- and long-term post-school aspirations and the degree to which job and subject choice corresponds to traditional patterns. There are few surprises in these results. Table 9.1 shows that the most popular subjects with girls are biology, French, home economics, and typing; only physics and chemistry attract similar proportions of boys. Table 9.2 and 9.3 show that a higher proportion of girls than boys intended to continue their education beyond the age of 16 and that very few of the nominated combinations of subjects are unusual among either boys or girls.

Fig. 9.1 shows that boys chose a smaller range than girls of popular job aspirations, that engineering is outstandingly popular with boys, and that only among boys is computing a popular aspiration. The absence of girls with aspirations to join the computer growth industries is surprising and may be taken as a warning for those with hopes that it has not yet become associated with either sex. It may also be found disturbing that more than 50 per cent of the response from boys is concentrated in engineering, construction and the forces. Perhaps the least satisfactory aspect of the tables is the indication that a large number of girls and boys cannot name either a job or selection of subjects for study after the age of 16.

Table 9.1 Number and percentage of respondents studying selected subjects

Subject	Girls (%)	Boys (%)
Physics	108 (21·3)	260 (58·3)
Chemistry	142 (28·0)	154 (34·5)
Biology	278 (54·8)	98 (22·0)
Other science	121 (23·9)	131 (29·4)
French	243 (47·9)	131 (29·4)
German	92 (18·1)	50 (11·2)
Family/child care	81 (16·0)	1 (0·2)
Office practice	56 (11·0)	14 (3·1)
Typing	173 (34·1)	8 (1·8)
Home economics	206 (40·0)	42 (9·4)
Needlecraft	73 (14·4)	1 (0·2)
Metalwork	5 (1·0)	138 (30·9)
Woodwork	3 (0·6)	121 (27·1)

Table 9.2 Which of the following do you hope to do on reaching age 16?

Aspiration	Girls (%)	Boys (%)
Further your education in college or at school	362 (71·7)	204 (46·3)
Get a job	117 (23·2)	184 (41·7)
Join a training scheme (e.g. YOP)	5 (1·0)	18 (4·1)
Don't know/other	21 (4·2)	35 (7·9)
Totals	505 (100)	441 (100)

Table 9.3 Subject combinations aspired to in school or college

Emphasis[1]	Girls	Boys
Mainly by girls	142 (53·6)	18 (10·1)
Mainly by girls and neutral	56 (21·1)	15 (8·4)
Neutral	20 (7·5)	16 (9·0)
Mainly by boys and neutral	33 (12·5)	51 (28·7)
Mainly by boys	14 (5·3)	78 (43·8)
Totals	265 (100)	178 (100)

Note:
1. The emphasis refers to stereotype. Subjects were classified according to DES statistics relating to boys and girls on courses in further education colleges. The table categorizes combinations by 'adding' boys' and girls' subjects.

212 *Option choice*

Fig. 9.1 Career aspirations: attitude scale respondents

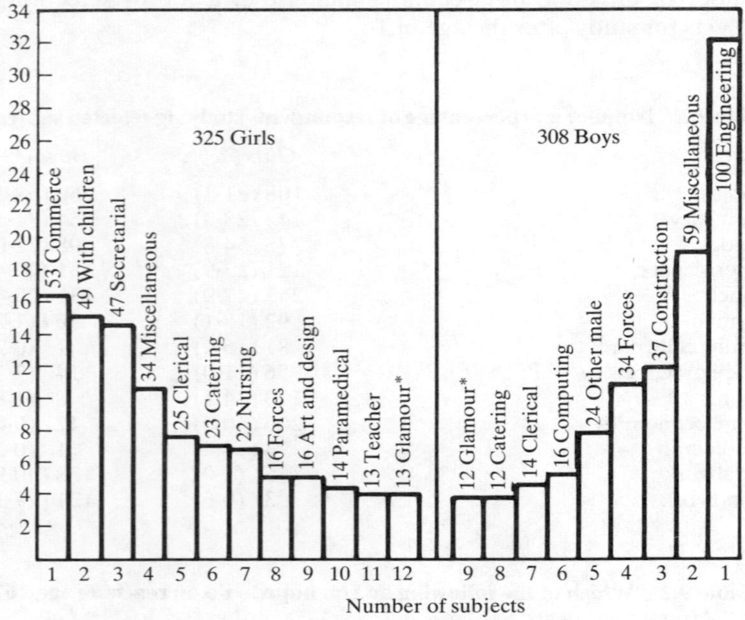

325 Girls:
- 1: 53 Commerce
- 2: 49 With children
- 3: 47 Secretarial
- 4: 34 Miscellaneous
- 5: 25 Clerical
- 6: 23 Catering
- 7: 22 Nursing
- 8: 16 Forces
- 9: 16 Art and design
- 10: 14 Paramedical
- 11: 13 Teacher
- 12: 13 Glamour*

308 Boys:
- 9: 12 Glamour*
- 8: 12 Catering
- 7: 14 Clerical
- 6: 16 Computing
- 5: 24 Other male
- 4: 34 Forces
- 3: 37 Construction
- 2: 59 Miscellaneous
- 1: 100 Engineering

Number of subjects

Note: 34·7% per cent of responses made no reply or said they didn't know
* includes: air hostess; footballer; stuntman; dancer, etc.

Agreement with EOC policy on good practice: 'Score P'

In Tables 9.4, 9.5 and 9.6 we have used a measure we called 'Score P'. It was constructed in the same way as 'Score T' of the teacher scale, but relates only to ten statements about school (see Appendix 6). These differences weaken conclusions based on comparison between 'Score P' and 'Score T'. Table 9.4 shows the 'Score P' distribution of all pupils compared with the 'Score T' distribution of all teachers in all schools in the survey. As the minimum 'Score P' is 10 and the maximum is 50 (1 or 5 × 10 statements) a score of 20 or under indicates strong agreement with the principles underlying EOC policy on good practice in schools; a score between 40 and 50 indicates strong disagreement. The table demonstrates that a much greater proportion of teachers than pupils agree with EOC policy and principles.

Table 9.4 'Score T' and 'Score P' distribution adjusted for comparison

Score		10–18 / 28–50	19–26 / 51–73	27–34 / 74–95	35–42 / 95–118	43–46 / 119–140	Base
Responses %	P	9·0	37·0	42·0	11·6	0·4	776
	T	20·9	54·9	21·4	3·1	nil	861

In addition, a much higher proportion of teachers than pupils is concentrated in the lowest category of score. This seems to suggest that stereotypical influence is a much greater force among pupils than teachers and that greater resistance to changes designed to introduce equal opportunity will be found among the pupils than the teachers.

Tables 9.5 and 9.6 show the distribution of 'Score P': column totals show the number of pupils who scored within 25 per cent, 50 per cent, 75 per cent and 100 per cent of the maximum score.

Table 9.5 Mixed schools in England and Wales: boys and girls

	10–22	23–26	27–31	32–46	Base
Girls	34·7	27·8	23·0	14·5	
	136	109	90	57	392
Boys	11·5	17·6	36	34·9	
	44	67	137	133	381

Table 9.6 Mixed schools in England and Wales: nominated and cluster

	10–22	23–26	27–31	32–46	Base
Nominated	24·6	22·5	28·7	24·2	
	130	119	152	128	529
Cluster	20·2	23·1	30·4	26·3	
	50	57	75	65	247

Girls are clearly represented in much greater proportions than boys in the first and second columns, thus generally adhering to the pattern of distribution among female and male teachers. Tables 9.4 and 9.5 taken together imply that it is boys rather than girls who will resist attempts to change practices in schools. On the other hand the distribution of scores in Table 9.6 suggests that pupils in nominated and cluster schools are not as distinct in their opinions as are their teachers. This may be an indication that a school environment has less impact on pupils than on teaching staff.

Boys and girls in school

This aspect of the survey was intended to provide a counterpart to the teacher survey. Although it contained only three directly comparable statements, it asks for agreement or disagreement with items of principle and practice which reflect EOC policy (see Appendix 8). Four statements attracted near unanimous agreement or disagreement which distinguished these results from all others. Pupils strongly agree with provision of mixed classes (77·6 per cent boys and 75·1 per cent girls); and that attitude extends to disagreeing with separating the sexes for some subjects (63·5 per cent boys and 63·8 per cent girls) and single-sex schools (61·8 per cent boys and 66·2 per cent girls). The response also overwhelmingly rejected the suggestion of separate playgrounds (92 per cent boys and 93·1 per cent girls).

The three statements on both teacher and pupil scales referred to the role of schools in reducing sex discrimination and practices relating to punishment and the provision of playground areas.

Table 9.7   Teacher and pupil responses to Statement 8

Statement 8   Schools should set an example in reducing sex discrimination.

Category	Strongly agree	Mildly agree	Unsure/ uncommitted	Mildly disagree	Strongly disagree	Base
Female	68·2	28·1	2·8	0·9	0·0	352
Girls	50·3	26·5	14·7	5·1	3·4	505
Male	55·4	34·5	5·4	3·0	1·8	502
Boys	30·0	35·8	21·2	7·7	5·4	444

Fewer pupils than teachers believe schools should set an example in reducing sex discrimination (see Table 9.7). Although a large proportion of pupils were uncertain, the proportions who feel schools are positively not the place for this principle are greater than those of teachers. As with 'Score P' the general pattern of responses shows that girls stand in relation to female teachers in much the same way as boys relate to male teachers.

Table 9.8   Teacher and pupil responses to Statement 4

Statement 4   The same punishment should be used for both boys and girls.

Category	Strongly agree	Mildly agree	Unsure/ uncommitted	Mildly disagree	Strongly disagree	Base
Female	48·6	25·0	6·0	13·9	6·5	352
Girls	30·9	32·7	8·3	14·7	13·5	505
Male	38·5	27·9	7·8	15·6	10·2	499
Boys	49·2	29·0	7·9	8·8	5·2	445

From the figures for *Statement 4* it is possible to detect naked self-interest as much as considerations of equal opportunity. Girls are far less comfortable than boys with the idea of equal punishment – a point which could be interpreted as meaning that girls have everything, and boys nothing, to lose by agreement (see Table 9.8).

Responses to *Statement 9* should provide ample evidence that girls and boys do not need separate playgrounds. Pupils overwhelmingly demonstrate that concern by some teachers is misplaced, although in an ideal world it should be possible to accommodate the very small number of pupils who could benefit from a separate area within a mixed playground. It is likely that the age of the pupil respondents has influenced these results which do not show that pupils of all ages prefer mixed playgrounds: younger pupils may have needs which imply single-sex playgrounds in the absence of sufficient space to accommodate all games.

Table 9.9 Teacher and pupil responses to Statement 9

Statement 9 Girls and boys need separate playgrounds at school.

Category	Strongly agree	Mildly agree	Unsure/ uncommitted	Mildly disagree	Strongly disagree	Base
Female	6·3	9·8	6·1	16·7	61·1	347
Girls	2·6	3·9	1·6	10·3	81·7	507
Male	3·2	6·3	5·5	14·2	70·8	506
Boys	2·7	2·5	1·8	10·4	82·7	444

We now turn to statements that were offered only to pupils. The first group deals with subjects and their suitability for boys or girls.

Statement 5 If boys and girls always studied the same subjects they'd be equally good at them.

Statement 13 There are no subjects better suited to either boys or girls.

Statement 7 Boys probably make better use than girls of their education.

Table 9.10 Responses to Statements 5, 13 and 7

Statement (number)		Strongly agree	Mildly agree	Unsure/ uncommitted	Mildly disagree	Strongly disagree	Base
5	Girls	17·0	26·7	17·4	23·3	15·6	506
	Boys	10·5	27·6	19·7	28·0	14·1	446
13	Girls	26·3	27·5	17·6	23·2	5·3	505
	Boys	15·0	20·9	18·6	28·4	17·0	440
7	Girls	2·2	6·3	4·8	17·4	69·3	505
	Boys	9·7	14·7	24·6	28·0	23·0	443

The statements' responses in Table 9.10 show that girls and boys strongly disagree on the relevance of subjects and education to both sexes. In particular, only just over a third of boys believe subjects are suited to both boys or girls, while a majority of girls do so (*Statement 13*); and nearly a quarter of boys compared with fewer than 10 per cent of girls believe boys make better use of their education. Fewer than half of the respondents believed that experience in a subject would result in equal skill levels. Generally more boys than girls believe some subjects are inappropriate for either sex and that there is little point in attempting to remove the barriers to experience; most girls, however, believe that no subjects are inappropriate, although they also believe that achievement may differ. Whatever the causes of these responses, they provide a case for developing teaching methods and school systems to overcome demotivation and barriers to achievement.

We also tested pupil attitudes in relation to the job market. In the responses to *Statements 11* and *14* we can see a continuation of the belief in freedom of access which girls exhibited in relation to subject choice (see Table 9.11).

Statement 11 Girls should be encouraged to consider taking jobs normally done by boys when they leave school.

Statement 14 Boys should be encouraged to consider taking jobs normally done by girls when they leave school.

Table 9.11 **Responses to Statements 11 and 14**

Statement (number)		Strongly agree	Mildly agree	Unsure/ uncommitted	Mildly disagree	Strongly disagree	Base
11	Girls	17·6	44·6	15·8	15·0	7·1	506
	Boys	7·9	36·2	21·3	24·7	9·9	445
14	Girls	10·5	39·9	15·8	20·4	13·4	507
	Boys	5·2	19·5	18·9	29·3	27·0	440

Clearly, most girls believe they should be encouraged to extend the range of jobs under consideration to those traditionally done by boys (62·6 per cent), although fewer girls would extend a similar opportunity to boys (50·4 per cent). On the other hand boys are hostile to the idea that they should consider traditionally girls' jobs and are considerably less enthusiastic than girls at the thought of girls entering 'their' job market.

In the above two groups of statements there is a nearly uniformly high proportion of responses in the unsure/uncommitted category. The only certainty is exhibited by girls in believing they make equal use of their education (*Statement 7*). In our opinion this is particularly important in relation to *Statements 13* and *7*: boys and girls should be clear that school subjects and the value of schooling have equal application for boys and girls. This observation can be extended to *Statement 5*, except that the proportion of pupils believing experience in a subject will not overcome 'natural' aptitudes overshadows other considerations.

The next statement concerned the thorny question of whether boys and girls should do the same sports and games at school. Our teacher respondents had indicated a nearly unanimous belief that physical differences dictate separation of girls and boys for physical education.

Statement 1 Girls and boys should do the same sports and games at school.

	Strongly agree	*Mildly agree*	*Unsure/ uncommitted*	*Mildly disagree*	*Strongly disagree*	*Base*
Girls	14·0	59·3	5·9	17·4	3·4	506
Boys	10·1	43·5	8·1	30·7	7·4	446

The clear evidence from *Statement 1* responses is that boys and girls wish to enjoy the same sports; surprisingly, perhaps, it is the girls among whom we find most support (73 per cent) but the majority of boys also agree (53.6 per cent). The impression we were given by teachers in case study schools is that boys would be enthusiastic for the idea and bad mannered during the event; in fact, 38·1 per cent opposed. The support from girls and boys is mainly mild, indicating that the subject is not a burning issue and the responses are speculative. Mild or not, these responses show that the practices which arise from the attitudes of teaching staff are not based on the interests of the pupils.

Outside influences

One aspect of the debate on equal opportunity concerns the need for positive action to overcome stereotypical influences from outside the school. It is argued that pupil perception of male and female roles precludes a free choice of subject or job. The influences are said to be present before school begins, to operate alongside the school environment and to extend to shaping images of adult life. Provision of equal opportunity therefore consists in freeing subjects and jobs from existing gender association as well as ensuring school systems and teaching methods do not contribute to the association.

Three components of our pupil survey were designed to test the existence and emphasis of this assumed stereotypical influence. We offered pupils a list of careers, another on home life and a third on personality characteristics (see Appendix 8), and asked pupils to attribute gender suitability to each. Provision was made for indicating degrees of gender suitability although results here were inconclusive and our figures show only the responses indicating an item was free of gender association. The definition of freedom varied with each category and where appropriate includes the responses '*don't know*', '*equally suitable for men and women*' and '*by men and women together*'.

The great majority of responses from boys and girls indicate gender association. On 56 per cent of the items less than 50 per cent of the responses from girls were free of gender association; 60 per cent or more of responses were free on only 30 per cent of items. The corresponding measures of responses from boys were 78 per cent and 22 per cent. These figures demonstrate the existence of stereotypical influence. The framework within which pupils take decisions includes beliefs concerning gender-appropriate jobs and careers, future roles within family life and the personal characteristics of men and women.

The responses indicate girls and boys bring the same general framework to bear on the majority of items. This suggests influences which shape attitudes have a similar impact, on boys and girls, though consistently fewer girls than boys associated listed items with either men or women.

Jobs and careers

Fig. 9.2 shows that a few jobs (including solicitors, politicians, dentists, TV newsreaders and computer programmers) form a small group to which fewer than 40 per cent of boys and girls attribute gender association (see Appendix 8). With the possible exception of newsreading, each profession contains a much higher proportion of men than women, and it is necessary to look beyond mere balance of numbers to explain the perceived neutrality. Although our survey did not set out to explain the views of pupils, a few pointers can be suggested; for example, the imbalance of men and women in politics may be outweighed as an influence by the existence of a female prime minister, or the promotion of computing as a subject suitable for boys and girls in schools may over-ride the computer programmer example. However, an important consideration must be that each item represents a profession and teachers have consistently impressed on us that the upper ability pupil is subject to fewer stereotypical limitations on choice. Thus the professional status of these items may demonstrate an awareness among all pupils of an implied connection between freedom of choice and academic achievement.

To examine this proposition we can identify the items which are heavily gender associated and make a comparison between their status and that of neutral items. The gender associated group includes

Fig. 9.2 Response on jobs and careers: percentage without gender association.

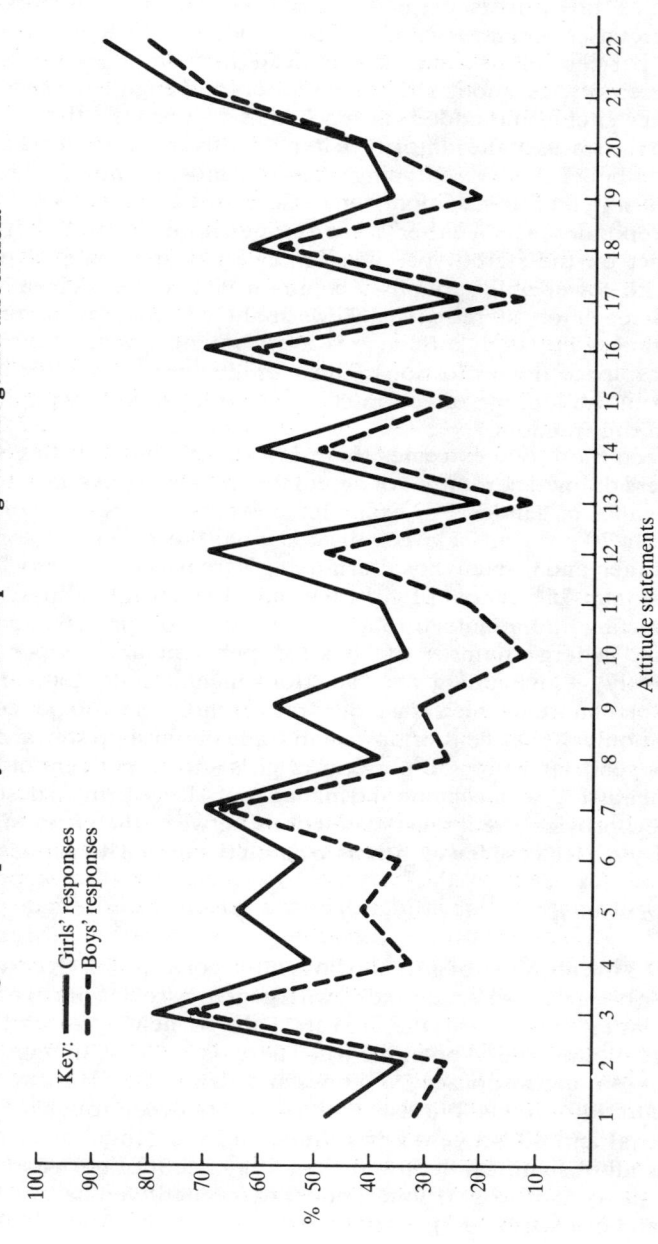

Key: —— Girls' responses
– – – Boys' responses

Attitude statements

Note: Percentages are derived from response to item 'Equally suitable for men and women'

Pupil attitudes 219

electricians, taxi drivers, car mechanics, office cleaners, farmers, private secretaries, engineers and fashion models: on each item more than 60 per cent of girls and boys indicated gender association. The firmest stereotypes among girls were farmers and engineers; boys also chose these items, but added car mechanics. In our view the contrast between the status of the majority of items in this and the neutral group justifies a belief that stereotyping of jobs is most pronounced in low status jobs. In addition, comparison between the two groups indicates that a preponderance of either women or men in any job need not have an impact on the stereotype. This implies that upper ability pupils share with lower ability pupils a common view of the relevance of gender to each job: stereotypical views are held in common across the ability range, but their influence is most potent among pupils who cannot aspire to the professions. Those in the upper ability bands are freed from the limiting effect on choice, and lower ability pupils are aware of this freedom.

Between these two extremes there is a variety of conflicting views and of less dramatic examples of agreement between boys and girls on the relevance of gender. For example, fewer than 50 per cent of boys and nearly 70 per cent of girls indicated a hairdressing job is appropriate for men and women; hospital nursing is free of gender association for more than 55 per cent of girls, but only 30 per cent of boys; while shop assisting and architecture are gender free for girls (60 per cent each) and a large number of boys (55 per cent and 48 per cent, respectively). Outstanding contradictions include management of a large firm — an item which is gender free for more than 60 per cent of girls, but only 40 per cent of boys; and trade union shop stewardship, which is gender free for 50 per cent of girls and 32 per cent of boys. Hospital nurses, car mechanic and manager of a large firm, in descending order, provide the largest distinctions between the views of boys and girls; in each case fewer girls associated the item with gender.

Men and women

In Fig. 9.3 the attitudes of girls and boys often correspond. Occasionally, fewer boys than girls responded with gender association; examples of the latter occur with the items: 'Tidy or neat', 'Careful' and 'Conscientious' (see Appendix 8). There is a large difference in emphasis among responses from boys and girls to the 'Hardworking' and 'Ambitious' items, but it is a difference between roughly 60 per cent (boys) and 80 per cent (girls) freedom from gender association. Perhaps more significantly, fewer than 50 per cent of boys and more than 60 per cent of girls attribute gender to competitiveness; and fewer girls than boys attributed gender to importance or kindness, although

Fig. 9.3 Responses to men and women: percentages without gender association.

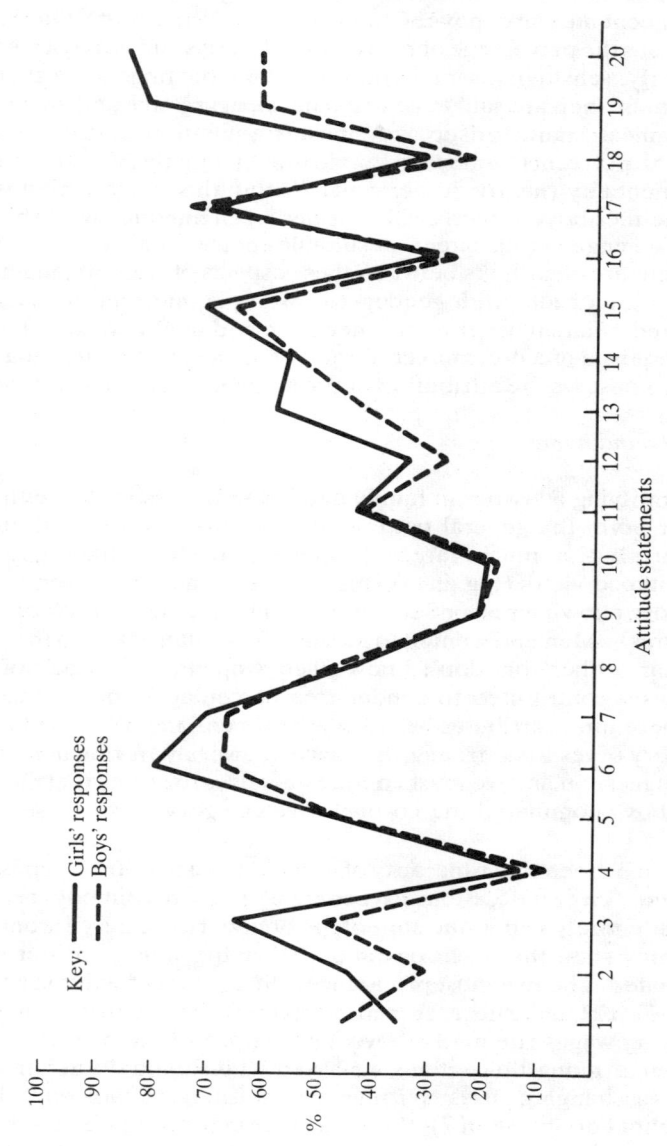

Key: —— Girls' responses
     - - - Boys' responses

Attitude statements

Note: Percentages are derived from responses to items 'Applies equally to men and women' and 'Don't know'.

the differences are small and both exceeded the 60 per cent measure on both items.

Of the items which were gender associated, only the responses 'talkative' provide an example of boys and girls on different sides of a 40 per cent measure (boys 30 per cent, girls 45 per cent). On six other occasions the percentage of responses from boys and girls corresponds, or nearly: sensitivity, sentimentality and nimble fingers are attributed to women; men are said to be mechanical, aggressive and violent. The mechanical characteristic was most frequently gender associated (85–90 per cent), followed by violence (roughly 80 per cent) and sentimentality (nearly 80 per cent). Within this framework it is clear that neither boys nor girls will consider an engineering workshop – let alone an engineering career – a suitable choice for a girl.

There are clear links between these aspects of stereotyping and the association of jobs with gender: for example, mechanical aptitude is required of an engineer or car mechanic and nimble fingeredness is a pre-requisite of a dressmaker. Perhaps the most noteworthy feature of the responses is the attribution of prestigious characteristics to men.

Family and home

In identifying activities in family and home life associated with either sex or both, the general patterns of response by boys and girls are similar, but a much larger proportion of boys than girls have stereotyped views (Fig. 9.4). This may be because we incorporated a category allowing respondents to nominate the items as co-operative ventures – 'Men and women together' – as an alternative to the by now familiar 'either' or 'don't know' (see Appendix 8). Each of these responses contributed to gender-free percentages and on five items co-operation contributes between 37 per cent and 58 per cent of this category of response from girls. However, we have no means of testing this suggestion and we must confine ourselves to noting that more girls than boys nominated the co-operative category in response to each item.

It can be seen that a majority of girls chose gender-free responses on six items, on two occasions exceeding 60 per cent; but boys remained almost entirely within the stereotype boundaries, emerging once only to firmly state that decisions about spending wages are not gender associated. The five most pronounced differences of opinion (items 1, 5, 6, 7, 12) indicate a shared stereotype except in the matter of spending wages (item 12): boys felt it appropriate for men; girls for women. Among these items we asked who should do minor repairs such as changing fuses, putting new washers in taps and clearing household drains (item 7); this is singular in drawing the most positive

Fig. 9.4 Responses on family and home: percentage without gender association.

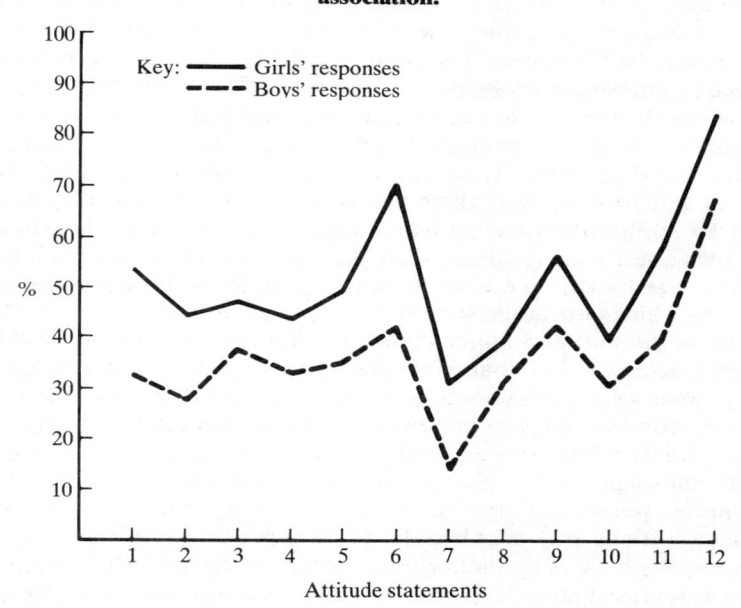

[Graph showing Girls' responses (solid line) and Boys' responses (dashed line) across Attitude statements 1–12, y-axis % from 0 to 100.]

Note: Percentages derived from responses to items 'By men or women – it doesn't matter', 'By men and women together', and 'Don't know'.

gender-associated response from boys and girls, and because it is distinguished by both from other household environmental chores and from interior decoration (item 11). When we asked who should take the baby out in its pram (item 6) we discovered a wide gulf between the opinion of boys and girls: 24 per cent of boys and 6 per cent of girls feel strongly that it is a job for women and nearly 40 per cent more girls than boys are happy to see dad taking baby for a walk. However, a high proportion of the gender-free responses indicates it is a co-operative venture (girls 40 per cent, boys 35 per cent).

Combating stereotypical influences

Chapter 8 showed that an active role in promoting equal opportunity is shunned by the majority of teachers in our study; the greatest number of voluntary comments by teachers on the attitude questionnaire concerns distaste for the term 'encourage(ment)' which we used throughout. Option schemes were frequently held to be an opportunity for free choice, systems were devised to minimize the impact of teachers on decisions and few careers staff were sympathetic to a suggestion that they should attempt to influence the pattern of career choice by girls and boys.

The results suggest, in our view, that the existence of stereotypical influence constitutes grounds for introducing corrective treatment whether that influence stems from inside or outside the school. We cannot agree with a view which accepts that pupils should be invested with the confidence to take decisions which will affect their whole lives, yet does not encourage those same pupils to reject unnecessary limits on their freedom to choose. In many case study schools the provision of subjects which encourage stereotypical images is based on an 'educational' argument; the upper ability pupil is, in fact, *encouraged* to widen her/his view of what are appropriate subjects or jobs; while the lower ability pupil faces academic and personal barriers to choice further constrained by *provision of routes* capable of fulfilling stereotypical roles.

The message is clear: the question is not whether teachers should encourage pupils, but how they should encourage them to take decisions in a framework which includes an appreciation of the external influences which limit their choice. Encouragement in this context means identifying the stereotypical barriers to motivation and interest in a subject as a preliminary to creating a remedial programme which will remove such barriers: it is the barriers at which coercive effort is aimed in a context analagous to identifying learning needs as a preliminary to creating teaching programmes. It is recognition of stereotypical influence as a barrier to development of aptitude and ability rather than a desirable socializing influence outside the educational terms of reference that is the key to legitimizing positive discrimination.

CHAPTER 10

Conclusions

In the course of this book we have seen that boys and girls differ in the subjects they choose at the age of 13+. More boys than girls take physical sciences and technical subjects, while more girls take biological and vocational subjects and languages. The pattern of choice, though not the pattern of provision, has changed little since the passing of the Sex Discrimination Act: there are few differences between our survey results in nine major academic areas and those from an HMI survey conducted in 1973 (GB. DES, 1975). On leaving school, pupils also exhibit differences in destinations according to sex. More boys than girls aspire to and achieve apprenticeships; more girls than boys aspire to and achieve secretarial jobs. The patterns are reflected in post-school education: secretarial, para-medical and teaching courses attract more girls than boys; engineering and scientific courses attract more boys. Our analysis showed that if pupils do take subjects non-traditional for their sex at school they are more likely to take up a non-traditional post-school course, but the sex of a pupil is a factor more statistically important in destination than the subjects studied. Thus, a girl taking sciences at school is more likely than other girls to follow a post-school science course, but less likely to do so than a boy who has not studied science.

Faced with these patterns of take up, and the fact of the Sex Discrimination Act, our study has shown that local authorities and schools appear to wish to be seen as taking the issue seriously, at least in their written responses to us. Most schools in our survey had discussed the issue in staff meetings, a large minority had considered it at meetings of governors and parent–teacher associations, though less than a sixth had given members of staff special responsibility or set up working parties on the issue. Very few made explicit reference to their policy in prospectuses.

In terms of school organization, over a third of schools claim to balance numbers of each sex in streams, which practice the EOC regards as unlawful, and most keep registers listing boys and girls separately. A few schools still restrict some subjects to one sex in defiance of the Sex Discrimination Act, but a high proportion offer all subjects to both, and teach most subjects including physical education and games and sex education in mixed groups, though in some schools some craft subjects are offered in single-sex groups to encourage and respond to non-traditional choice. Ninety per cent of schools offer a rotational craft system, many as a response to the Act, but few offer courses in women's studies or compensatory courses for pupils taking subjects non-traditional for their sex.

Overall, the picture appears to be that perhaps 75 per cent of schools conform to the letter of the Act, though do not particularly wish to go beyond this. Some 10 per cent have strong equal opportunities policies and some 15 per cent exhibit a number of features of 'bad practice'. This picture of overall school policies is a cause for both encouragement and concern. Protagonists of equal opportunities can feel encouraged that only a few schools actively discriminate on grounds of sex, and that the great majority show some features of good practice. But the existence of the minority who do discriminate and the apparently widespread belief that equal opportunities is simply a matter of not breaking the law suggests that much more needs to be done to encourage schools to embrace the spirit of the 1975 Act.

School policy and organization is not all. Does it have any effect? We show that there is little overall association between our measures of good practice and non-traditional subject take up in the major academic subjects. There is some suggestion that Rotational Craft Timetables encourage non-traditional craft take up, but the feature most associated with non-traditional take up is single-sex schools, though this may be because the schools we examined were mainly, or historically, selective.

We examined some of the features of school practice that may contribute to these findings. First we looked at the combinations of subjects that option systems permitted or prevented in a sample of 130 schools. This showed that in most schools the structure of the option system neither encouraged nor prevented sex-biased choice, though some schools had a system encouraging traditional patterns of take up and few made non-traditional combinations difficult. A large minority permit no science to be taken. When we compared the structure of schemes with take up we found that 'good' schemes are not associated with non-traditional take up overall, though some subjects appear to be affected to some extent. But the marked differences in take up cannot be explained solely by reference to formal rigidities of option systems.

We looked then at the influences within schools and their option systems which might affect pupils' choice of subjects. Firstly, we found that teachers frequently intervene in option choice advising on 'acceptable' or 'suitable' combinations of subjects for pupils. Secondly, some option schemes link subjects in ways which may be discriminatory, in that girls might find it more difficult to meet the conditions for acceptance such as in a craft subject because of a physics link. Thirdly, many schools introduce for lower ability groups para-science courses which are effectively sex-stereotyped. Fourthly, Rotational Craft Timetables are often badly implemented, being offered in an abbreviated form, or irrelevant to examination subjects, and so offer an inadequate experience base for pupils to make a serious choice. Lastly, we found that option forms themselves are often effectively restrictive on choice because of the way they are structured and applied. Many list subjects in multi-disciplinary blocks reflecting the school timetable, thus fitting pupils to timetable rather than timetable to pupils' choices. Some are so complicated as to be almost incomprehensible. Schools often defend their arrangements on grounds of inadequate resources, or discipline problems arising from compulsion to study non-traditional subjects. We found that although these arguments have force, schools with commitment manage to cope with the problems. Our examination of practices in case study schools suggested features of a good practice option scheme that should be within the capacity of any school to maintain, for all its features are found in schools somewhere, sometimes in schools without specific commitment to equal opportunities.

Another major factor influencing subject take up is the way in which subjects are presented to pupils at option choice time, and subsequently the ways in which they are taught. In formal literature, such as option booklets, over half the schools made it clear that both boys and girls were welcome in some subjects, but only one in nine stated that all subjects were open to all pupils. Some craft subjects were presented as for one sex; science descriptions often demonstrated a hierarchy of difficulty, though some schools specifically encouraged girls to choose physical science.

Our case studies showed that there is a wide variety of practices in schools, some of which encourage equal opportunities, others of which positively hinder it. Staff often hold strong views on the issue, perhaps the main evidence from the case studies was of the contrast between those who were attempting to reduce disparities in take up and improve teaching practices and those who said it could not be done. Thus, for example, in the physical sciences we were offered more explanations of the problems than solutions. Many teachers ascribed the failure to follow physical sciences to the pupils and influences on them, but many also believed that there is no career relevance in the subjects for girls. In other schools we came across examples of ways of tackling the problem, including creating girls' physics classes, and revision of syllabuses. The school most successful in getting a majority of girls to study a physical science to 16 had a core curriculum science programme, and seemed to surmount the problems which most teachers expressed in their opposition to the idea of a core curriculum science. Similarly, in craft subjects we found a disturbing incidence of reluctance by teachers to encourage non-traditional choice, more among technical craft than home economics teachers. The introduction of design and technology courses rather than traditional crafts in some case study schools allowed widening of opportunities for both sexes, but was often greeted with hostility by some members of staff.

Conflicting views of teachers were also a feature of the pattern of careers teaching. This is an important factor in option choice, as most schools suggest that pupils consider possible careers when choosing their subjects at 13+. Our survey revealed that a large number of schools consider equal opportunities in relation to careers teaching and had made use (with mixed results) of equal opportunities orientated literature, and introduced features on their programmes such as speakers providing non-traditional role models. Some schools incorporated topics on sex roles and equality in core subjects such as English or social studies. Case study schools did not reveal the same commitment. Only four out of fourteen provided careers advice before option choice, and most took a passive attitude to post-option advice, limiting themselves to providing material and timetabled careers lessons. Only two employed positive equal opportunities features. Many teachers expressed the view that schools should remain 'neutral' in this area, as in curriculum choice. And we found that some schools, and in particular one careers office, colluded with employers to channel pupils into jobs of a traditional nature.

The idea of 'neutrality' emerged again in our study of teacher attitudes. Most teachers were committed to equal opportunities in principle, though they showed decreasing enthusiasm for practical implementation of the principles. Their views were to an extent associated with their sex, but more strongly with subject, with teachers of traditionally stereotyped subjects such as physical sciences and crafts often holding strong stereotyped views. The minority opposed to equal opportunities argued in their comments that schools should not positively intervene in the process of choice by pupils – they should supply 'neutral' information and let the pupils decide. In our view this stance denies the existence and importance of the factors promoting stereotyping which we have discussed, and it also fails to take account of the attitude of pupils.

Our attitude study of pupils showed that in many ways the problems of achieving equal opportunities in education derive from them. Pupils are even less likely to agree with equal opportunities principles than teachers and boys less likely than girls. But there were striking contrasts in pupils' attitudes. Most pupils agreed that schools should set an example in reducing sex discrimination, yet in specific respects many boys, and to a lesser extent girls, showed themselves opposed to equal opportunities. Fewer than half of pupils believed that boys and girls could be equally good at all subjects. Pupils identified many jobs, careers, personal qualities and activities in the home with one sex, again, boys more consistently than girls. If pupils are to have equal opportunities these presuppositions have to be confronted. This is not to argue that they must be made to conform to some other view, but they must, if education is to be anything other than a predictable channelling mechanism, be considered, examined and where necessary challenged.

Given our findings, we suggested in the course of this study specific remedies to deal with some of the problems of implementing equal opportunities in schools. These proposals are of different kinds and concern different people operating at different levels. At the level of school policy, it is clear that some schools still have to consider the issue of equal opportunities, and that most schools fail to make policy explicit in their prospectuses. We suggest that all schools should, at meetings of governors, staff and parent–teacher associations consider – and from time to time reconsider and appraise – their policy towards equal opportunities. This should involve recognition and analysis of the differences in the subjects studied by pupils, the pressures towards sex stereotyping and the school's attitude to confronting them, and the steps the school intends to take to deal with them. The policy should be set out in the prospectus and other school literature, especially option booklets. When these documents are being compiled a senior teacher or working group should be responsible for ensuring that individual contributions are consistent with school policy. The production of option booklets particularly requires scrutiny, as many that we examined contradicted school policy and in some cases the law. Nor do we believe that such literature should be 'neutral'. It must, without browbeating the pupils, outline the possible benefits of non-traditional subject choices. 'Neutrality' maintains the status quo, with its evident differentiation and stereotyping.

The main point at which sex differentiation occurs is at the time of option choice. The organization and administration of option schemes is a crucial component of school policy on equal opportunities. We would mention the need for clarity and simplicity, and the importance of designing the timetable to fit option choices (so far as reasonably possible) rather than fitting choices to a timetable. Subjects should not be linked, especially in ways that imply sex stereotypes; para-science subjects should be avoided: and it seems to us self-evident (yet surprisingly overlooked in some schools) that some careers advice should precede option choice.

The proposals we have made so far are mainly matters of organization and administration, sometimes at a level of detail. The importance of these items should not be underestimated.

The ethos of a school is manifest through such features. Nor should administrative arrangements, such as the way subjects are grouped on an option form, be overlooked as 'mere' administration; they can affect subject choice. True, they are not the *only* place where an equal opportunities policy must be implemented, but they are part of the process of implementation and must be consistent with the aims of policy. The administrative and organization structures of a school enforce a hidden curriculum as much as the hidden values and assumptions of the teachers and the system.

Administrative and procedural reforms of this kind will not, of course, eliminate stereotyping on their own. Schools and their staffs need to reassess their attitudes, educational practices and educational philosophies. Such a process can take place at several levels. At the minimum, teachers need to ask, subject by subject, whether their approaches and practices do offer pupils of either sex a worthwhile educational experience. In many cases this will be a new experience for the teachers. We were struck by the inability of many teachers we talked with to offer any account at all of what it was that their subject offered to pupils that others did not. This process would lead, we believe, to some searching reappraisal of classroom practices and attitudes and also to redevelopment of existing syllabuses. The subject areas in which such reform seemed most needed include not only the more obvious sciences, crafts and technical subjects, but also some core subjects like English and the humanities. Very often, progress towards equal opportunities arises from curricular reforms which seek to avoid excessive subject specialization, like the creation of integrated science courses and the emergence of design and CDT courses.

The general employment of an approach to curriculum which regarded it as a means to ends and identifying what these ends are, would, we believe, lead to specific benefits for equal opportunities in traditionally stereotyped subject areas. In crafts, for example, the skills taught are often sex stereotyped. Yet they can be identified and taught as general and transferable. For example, manual dexterity is learned in both needlework and metalwork; the translation of two- and three-dimensional representations is common to both. By formulating an array of skills in these general terms, as has been done by, for example, the Further Education Unit's *A Basis for Choice*, (1979), it is possible to develop them in non-stereotyped ways. A similar analysis, at a more general level, has been done by the City and Guilds of London Institute (1982) which lists 14 basic abilities covering communication, practical and numerical, social and decision-making abilities. if a series of abilities such as these are established, it becomes possible to identify what activities, or conventional subject teaching, might contribute to their development. Moreover identifying what pupils will be able to do (the ends), rather than the subject areas they have been acquainted with (the means), places an emphasis on skills rather than knowledge, which, if nothing else, is important in assisting pupils in the narrow concern of seeking employment.

The need for this kind of reappraisal exists also in schools which have already made efforts to reform curricula and procedures. They need to ensure that programmes are properly implemented and to find ways of assessing whether the changes they have made are having any beneficial effects. The failure of many existing rotational craft schemes is due to poor practices. Similarly, schools should examine carefully the many para-scientific courses for lower ability pupils, which appear to us to be deficient in general educational, as well as equal opportunities, terms.

But we suggest, further, that teachers ought to think in terms, not just of importing equal opportunities into existing curricula, but rather of creating courses afresh that start from the needs and interests of both boys and girls, not from the 'demands of the subject' or the predictions and presumptions of teachers about pupils' needs. We take this approach because of our growing conviction that good equal opportunities practice follows from, indeed is identical with, good educational practice. This has, of course, been a feature of the EOC's beliefs for some time, but it needs a word of explanation. It is meant here in the sense that stereotyping is essentially treating pupils not as individuals, but as members of a group. Where we found good practice, it invariably involved considering the needs of pupils as people, rather than as members of one or other sex, and considering what they might need to equip them for the vicissitudes of future life. Our view is that reforming curriculum for equal opportunities involves a fundamental reassessment of schools' educational philosophies. This conviction was reinforced by the relatively slow progress that has been achieved since the passing of the Sex Discrimination Act. Our feeling is that thinking has to get outside the frame of what schools currently do. In considering new approaches we found ourselves questioning the idea that education should consist of discrete academic subjects. In a somewhat tautological sense, sex stereotyping in education arises because we have separate subjects. If there was no 'physics', boys and girls could not choose whether or not to study it. This is not entirely trivial.

Subjects reflect a structuring of knowledge and impose structures on schools which encourage stereotyped choice because of their associations and implications for pupils of either sex.

Subjects have other implications. They tend to deny the importance, sometimes the existence, of skills. Certainly, we frequently encountered the explicit or implicit view that skills are relevant only to specific jobs. Skill training is somehow viewed as inferior to 'education'.

A new approach could, in our view, be based on the development of qualities and general competencies in pupils to help them cope with and control their own lives in the world after school. We point to the work of Raven (1977 and 1982), Burgess and Adams (1980) and others as a basis for developing a competency-based education that is particularly appropriate for the children we are concerned with in this study who are beginning to formulate (indeed are obliged to decide) their views on future careers and the educational paths that will help them in pursuing those choices. Raven's work has shown that schools concentrate on 'academic goals' to the detriment of wider, and, moreover, widely accepted, educational goals. In fact 'academic goals' can be regarded as a sub-set of the wider educational goals. Raven shows that 'most teachers, parents, pupils and employers think that secondary schools should be concerned with developing the whole person'. Specifically, this involves fostering such qualities as

> the willingness and the ability to take the initiative in introducing change in their society, independence, the ability to make their own observations and learn without instruction, the ability to apply facts and techniques to new problems, to develop their characters and personality and to ensure that they leave school intent on being master of their destinies.

These qualities are 'characteristics and abilities which will enable people to reach their value goals – whatever these goals may be and whatever the social structure in which these people live and work'. They thus offer a basis for developing a *general* educational approach, which is particularly pertinent for the pupils we are concerned with in this study.

The formulation of clear objectives for education is a key part of this approach and particularly important for equal opportunities. It involves the recognition by pupils and teachers of the pressures and prejudices that face pupils. It is thus part of the process for girls or boys to recognize and confront the disparities in culture and circumstances that face them because of their sex, and to devise programmes of education to challenge, accept or avoid them. The competencies that Raven described can be seen as skills, knowledge, experiences, abilities that enable pupils to tackle these and other problems in the real world that they face currently and anticipate in later life.

Raven (1977) shows how his ideas could be developed within subjects as they are currently organized, and itemizes ways in which specific subjects could be presented to pupils to encourage the development of competencies, using a variety of different inputs geared to different objectives. Much more use could be made of both individual and group project work, structured to ensure that whatever pupils work on is relevant to their needs and differs from one pupil to another.

Of course, if education is seen as a way of meeting the individual needs and problems of pupils (of either sex), then two further issues are raised. Firstly, it suggests that individual needs can only be met by individual educational programmes. Secondly, it suggests that pupils themselves should be involved in formulating their problem and their programmes. Programmes of independent study are already established and working at post-school level in the UK and elsewhere. There is no reason why they should not be attempted at school level. We are not alone in arguing for their development. Burgess and Adams (1980) show how such programmes for the last two years of compulsory education can be devised, and Raven's work (1977 and 1982) suggests that these ideas are not as fanciful as they seem.

The education system is, perhaps inevitably, beginning to recognize the force of some of these arguments. Equal opportunites in education would be enhanced, in our view by implementation of some of the recommendations of such bodies as the Schools Council for increased personal and social education. In a recent report Kenneth David (1983) urges every secondary school to carry out, as a matter of urgency, a constructive and co-ordinated review of personal and social education – an 'umbrella' term covering overlapping areas of the curriculum such as morality, religion, politics, health and careers. These topics should form part of a basic curriculum alongside the traditional subjects in secondary schools, rather than be optional extras for just a handful of pupils.

We emphasized one particular area of school curriculum needing attention. This is careers teaching, which is important, not only because of the obvious breaches of the law. Since so much can hinge on a pupil's choice of subjects at 13+, it does seem to us incumbent upon schools to offer pupils some positive assistance with that choice. It is no great discovery that careers guidance is a 'Cinderella' of education: insufficient time and resources are devoted to it. As a minimum, this needs to be remedied. This may require radical reforms of school timetables, since by the time pupils get to 13, they have perhaps been exposed to inadvertent and subtle pressures and stereotyping for at least eight years. A couple of hours a week is hardly too much to attempt to remedy this. But even this may be insufficient. If pupils are to be obliged to make these far-reaching decisions, they need help to develop decision-making skills; experience in considering arguments, the consequences of alternative courses of action; help in evaluating evidence; assistance in researching and examining their self-images and the pressures upon them. Few, if any, schools offer this kind of experience.

We also suggest that schools examine carefully the benefits of work experience programmes, which often force schools into sex-biased allocation to places. We recommend that these and other questions should be considered by the Equal Opportunities Commission concurrently with internal and external career service attempts to negotiate change. Local authority associations, employers, business organizations and local authorities themselves should be persuaded to offer placements and influence offers of placements. This implies a commitment of time and organization which at present may not be available, but simply adds to the inadequate resources and lack of support experienced by teachers involved in careers advice.

We identified in Chapter 7 many ways in which attitudes and practices in the teaching of subjects should be changed, and we need not repeat these here. We would mention, however, the apparent importance of protecting small numbers of pupils of one sex in a class predominantly composed of the other. There seems to be a 'threshold' – of about four or five pupils – below which, minority pupils are prone to give up an option, but if this is surmounted others will be encouraged to follow. Most schools keep small numbers of, for example, girls in physics classes together, rather than splitting them between different classes. Similarly, some schools have made successful use of single-sex classes – for a limited period – for non-traditional subjects such as home economics for boys.

This study has shown that most of the objections to implementing an equal opportunities policy are invalid. (This is not an argument about the principle of equal opportunities, which ultimately remains a matter of value, though now constrained by law.) The main objections to practice were that 'it can't be done' for administrative, economic, educational or discipline reasons. Yet for every objection we found an instance where some other school had managed to cope with the problem. So good practice may be difficult, but it is not impossible.

This last point raises the question: whose job is it to ensure equal opportunities? One trite, though true answer is, of course, everyone's. But there are specific responsibilities within the education service, and it is to these that we now turn. Implementing equal opportunities is a responsibility of both Local Education Authorities and schools. Local authority officers, head teachers and teachers should know what equal opportunities imply; some evidently do not. Although governing bodies usually have responsibility for the overall conduct and curriculum of the school, it is the head who is responsible for day-to-day management and therefore has the prime responsibility for ensuring that pupils have equal opportunities, regardless of their sex. Local authorities, apart from having overall responsibility for what goes on in their schools, are responsible for ensuring that the Sex Discrimination Act is complied with. There are a number of instances reported here where they fail in this duty. It is worth recalling that LEAs are under a general duty under Section 25 of the Act as well as specific duties under Sections 22 and 23 to ensure that the facilities they provide for education and any ancillary benefits are provided without sex discrimination. More positively, LEAs have been exhorted from time to time by the Secretary of State not just to avoid discrimination but to help redress disparities in take up of subjects and to embark on other more positive equal opportunities policies. Since schools are among the facilities they provide, there is an obligation on LEAs to ensure that equal opportunities are encouraged in their institutions through school policies and practices. This is significant because of the provisions of the Education Act 1980 and the procedures proposed for LEAs to develop and monitor their own and their schools' curricular policies in Circular 6/81. In implementing the procedures outlined in that circular, LEAs have an opportunity to encourage schools to scrutinize their practices in respect of equal opportunites and to develop positive policies, and as they reappraise these policies as proposed in the circular, to develop and amend them. Our findings suggest that they might take more interest in identifying the schools exhibiting good and bad equal opportunities practices and disseminating the former. We suggest that the EOC should embark on discussions with the Society of Education Officers and the local authority associations to use this mechanism to the full to benefit equal opportunities.

But equal opportunities will not happen just because LEAs say they should. Our findings suggest to us that the head has a crucial task in management of policy. Yet good management is unlikely to happen of its own accord. There is a considerable responsibility on the head to ensure that the issue is one of concern in his or her school, and to ensure that all aspects of school organization and practice reflect the aims of policy. In most schools there will be a need to ensure the commitment of staff to this aim as to any other. We should not encounter the kinds of conflict between departments or individuals that were a disconcertingly frequent feature in our case studies. In one school, where policy was widely implemented, this had been achieved by the head's use of a wide range of management devices to 'carry' the staff with her. Instead of imposing an equal opportunities policy by *fiat*, she had initiated curriculum development groups, who (no doubt with the help of sympathetic teachers) had devised new curricular policies consistent with equal opportunities. The effect can be to make staff, who are initially unsympathetic, committed to the new ideas because they have themselves been a part of them. It is a cliché in some respects, but it does work. At any rate, no school will have a successful policy if staff are opposed to it. So, it is to the views and attitudes of teachers that we now turn.

The main purpose in identifying teacher attitudes was to illuminate sources of promotion or inhibition of equal opportunity, rather than to identify any group on a scale of culpability for bad practice. Teachers respond to the logic of their environment and influence the organization of a school in a manner reflecting that logic. The impact of this influence may vary with their responsibility within the system; or the policy of a school may be neutralized at classroom level where individual teachers on any scale or in any post may communicate an unsympathetic attitude to aspects of equal opportunity.

Our attitude study and our discussions with staff in case study schools suggest that it is important to pursue the train of thought which takes into account the teacher as agent and initiator in the educational system. We encountered two key objections from teachers to their active involvement in equal opportunities policies.

Many teachers tried to explain to us that they and the system are 'neutral'. We reject this view: the teacher shapes the environment as well as operates within it and is not – and cannot be – 'neutral'. Similarly, many teachers argued that practices which disadvantaged pupils of one or other sex were necessary on 'educational' grounds. This too we reject. There is sometimes a logic for the practices, but it is not evidently 'educational'. For example, consider the clear distinction that appears to exist between the attitude to girls among teachers of 'innovative' subjects (such as design) and teachers of bench-based craft subjects; in both groups males predominate, but the former express a wish to encourage girls to adopt their subject while the latter are mainly opposed to non-traditional choice. Can either group justifiably claim to argue their case for exclusion/inclusion of girls solely on the basis of educational priorities, without reference to vested interest? We would suggest that each group has taken a *rational stance* in relation to equal opportunity based partly on their perception of their personal interest, and it is important to recognize this: on the one hand, bench-based subjects are accorded a professional status such that change of syllabus or introduction of girls will threaten that status, and on the other, design teachers are promoting their innovative approach in competition with traditional views in order to create a niche for their subject.

The influences are of course much more diverse than this. They may result in firm agreement with option schemes which produce imbalance between sexes in science lessons; similarly, our case studies uncovered a persistent argument that science in the core curriculum, or compulsory choice of a physical science, will lead to problems of indiscipline. The question is: is this an educational argument? We think not: indiscipline is a matter of classroom management and syllabus development, of changes in teaching method and innovation to overcome the indiscipline. Schools in which a physical science is encouraged or is compulsory have developed syllabuses, have changed teaching method: they have seen the reasoning of treating indiscipline as an outcome of educational practice; it is an indicator of a need for change, to be confronted rather than avoided.

This is the crux of the problem for many teachers: the apparent contradiction between good educational practice and good equal opportunity practice. Head teachers with whom we talked explicitly enunciated this problem; other teachers referred to it most frequently when alluding to the examination system as an obstacle course on career routes. It results in paralysed inactivity where an observed inequality remains for want of reconciliation of the 'opposing' demands of equality of opportunity and educational goals. We believe this is a self-imposed dichotomy: it is not universally accepted by teachers; it has its roots in concerned individuals' frustration with the priorities of the system (e.g. the metalwork teacher who called his school an 'exam factory'); and it represents use of the educational system as a scapegoat for teachers' educational goals which are rapidly becoming indefensible. For how long will schools continue preparing pupils only for a local job market? Or encourage subject choice leading to a narrow focus of skills useful to a single career? Or ignore that stereotypes used as a basis for 'sensible' skill acquisition are inappropriate for a present and possible future in which roles may be blurred by unemployment and rapidly changing social demands?

In saying this, we are, nevertheless, wary of excessively criticizing teachers as a group. The topic of equal opportunities has overtaken the teaching profession, but seems still to be less significant than other pressures and responsibilities to which teachers must respond. There were, however, helpful findings from our study, too. Though their views were often contradictory, it is clear that most teachers are in principle against discrimination or disadvantage on grounds of sex, though they are decreasingly sure about equal opportunities and positive discrimination policies. They recognize that children bring stereotypes with them into schools, and that teachers sometimes support and may even encourage these, even if they believe that they are inappropriate. Some teachers hold stereotyped views more than others but our abiding impression was that teachers are looking for a clear lead on the topic of equal opportunities. They were unhappy at the dissonance between their beliefs and their practices. But the nature of the lead is crucial. Clearly, present initiatives do not satisfy them, for a variety of reasons, again probably contradictory – some teachers resent the 'harrassment' of the EOC, others are hardly aware of it.

These problems can be viewed as part of a general dichotomy between the views that teachers hold about the purposes of education and the practices that actually follow. This dichotomy has been documented by Raven (1977), who found that when asked what they thought the objectives of education ought to be, teachers, pupils and parents were in broad agreement, but when asked what aims were implied by their actual teaching teachers reported that they implemented quite different ones. All this suggests a need to establish a sound academic basis for what teachers believe should be taught, both in general educational terms and in terms of equal opportunities, and we have outlined earlier how this might be developed. In all this the local authorities have a role to play by encouraging in-service training and examining the role this could play in providing teachers with more support in deciding the priorities of the school policies. It is not reasonable to suggest that teachers should be faced with decisions on issues on which they are potentially the least informed and yet most directly responsible.

It is also important that teachers entering the profession should be familiar with the problems and issues and some of the ways of tackling them. At present, the government and many teacher-training institutions regard equal opportunities as a topic to be dealt with only by in-service education – or at least as an option in initial training. We recommend that these bodies reconsider this view. It should be a central component of any initial training course since, as this study shows, equal opportunity for boys and girls is an essential feature of good educational practice.

APPENDIX 1

Response rate and representativeness of samples

Response rate (%)

Cluster	Nominated	Overall
57	73	63

Representativeness

The samples were tested for representativeness of: LEAs with a selective system, age range, proportion of single-sex schools, type of authority (London, metropolitan, county), geographical location, level of financial provision for secondary education in the LEA, political control of the LEA.

Nominated sample

Schools in Labour and urban areas are over-represented in this sample. The schools nominated were almost exclusively mixed comprehensives (three girls' schools were nominated, no boys' schools), although in terms of the degree to which the LEAs in the sample operate a selective system the sample is representative of the country as a whole. Geographical location is representative. There is a slight tendency for authorities with higher financial provision to be over-represented.

The cluster sample

The English and Welsh sample is representative of financial provision, extent to which a selective system operated and numbers of single-sex/mixed schools. There are slight tendencies for Labour authorities to be under-represented and county districts to be over represented. Northern and southern schools are under-represented compared to middle region schools. There is also a slightly larger proportion of 11–14 and 14–18 schools than in England and Wales as a whole.

The addition of a Scottish authority increases the bias towards rural schools and decreases the bias towards middle region schools. The level of financial provision was proportionate. It will become clear later in this appendix that the features taken into account in assessing representativeness are not, on most variables, strongly associated with differences in the extent to which schools promote equal opportunities or in differences in non-traditional subject take up (except in the case of single-sex schools).

Case study schools

MIXED SCHOOLS ENGLAND NOMINATED SAMPLE

'Midland Comprehensive' 11–18 comprehensive; 720 pupils; Midland; city centre catchment; Labour LEA; amalgamation of two single-sex schools; poor situation and catchment; 50 per cent of pupils non-European background; positive discrimination policy towards non-traditional choice, pioneered by headteacher.

'Freelist Comprehensive' 11–18 comprehensive; nearly 1,300 pupils; prosperous southern suburban catchment; Labour LEA; claims to have adopted equal opportunities policy before 1975 and active in promoting it, though drew attention to its failures.

'Inner City Comprehensive' 11–18 comprehensive; 850 pupils; London city centre catchment; Labour LEA; popular school with active equal opportunities policy promoted by dynamic headteacher and widely supported by staff.

'Northern Modern' 11–16 secondary modern; 760 pupils; mainly council estate catchment; northern region; Conservative LEA; head least sympathetic to equal opportunities of all we visited.

MIXED SCHOOLS ENGLAND CLUSTER SAMPLE

'Smallchange Secondary' 12–18 secondary modern; 720 pupils; in southern rural catchment; Conservative LEA; passive view of equal opportunities.

'Northern Comprehensive' 11–18 comprehensive; 1,540 pupils; northern suburban catchment, mostly council estate; Labour LEA; little equal opportunities commitment with exception of one craft teacher fighting special request system.

'New View Comprehensive' 13–18 comprehensive; 1,100 pupils; prosperous southern rural catchment; Conservative LEA; compulsory core curriculum claimed to promote equal opportunities through educational achievement.

'Midshire Upper School' 14–18 comprehensive; 1,460 pupils; prosperous Midland rural catchment; Conservative LEA; strong academic tradition; no obvious equal opportunities initiatives.

'Daleview Comprehensive' 11–18 comprehensive; 1,520 pupils; prosperous northern rural catchment; Labour LEA; popular school on academic record; head teacher unsympathetic to EOC aims.

SINGLE-SEX SCHOOLS NOMINATED SAMPLE

'Seatown Girls' 11–18 comprehensive, but recently grammar; 1,100 pupils; southern mainly council estate catchment; head teacher has pioneered curriculum containing craft, design and technology, computer science, compulsory science and linkcourses in technical subjects.

SINGLE-SEX SCHOOLS CLUSTER SAMPLE

'Oldboys Grammar' 11–18 grammar school in prosperous London Suburb; 700 pupils; Conservative LEA; highly traditional atmosphere and emphasis on academic excellence; little concern with equal opportunities.

'Suburban Girls Modern' 11–18 secondary modern in same authority as 'Oldboys Grammar'; 700 pupils; equal opportunities regarded as not relevant in single-sex schools, though has some links with boys schools.

SCOTTISH SCHOOLS CLUSTER SAMPLE

'Scottish secondary' 12–16 co-educational school; comprehensive intake creamed off to other schools in third year; 990 pupils; mainly council estate catchment; some commitment to equal opportunities.

'Scottish Academy' 12–18 comprehensive in same authority as 'Scottish Secondary'; 1,360 pupils in rural catchment; strong academic tradition; little commitment to equal opportunities, though with some examples of good and bad practice.

APPENDIX 2

Good practice in schools

School policy

Good practice here involves a commitment by the school as a whole to avoid limiting the educational opportunities of boys or girls. This is evidenced by such features as the following.

- The school prospectus contains a statement that the school is committed to the principle of equal opportunity.
- Governors, parent–teacher associations and staff meetings discuss the subject and are kept aware of progress.
- A teacher is appointed with special responsibility for monitoring and promoting equal opportunities – or a teacher or group of teachers undertakes this voluntarily.
- The school has posters and wall displays concerning equal opportunities.
- The school has a policy to encourage women to take senior positions especially outside counselling and pastoral functions.
- Inservice courses on sexism and education are attended by teachers.
- The school has women teachers for traditionally male subjects.
- The school has a policy that resource allocation between subjects should not be discriminatory.
- Registers do not list pupils separately by sex.
- Playgrounds are mixed.

Option schemes

Good practice includes:

- non-sexist language used in options booklets; encouragement for pupils to take non-traditional subjects in option booklets; a statement in option booklets that all subjects are open to both sexes;
- no subjects closed to pupils of either sex, except under the special

circumstances prescribed in the Sex Discrimination Act;
- optional subjects grouped in such a way that non-traditional choices are encouraged or compulsory;
- a core curriculum in which pupils are encouraged or compelled to choose at least one subject in defined discipline areas, such as general science and/or two science subjects, and/or maths, and/or a Craft, and/or languages. (Note: this and the previous item raise the prospects of discipline problems caused by forcing children to study what they don't like and possibly also of resource problems);
- traditional boys' and girls' subjects not timetabled against each other, or grouped in option blocks so that the choice of one precludes the choice of the other;
- avoidance of pre-emptive choices, e.g. a pupil may not choose metalwork in the fourth year unless he/she has studied it in the third year, but girls are not offered it in the third year. It can be argued that these conditions are bad practice even if metalwork is available for third-year girls as they may not choose it then, but may wish to choose it in the fourth year;
- allocation of places to option subjects where resources are limited irrespective of sex, both directly and indirectly, e.g. not preferring pupils with career aspirations which tend to favour either sex, such as boys in motor vehicle engineering;
- or excluding craft subjects from the curriculum of the lower school, so that pupils have to make positive choices, rather than drifting into them and the jobs they lead to;
- a Rotational Craft Timetable preceding option choice;
- a 'crash course' to enable pupils with inadequate backgrounds in particular subjects to prepare for their study after option choice.

Allocation to classes or streams

Good practice includes:

- making no attempt to balance the composition of classes or streams according to sex; it is good practice to group together small numbers of pupils of either sex in a non-traditional subject to avoid isolation;
- making pupils work together in mixed sex groups, when there are sufficient numbers, particularly in science laboratories.

Subject teaching

Generally good equal opportunities practice involves making all subjects equally attractive to boys and girls. This may involve substantial curriculum change.

In specific subjects this includes considerations such as:
- taking a wider view of the value of craft subjects than as career routes in engineering for boys or as training for housework for girls;
- including topics in craft subjects which might promote non-traditional choice, e.g. jewellery in metalwork, or unisex or boys' clothes in needlework;
- revising option syllabuses, so that traditional emphases are eliminated, e.g. converting needlework to textiles;
- avoiding excess theoretical emphasis in the physical sciences which tends to deter girls;
- widening and updating biology syllabuses to make them more attractive to boys, covering topics such as ecology and the environment;
- giving special help to pupils in non-traditional subjects, so that they are not deterred by additional difficulties;
- making pupils work in mixed sex groups in science laboratories, when there are sufficient numbers;
- offering mixed sex physical education and games and non-traditional sports teams, e.g. girls' football;
- providing compulsory mixed sex parenthood courses;
- linked courses in local further education colleges which include subjects traditionally taken by girls, such as hairdressing.

Careers education

Good practice includes the following:
- Careers education is offered before option choice as well as afterwards, so that pupils can be made aware of the career implications of their choices (see Option schemes on pages 242–3);
- Careers education includes analysis of sex roles in society;
- Visitors with occupations non-traditional for their sex are invited to talk to pupils;
- Work visits and work experience schemes are open to both boys and girls and/or positive encouragement is given for pupils to choose non-traditional work;
- Careers interviewers point out that many traditional female occupations are jobs rather than careers, and generally suggest and encourage non-traditional careers;
- Careers literature is not sex stereotyped;
- Careers staff liaise with local industry to encourage acceptance of applicants to jobs non-traditional for their sex;
- Careers education is conducted in mixed groups.

Single-sex schools

- Single-sex schools should have adequate provision of science laboratories.
- If a subject is unavailable in the school arrangements should be made for pupils to study the subject in another school.
- Such schools could have teaching non-traditional subject areas – e.g. home economics in a boys' school, electronics in a girls' school.
- Girls' schools could have an industry link scheme.

Extra-curricular activities

Good practice includes:

- a range of school clubs and societies open to both sexes;
- sports teams open to both sexes;
- school visits and trips open to both sexes.

APPENDIX 3

Aspirations, destinations and hobbies of pupils from case study schools

Job aspirations of 430 boys
Mixed schools

Technical apprenticeship (includes electrical, engineering, building, welding, joinery, carpentry, panel beating, plumbing, motor mechanics, printing, construction)	181
Engineer (all levels)	64
Forces	71
Catering/chef	17
Draughtsman, sales/shop, technician/laboratory assistant/scientific	14 each
Police	13
Bank, clerical	10 each

Others, less than ten each:
Agriculture/horticulture/forestry
Teacher, don't know
Postman, lorry driver, work outdoors, computing
Designer, fire service, artistic
Factory
Music (playing/sales), warehouse/stores, airline, photography, acting
Management, animals, vet, hairdresser, accountant, bus driver
Unspecified further study, lawyer, architect, painter, messenger
Gamekeeper, medical, hospital porter, museum, ornithologist, golfer, sport, nurse, commercial, don't know, chemist, archivist, technical illustrator, astronomy, meat packer, refuse collector, cobbler, slaughterhouse, prison officer, blacksmith, social work, machine operator, glazier, metalwork, car sales, health inspector.

Job aspirations of 421 girls
Mixed schools

Secretarial/office/clerical	136
Hairdresser	56
Nanny/nursery nurse/with children	51
Nurse	48
Sales/shop assistant	46
Catering/hotel work	44
Police	21
Para-medical	21
Bank	29
Telephonist/receptionist	18
Art/design	17
Social work/welfare	16
Forces	15
Teaching (not scientific or technical)	14
Fashion design/manufacture/selling	13
Factory	11
Unspecified further study, air hostess, beautician, animals/horses/kennels	10 each

Others less than ten each:
Accountant
Computing, model, agriculture/horticulture
Pharmacy, actress, languages/translator, dancer, photography
With travel, don't know
Engineering, floristry, draughtswomen, travel agent, probation officer, psychiatrist
Film director, swimbath attendant, politician, WRVS, waitress, civil service, business, library, architect, with people, doctor, music journalist, buyer, social security officer, laboratory technician, prison officer, retail jeweller, physical education teacher, media, science teacher, marine biologist, study physical science, dentist, veterinarian.

Aspirations of 52 girls
Girls' schools

Higher education courses		17 girls with maths, physics or chemistry in their A-levels	No higher education		17 girls with maths, physics or chemistry in their A-levels
Humanities/arts	12	2	Nurse	3	0
Social service management	4	3	Forces	2	0
Child psychology/psychology	3	2	Beauty therapist	1	0
PGCE/BEd	10	2	Civil Service	6	0
Accountancy	1	1	Local Government	1	0
Law	1	0	Police	1	0
Languages	4	0	Ground hostess	1	0
Biology	2	2	Catering	1	0
Para-medical	3	3	With people	1	0
Health administration	2	0	Office	4	1
Doctor	1	1	Artist	1	0
Chemistry	1	1	Building society	1	0
Media studies	5	1	LRAM	1	1
Physics	1	1			
Engineering	1	1			
Mathematics	5	5			
Unspecified	3	0			

Jobs/further education destinations for 532 boys
Mixed schools

Apprenticeship	94
Unspecified further study	77
Forces	23
Unspecified work experience/training	23
Agriculture/horticulture, storeman/warehouse	22
Engineering	30
Building	17
Chef/catering/hotel, unemployed	16 each
Clerical	15
Shop/sales	14
Further study non-scientific	10

Others less than ten each:
Labourer
GPO, factory
Further study scientific/technical
Groundsman
Bank clerk, machine operator, British Nuclear Fuels Ltd
Hairdresser, milkman, pre-nursing, management, window making firm
Music, gamekeeper, police, porter, miner, sculptor, fire service, double glazing firm, postroom, foundry, butcher, cobbler, pest killer, sawmill, swimming pool attendant, railway, environmental health officer, art studio, messenger, laboratory assistant, computing, paint sprayer, trainee manager.

Jobs/further education destinations of 486 girls
Mixed schools

Unspecified further study	103
Office	106
Shop assistant	85
Factory	36
Hairdresser	29
Unemployed	17
Catering/home economics	15

Others less than ten each:
Secretarial course
Pre-nursing course
Unspecified YOP/WEP, nursery nurse/children
Study of biology, study of physical science or maths
Domestic assistant, dental nurse, bank
Jewellery, computing, beautician, further study with no science, receptionist, business studies course, telephonist, waitress
Labourer, police, study of art, warehouse, pharmacist, study of floristry, newspaper messenger, baths attendant, study of photography, study of ballet, study of sociology, library assistant, accounts clerk, cleaner.

Destinations of 52 girls
Girls' school

Higher education courses

Unspecified	3
Teaching	3
Humanities/social science	10
Arts/Languages	5
Management service/business studies	4
Law	2
Music	3
Medicine	3
Para-medical	3
Physics/astrophysics	1
Mathematics/computing	2

Non-higher education

Bank	3
Timber firm	1
HND catering	1
Journalism	1
Civil Service	2
Solicitors' office	1
Architects' department	1
Temporary au pair	1
Shop management	1
Badminton coach	1
Nursing	3

Destinations of 50 boys
Boys' school

Social science/humanities at university (including accountancy)	9
Engineering	6
Arts at university/higher education	6
Banking	6
Biological science at university	5
Police	3
Physical science in higher education, trainee manager, printer	2 each
Surveying, builder, accounts clerk, electrical, car mechanic, sales, English at university	1 each

Hobbies of 441 boys
Mixed schools

Football, 63; Sports, 45; Music, 37; Youth club, 35; Swimming, 34; Cycling, 30; Fishing, 28; Cars, 27; Badminton, model making, motorbikes, 21 each; Art/drawing, 17; Cricket, 16; Animals/pets, 14; Table tennis, cadets/air training corps, 13 each; Electronics, 12; Reading, camping, 11 each; Rugby, 10.

Others, less than ten each:
Golf, drama, squash, snooker, tennis, gardening, parties, shooting, cooking, athletics, TV, scouts, walking, collecting, karate, dancing,

basketball, young farmers, rock climbing, photography, bridge, stamps, ferreting, computers, darts, weights, sailing, chess, coins, skating, Duke of Edinburgh, boxing, collecting military items, horses, crosswords, jogging, flying, canoeing, skiing, keep fit, housework, judo, astronomy, birdwatching, cinema, bowling, budgies, dead animals, bottles, bricklaying, films, keep livestock, volleyball, house repairs, water skiing, railways, chickens, radios, church, children, lacrosse, woodwork, pigeons, outdoors, pipe band, pottery, travel, graphical drawing, Shakespeare, snakes, kart racing, helping mentally handicapped, study, trampoline, social work, writing, Boys Brigade, Salvation Army, fly tying, gymnastics.

Hobbies of 447 girls
Mixed schools

Swimming, 64; Cooking, 57; Music, 54; Dancing, 49; Knitting/sewing, 40; Youth club, 35; Reading, 32; Art/drawing, 31; Horses, 27; Ice skating, 26; Sports, 25; Children/babysitting, 21; Badminton, tennis 18 each; Animals, walking, 16 each; Parties, 15; Camping, 12; Discos, 11; Cinema, 10.

Others less than ten each:
Photography, hockey, drama, cycling, writing, stamps, singing, friends, table tennis, gardening, athletics, keeping fit, sailing, rock climbing, squash, scouts/guides, TV, crosswords, tidying up, fashion, collecting, guides, shopping, football, boys, social work, hairdressing, pool, volleyball, ballet, Christian Union, coins, dogs, games, running, Duke of Edinburgh, archery skiing, canoeing, agriculture, gymnastics, cadets, cars, interior design, nature, preserving old buildings, first aid, pipe band, youth fellowship, Sunday school, butterflies, walking, current affairs, chess, house repairs, motorbikes, hairdressing, water skiing, pubs, poetry, roller skates, judo, housework, helping disabled people, netball.

Hobbies of 52 Girls
Girls' school

Music	22
Swimming	21
Reading	20
Tennis	17
Badminton	9
Cookery, drama	8 each
Sewing, riding, scouts or youth leaders, squash	7 each
Cycling, travel, church	6 each
Ice skating, sport, guides, walking	5 each

252 *Option choice*

Others less than five each:
Dance, windsurfing, camping, hockey, youth clubs
Table tennis, drawing, painting
Singing, hang-gliding, rock climbing, helping with Brownies, sailing, karate
Collecting coins, poetry, yoga, netball, keep-fit, photography, water skiing, politics, jogging, archery, playgroup, judo, cinema, art, helping blind people, typing, mountaineering, animals, skiing, rollerskating, decorating, baby sitting, Girls Brigade.

APPENDIX 4

Classification of non-traditional subjects, careers and hobbies

Girls

Subjects	Aspirations	Destinations
Technical drawing	Science teacher	Trainee jewellery maker
Physics	Draughtsman	Trainee electrician
Motor vehicle engineering	Computing	Engineer
Woodwork	Medicine (doctor)	Doctor
Metalwork	Barrister	Chemistry/higher education
Design and technology	Accountant	Mathematics/physics course
	Politician	Computing
	Mathematics course	Labourer
	Physics course	
	Engineering	
	Law	
	Architect	

Hobbies
Football
Pool
Cars
Motorbikes

Boys

Subjects	Aspirations	Destinations
Family life	Chef/catering	Catering
Cooking	Cookery teacher	French A-level
Office practice	French A-level	Hairdressing
Typing	Hairdresser	Pre-nursing course
Human biology	Work with animals	English at University
Housecraft	Youth and community work	
Home and community	Typing	
	Social work	
	Languages	

Hobbies
Cooking
Mental handicapped helper
Pets
Animals
Dancing

APPENDIX 5

Categorization of subjects for option tests

Science includes:
Physics
Chemistry
Physical science
Biology
Human biology
General science

Physical science includes:
Physics
Chemistry
Physical science

Technical includes:
Rural studies/science
Technical drawing
Woodwork
Metalwork
Building
Motor vehicle engineering
Engineering
Electronics
Technology
Design and Technology
Additional mathematics
Statistics

Vocational includes:
Shorthand
Typing
Commerce
Typing and office practice
Office practice
Needlecraft
Child care
Home economics (cookery)
Home economics (general)

Note: Title variations were categorized on these principles.

APPENDIX 6

Careers associated with subjects in option booklets in mixed schools

	Nominated	Cluster
Physics		
Technical	34	24
Engineering	31	14
Para-medical	17	7
Scientific	14	9
Medical	16	6
Forces/police	4	7
Law/architect	3	2
Many jobs	5	0
Further study	4	2
Teaching	1	1
Local authority civil service	1	1
Arts/media	1	1
Industry	1	1
Self employed	1	0
Commerce	1	0
Personal interest	0	1
Chemistry		
Medical	23	17
Para-medical	26	21
Food	17	10
Scientific	19	5
Engineering	9	6
Technical	10	3
Agriculture	6	4
Science (biological)	3	2
Further study	2	3
Fashion/beauty	2	2
Teaching	1	2
With animals	1	1
Local authority/civil service	1	0

	Nominated	Cluster
Industry	1	0
History/library	1	0
Law/architect	1	0
Many jobs	1	0
Further study of biology	10	9
Biology		
Medical	27	8
Para-medical	20	23
Agriculture	10	13
Food	4	10
Scientific	3	5
Science (biological)	6	1
With animals	5	1
Teaching	3	1
Social services	4	0
Further study	2	1
Fashion/beauty	0	2
Many jobs	1	0
Industry	0	1
Technical	0	1
Local authority/civil service	1	0
Human biology		
Para-medical	19	0
Social services	6	0
Medical	3	0
Science (biological)	1	0
Food	1	0
Fashion/beauty	1	0
Three sciences		
Medical	14	3
Scientific	3	0
Engineering	2	0
Para-medical	1	0
Technical	1	0
Agriculture	1	0
Science subjects generally		
Scientific	0	3
Personal interest	0	1
Technical	0	1
Engineering	0	1

	Nominated	Cluster
Double science/SCISP		
Medical	0	5
Scientific	0	3
Engineering	0	1
Para-medical	0	1
Technical	0	1
General science		
Technical	3	0
Personal	1	0
Medical	1	0
Engineering	1	0
Applied science		
Technical	0	1
Engineering	0	1
Rural science/studies		
Agriculture	1	8
Further study	0	1
Mathematics/statistics		
Commerce	8	0
Scientific	5	2
Technical	2	5
Many jobs	2	3
Engineering	2	2
Forces/police	1	1
Para-medical	0	2
Arts/media	0	2
Agriculture	0	1
Computer studies		
Commerce	11	3
Scientific	5	0
Engineering	3	0
Retail/shop	3	0
Local authority/civil service	2	0
Office work	0	1
Para-medical	1	0
Personal interest	1	0
History/library	0	1
Technical	1	0
Agriculture	1	0
Law/architect	1	0

	Nominated	Cluster
Technical (includes: metalwork, MVE, woodwork, electronics, building, design and technology, design, engineering)		
Technical	55	17
Engineering	17	8
Personal interest	9	3
Further study	3	4
Planning/surveying	3	0
Teaching	3	0
Transport	2	0
Industry	0	2
Scientific	1	0
Forces/police	1	0
Technical drawing		
Technical	25	8
Engineering	11	3
Design	7	0
Planning/surveying	4	0
Law/architecture	3	0
Further study	3	0
Teaching	2	0
Personal interest	0	1
Industry	2	0
Scientific	0	1
Many jobs	1	0
Child care		
Social services	11	7
Personal/home	7	2
Para-medical	4	3
Teaching	2	0
Further study	0	1
Home economics		
Food	30	30
Para-medical	11	5
Personal/home	8	2
Social services	2	5
Teaching	2	3
Further study	3	2
Fashion/beauty	1	0
Commerce	0	1
Forces/police	1	0
Many jobs	1	0

	Nominated	Cluster
Needlework		
Fashion/beauty	13	9
Personal	13	2
Retail/shop	2	1
Further study	1	2
Jobs with manual dexterity	1	0
Social services	1	0
Lower level commercial		
(includes: shorthand, typing, office practice)		
Office work	35	14
Personal/home	11	4
Commerce	5	0
Many jobs	3	3
Further study	3	0
Arts/media	2	0
Food	1	0
Scientific	1	0
Forces/police	1	0
Local authority/civil service	1	0
Higher level commercial		
(includes: business studies, commerce, accounts)		
Commerce	12	10
Office work	3	5
Further study	1	3
Personal	2	1
Retail/shop	1	1
Local authority/civil service	2	0
Law/architecture	1	0
Industry	0	1
Forces/police	1	0
Many jobs	0	1
Economics		
Commerce	17	5
Office work	1	3
Further study	4	1
Industry	4	0
Arts/media	2	0
Local authority/civil service	2	0
Scientific	1	0
Many jobs	1	0
Teaching	1	0

	Nominated	Cluster
Sociology		
Further study	4	2
Social services	2	3
Office work	1	0
Commerce	1	0
Para-medical	0	1
Teaching	0	1
History		
Law/architecture	1	5
Arts/media	0	5
History/library	4	1
Local authority/civil service	2	3
Commerce	1	1
Para-medical	2	0
Teaching	2	0
Many jobs	2	1
Plan/survey	0	2
Personal	0	1
Further study	0	1
Industry	0	1
Community service		
Paramedical	1	0
Social services	2	1
Geology		
Scientific	2	2
Engineering	1	2
Personal	0	1
Foreign	0	1
Scientific (biology)	0	1
Languages		
Foreign	21	8
Further study	10	9
Office	10	5
Commerce	7	12
Personal	4	1
Food	3	2
Teaching	3	3
Scientific	5	2
History/library	4	0
Many jobs	6	0

262 Option choice

	Nominated	Cluster
Law/architecture	1	2
Industry	1	2
Local authority/civil service	0	2
Arts/media	0	2
Technical	1	1
Transport	0	2
Forces/police	0	1
Fashion/beauty	0	1
Para-medical	1	0
Retail/shop	1	0
Social services	0	1
Religious education		
Para-medical	2	1
Further study	1	1
Teaching	0	2
Commerce	2	0
Many jobs	0	2
Social services	0	2
Office	1	0
With animals	1	0
History/library	1	0
Forces/police	1	0
Geography		
Foreign	5	5
Many jobs	4	4
Plan/survey	3	1
Scientific	3	0
Commerce	1	2
Local authority/civil service	2	1
Office	1	0
Teaching	1	0
Arts/media	1	0
Agriculture	0	1
Transport	1	0
Scientific (biology)	1	0
Forces/police	1	0
Physical education		
Para-medical	0	2
Teaching	1	1
Personal	0	1
Further study	0	1

	Nominated	Cluster
Latin		
Various university courses	12	4
Humanities		
History/library	2	0
Many jobs	1	1
Arts/media	1	0
Law/architecture	1	0
Local authority/civil service	1	0
European studies		
Transport	0	1
Foreign	0	2
Visual arts (includes: photography, art and design)		
Arts/media	17	9
Technical	5	5
Further study	6	6
Fashion/beauty	8	1
Design	7	0
Law/architecture	2	3
Teaching	2	2
Personal	2	0
Retail/shop	2	0
Plan/survey	1	0
Many jobs	1	0
Food	0	1
Performing arts		
Arts/media	3	2
Teaching	4	1
Further study	3	0
Fashion/beauty	2	0
Many jobs	0	2
History/library	0	1
Retail/shop	0	1
Personal	1	0

APPENDIX 7

Teacher attitudes: statements about school

1. Girls and boys should do the same sports and games at school.
2. Schools should encourage boys to study subjects mainly studied by girls.
3. Girls and boys work best in single-sex schools.
4. The same punishment should be used for both boys and girls.
5. If boys and girls always studied the same subjects they'd be equally good at them.
6. Schools should put boys and girls in separate classes for some subjects.
7. Boys probably make better use of their education than girls.
8. Schools should set an example in reducing sex discrimination.
9. Girls and boys need separate playgrounds in school.
10. All girls should study woodwork and metalwork at school.
11. Girls should be encouraged to consider taking jobs normally done by boys when they leave school.
12. Schools should ensure that all classes contain boys and girls.
13. There are no school subjects better suited to either boys or girls.
14. Boys should be encouraged to consider taking jobs normally done by girls when they leave school.

Responses available: Agree strongly
Agree to some extent
Unsure or don't know
Disagree to some extent
Disagree strongly

APPENDIX 8

Pupil attitudes: items on careers, home life and personality characteristics

Jobs and careers

1. Police constable
2. Electrician
3. Solicitor
4. Trade union shop steward
5. Manager of a large firm
6. Ballet dancer
7. Politician
8. Taxi driver
9. Hospital nurse
10. Car mechanic
11. Office cleaner
12. Hairdresser
13. Farmer
14. Architect
15. Private secretary
16. Dentist
17. Engineer
18. Shop assistant
19. Fashion model
20. Radio disc jockey
21. Computer programmer
22. Television newsreader

Responses available: Only suitable for men
More suited to men than women
Equally suitable for men and women
More suited to women than men
Only suitable for women
Don't know

Tasks in the family and home

1. Going out to work to support the home or family.
2. Bathing small babies.
3. Doing the food shopping.
4. Cooking family meals.
5. Making beds.
6. Taking baby out in its pram.

7. Doing minor repairs such as changing fuses, putting new washers in taps, clearing household drains.
8. Cleaning the home.
9. Making sure household bills are paid.
10. Staying at home to look after young children.
11. Doing interior decoration such as painting and paper hanging.
12. Deciding how the wages should be spent.

Responses available: By men only
   By men more than women
   By men or women – it doesn't matter
   By women more than men
   By women only
   By men and women together
   Don't know

Qualities applicable to men and women

1. Tidy or neat	7. Loyal	14. Patient
2. Talkative	8. Careful	15. Kind
3. Competitive	9. Sentimental	16. Nimble fingered
4. Mechanical	10. Violent	17. Conscientious
5. Lazy	11. Spiteful	18. Aggressive
6. Important	12. Sensitive	19. Ambitious
	13. Rude	20. Hardworking

Responses available: Applies to men more than women
   Applies equally to men and women
   Applies to women more than men
   Don't know

Reference list

ACKER, S. (1980). *Feminist perspectives and British sociology of education*. Paper presented at the BSA Annual Conference.
BARKER, D. L. and ALLEN, S. (1976). *Sexual Divisions and Society: Process and Change*. London: Tavistock.
BENN, C. and SIMON, B. (1972). *Half Way There*. Maidenhead: McGraw-Hill.
BRIDGES, D. (1974). 'Feminism and education', *New Era*, **55,** 6, 134–37.
BRIDGES, D. (1977). 'Education, women and human nature', *Proceedings of the Philosophy of Education Society of Great Britain*, **11,** 136–43.
BRIERLEY, J. (1975). 'Sex differences and education', *Trends in Education*, **1**.
BUCKLEY, A. (1979). Sex discrimination in secondary education: a case study of the subject choice of boys and girls in two mixed comprehensive schools. Unpublished MA thesis, City of London Polytechnic.
BURGESS, T. and ADAMS, E. (1980). *The Outcomes of Education*. London: Macmillan.
BYRNE, E. M. (1975). 'Inequality in education', *Educ. Rev.*, **27**, 3, 179–91.
BYRNE, E. M. (1978). *Women and Education*. London: Tavistock.
CENTRE FOR CONTEMPORARY CULTURAL STUDIES (1978). *Women Take Issue*. London: Hutchinson.
CHETWYND, J. and HARTNETT, O. (1978). *The Sex Role System*. London: Routledge and Kegan Paul.
CITY AND GUILDS OF LONDON INSTITUTE (1982). CGLI profiling: project 2 report.
COLEMAN, G. E. (1977). An investigation of girls' job perceptions. Unpublished MEd thesis, University of Liverpool.
CRAC (Annual). *Your Choice at 13+*. Cambridge: CRAC.
CROWTHER REPORT. GREAT BRITAIN MINISTRY OF EDUCATION. CENTRAL ADVISORY COUNCIL FOR EDUCATION (ENGLAND) (1959). *15–19*. (Vol. 1, Report; Vol. 2, Survey). London: HMSO.
DALE, R. R. (1971). *Mixed or Single Sex School? Vol. 2: Some Social Aspects*. London: Routledge and Kegan Paul.
DALTON, P. (1980). Issues in the role and status of needlecraft. Unpublished MEd thesis, University of Sussex/Brighton Polytechnic.

DAVID, K. (1983). *Personal and Social Education in Secondary Schools.* London: Longman.
DAVIES, L. (1978). 'The view from the girls', *Educ. Rev.*, 30, 2.
DAVIES, L. and MEIGHAM, R. (1975). 'A review of schooling and sex roles, with particular reference to the experience of girls in secondary schools', *Educ. Rev.*, **27,** 3.
DEEM, R. (1978). *Women and Schooling.* London: Routledge and Kegan Paul.
DEEM, R. (1980). *Schooling for Women's Work.* London: Routledge and Kegan Paul.
DELAMONT, S. and DUFFIN, L. (Eds) (1978). *The Nineteenth Century Woman.* London: Croom Helm.
FRAZIER, N. and SADKER, M. (1973). *Sexism in School and Society.* New York: Harper and Row.
FREEMAN, H. (1977). 'On Women's Education', *Proceedings of the Philosophy of Education Society of Great Britain*, **11**, 113-35.
FURTHER EDUCATION UNIT (1979). A Basis for Choice.
GALTHORNE-HARDY, J. (1977). *The Public School Phenomenon.* London: Hodder and Stoughton.
GREAT BRITAIN. DEPARTMENT OF EDUCATION AND SCIENCE (1975). *Education Survey 21: Curricular Differences for Boys and Girls.* London: HMSO.
GREAT BRITAIN. DEPARTMENT OF EDUCATION AND SCIENCE (1977). *Education in Schools: A Consultative Document.* London: HMSO.
GREAT BRITAIN. DEPARTMENT OF EDUCATION AND SCIENCE (1979). *Aspects of Secondary Education in England.* London: HMSO.
GREAT BRITAIN. DEPARTMENT OF EDUCATION AND SCIENCE (1980a). *Girls and Science.* London: HMSO.
GREAT BRITAIN. DEPARTMENT OF EDUCATION AND SCIENCE (1980b). *Statistics of School Leavers.* London: HMSO.
GREAT BRITAIN. DEPARTMENT OF EDUCATION AND SCIENCE (1981). *Statistics of Education, Vol. 1, Schools.* London: HMSO.
GREAT BRITAIN. EQUAL OPPORTUNITIES COMMISSION (1979). *Do You Provide Equal Opportunities?* Manchester: Equal Opportunities Commission.
GREAT BRITAIN. EQUAL OPPORTUNITIES COMMISSION (1980). *Breakthrough: A Pictorial Record of Five years' Progress Towards Sex Equality in Employment.* Manchester: Equal Opportunities Commission.
GREAT BRITAIN. EQUAL OPPORTUNITIES COMMISSION (1982). *Equal Opportunities in Home Economics.* Manchester: Equal Opportunities Commission.
HANNAN, D. F., BREEN, R., MURRAY, B. and O'HIGGINS, K. (1981). Sex Differences in Subject Provision and Choice in Irish Post-primary Schools. Unpublished paper, Economic and Social Research Institute, Dublin.
HANNON, V. (1981). *Ending Sex Stereotyping in Schools: A Sourcebook for School-based Teacher Workshops.* Manchester: Equal Opportunities Commission.
HURMAN, A. (1978). *A Charter for Choice: A Study of Options Schemes.*

Windsor: NFER-NELSON.
ILEA (1975). *Careers Opportunities for Women and Girls.* London: ILEA.
JACKSON, S. (1978). 'How to make babies: sexism in sex education', *Women's Studies International Quarterly*, **1**, 341–52.
KELLY, A. (1976). 'Women in science: a bibliographic review', *Durham Research Review*, **7**, Spring, 1092–1108.
KELLY, A. (1979). 'Why girls don't do science', *Collaborative Research Newsletter*, **4**, 61–8.
KEYS, W. and ORMEROD, M. B. (1977). 'Some sex related differences in the correlates of subject preference in the middle years of secondary education', *Education Studies*, **3**, 2.
KING, R. A. (1981). 'Secondary schools: some changes of a decade', *Educational Research*, 23, 3.
KING, R. A. (1982). 'Organisational change in secondary schools: an action approach', *British Journal of Sociology of Education*, **3**, 1.
KUHN, A. and WOLPE, A. M. (1978). *Feminism and Materialism.* London: Routledge and Kegan Paul.
LOBBAN, G. (1975a). 'Sex roles in reading schemes', *Educ. Rev.*, 202–9.
LOBBAN, G. (1975b). 'Sexism in British primary schools', *Women Speaking*, **4**, 10–13.
LOBBAN, G. (1978). *The Sex Role System.* London: Routledge and Kegan Paul.
LOVE, C., SMITH, D. and TURNBULL, A. (1980). 'Women in the making', *South Bank Sociology Occasional Paper 2.* Polytechnic of the South Bank.
MILES, H. B. (1979). 'Some factors affecting attainment at 18+', Oxford: Pergamon.
MITCHELL, J. and OAKLEY, A. (1976). *The Rights and Wrongs of Women.* London: Penguin.
MURPHY, R. J. L. (1980). 'Sex differences in GCE examination entry statistics and success rates', *Educational Studies*, **6**, 2, 169–78.
NAVA, M. (1980). 'Gender and education: a discussion of two recent books', *Feminist Review*, **5**,
NEWSOM REPORT. GREAT BRITAIN. MINISTRY OF EDUCATION. CENTRAL ADVISORY COUNCIL FOR EDUCATION (ENGLAND) (1963). *Half our Future.* London: HMSO.
NICHOLSON, J. (1977). *What Society Does to Girls.* London: Virago.
NORWOOD REPORT. GREAT BRITAIN. BOARD OF EDUCATION (1943). *Report of the Committee of the Secondary Schools Examination Council on Curriculum and Examinations in Secondary Schools.* London: HMSO.
NUT/EOC (1980). *Promotion and the Women Teacher.* Equal Opportunities Commission.
OECD (1980). Press release a(80) 26, 17 April. Paris: OECD.
PARSONS, G. (1979). 'Set books and static curricula: the case of English literature', *Journal of Curriculum Studies*, **11**, 4, 338–40.
PARSONS, G. (1980). Antiquated themes in English Literature syllabuses. Unpublished paper, Department of Sociology, University College, Cardiff.
PARSONS, G. (Forthcoming). 'English literature: its educative classification and wider implications', *Education for Development.*

PITT, A. W. H. (1973). 'A review of reasons for making a choice of subjects at the secondary school level', *Educ. Rev.*, **26**, 1.
PLOWDEN REPORT. GREAT BRITAIN. DEPARTMENT OF EDUCATION AND SCIENCE. CENTRAL ADVISORY COUNCIL FOR EDUCATION (ENGLAND) (1967). *Children and their Primary Schools.* London: HMSO.
RANCE, S. (1978). 'Going all the way', *Spare Rib*.
RAUTA, I., and HUNT, A. (1975). *Fifth Form Girls: Their Hopes for the Future.* London: HMSO.
RAVEN, J. (1977). *Education Values and Society.* London: H. K. Lewis.
RAVEN, J. (1982). 'Broadening the base of educational assessment: some reasons, some problems and some suggestions', *Bulletin of the British Psychological Society*, **25**, 332–44.
RICKS, F. A. and PYKE, S. W. (1973). 'Teacher perceptions and attitudes that foster or maintain sex role differences', *Interchange*, **4**, 26–33.
ROBINSON, P. D. (1973). 'Physical activity and femininity', *British Journal of Physical Education*, **4**, 4, 59–60.
SAWDON, A., PELICAN, J. and TUCKER, S. (1981). *Study of the Transition from School to Working Life.* Leicester: Youthaid.
SHARMA, S. and MEIGHAM, R. (1980). 'Schooling and sex roles: the case of GCE O level Mathematics', *British Journal of Sociology of Education*, **1**, 2, 193–206.
SHARPE, S. (1976). *Just Like a Girl: How Girls Learn to be Women.* London: Penguin.
SHAW, B. (1979). 'Sex discrimination in education: theory and practice', *Journal of Philosophy of education*, **13**.
SMITHERS, A. G. (1976). 'A psychological study of girls specialising in science in the sixth form', *SSRC*.
SPENDER, D. (1981). 'Sexism in schools', *The Listener*, 31 December, 816.
STACEY, J., BEREAUD, S. and DANIELS, J. (1974). *And Jill Came Tumbling After: Sexism in American Education.* Dell.
STAMP, P. (1979). 'Girls and mathematics: parental variables', *Br. J. Educ. Psychol.*, **49**, part 1, 39–50.
TAYLOR, J. (1979). 'Sexist bias in physics text books', *Physics Education*, 14, 277–80.
TEACHERS ACTION ALLIANCE (1980). *Sexism in Irish Education.*
WARDLE, D. (1978). 'Sixty years on: the progress of women's education 1918–1978', *Trends in Education*, **4**, 3–7.
WOLPE, A. (1974). 'The official ideology of education for girls'. In: FLUDE, M. and AHIER, J. *Educability, Schools and Ideology.* London: Croom Helm.
WOLPE, A. (1977). *Some Processes in Sexist Education.* London: Women's research and resources centre.
WOMEN IN THE NUT (undated). *Sexism in School: Discussion Document.*
WOOD, R. (1976). 'Sex differences in mathematics attainment at GCE ordinary level', *Educational Studies*, 2, 141–60.
WOODHALL, M. (1973). 'Investment in women: a reappraisal of the concept of human capital', *International Review of Education*, **19**, 1, 9–29.

Further reading

BENN, C. (1973). 'Some aspects of sex inequality in education', *Journal of Applied Education Studies*, 12–19.
BIOLETTI, P. A. (1976). The influence of a girl's school on the socialisation of its fourth year pupils. Unpublished MEd. thesis, University of Newcastle.
BYRNE, E. M. (1974). *Planning and Educational Inequality*. Windsor: NFER-NELSON.
DALE, R. R. (1975). 'Education and sex roles', *Educ. Rev.*, 27, 240–8.
DRIVER, G. (1980). 'How West Indians do better at school (especially the girls)', *New Society*, 17 January, 111–114.
DYHOUSE, C. (1978). 'Towards a "feminine" curriculum for English schoolgirls: the demands of ideology 1870–1963', *Women's Studies International Quarterly*, 1, 291–311.
ELLIOTT, J. (1974). 'Sex role constraints on freedom of discussion: a neglected reality of the classroom', *New Era*, 55, 147–55.
FLUDE, M. and AHIER, J. (1974). *Educability, Schools and Ideology*. London: Croom Helm.
FULLER, M. (1978). Dimensions of gender in a school. Unpublished PhD thesis, University of Bristol.
HARTNETT, O., BODEN, G. and FULLER, M. (1979). *Sex Role Stereotyping*. London: Tavistock.
HEARN, M. (1979). 'Girls for physical science: a school based strategy encouraging girls to opt for the physical sciences', *Education in Science*, 82, 14–16.
HUTT, C. (1979). 'Why do girls underachieve?', *Trends in Education*, 4, 24–8.
KELLY, A. (1975). 'Why do girls study biology?', *School Science Review*, 628–32.
KELLY, A. (1978). 'Science for girls', *Woman's Studies International Quarterly*, 1, 4.
KELLY, A. (1981). 'Research on sex differences in schools in the UK'. UK National Report for the Council of Europe Educational Research Workshop on Sex Stereotyping in Schools, held at Hønefoss, near Oslo, 5–8 May 1981.
LOMNICKA, E. (1978). 'Education and the Sex Discrimination Act 1975', *New Community*, 5.

ORMEROD, M. B., BOTTOMLEY, J. M., KEYS, W. P. and WOOD, C. (1979). 'Girls and Physics Education', *Physics Education*, **14**, 5, 271–77.

PATTERSON, E. and MARLAND, M. (1980). Sex differentiation and Schooling: A Bibliography. Paper prepared for conferences at Churchill College, Cambridge.

READER-HARRIS, D. (1974). 'The same for both sexes?', *Conference*, **11**, 2.

ST JOHN-BROOKS, C. (1980). 'Sociologists and education: A for effort, B for achievement', *New Society*, **53**, 929.

SMITH, G. L. (1974). 'The education of women in secondary schools', *New Era*, 140–4.

WOOD, R. (1978). 'Sex differences in answers to English language comprehension items', *Educational Studies*, **4**, 157–65.

WOODS, P. (1976). 'The myth of subject choice', *British Journal of Sociology*, **27**, 2.

WOODS, P. (1979). *The Divided School*. London: Routledge and Kegan Paul.

Index

ability grouping *see* pupils, lower ability
Army Cadet Force   153
attitudes *see* parents, pupils, teachers
aspirations (of pupils)   2, 99, 44–47, 67, 102, 113, 116, 121, 122, 162, 212, 225, 246–252, 253–254

bad practice   2, 4, 67, 68–69, 75, 79–80, 226 *see also* good practice
balancing by sex *see* schools: quota systems
BBC publications   155, 158
books, school   15–16, 65, 152, 153

Careers
 education   16–17, 21, 24–25, 99, 124, 154–165, 167, 172–174, 185–187, 197, 228, 230, 233–234, 244
 lessons   155–165 *passim*
 literature   15
 neutrality in   159
 offices   2, 3, 4, 45, 52, 160, 162
 of pupils   2, 8–10, 16, 17, 44–53, 59, 61, 129, 216, 224, 248–250, 253–254, 256–263
 records   26, 44–45, 53
 service   163, 172, 173, 234
 teachers   3, 4, 16–17, 24–25, 102, 172

Careers Research and Advisory Centre   157, 163
Chief Education Officers   3, 54–56, 78, 82, 84, 151, 177
Circular 6/81   235
City & Guilds of London Institute   230
classes
 mixed sex   59, 83, 129, 144, 150, 156, 226, 243
 single sex   11, 12, 13, 22–23, 69, 83, 110, 111, 133, 149, 152, 153, 156, 159, 173, 201–203, 217, 226, 228, 234
courses
 compensatory   21, 24, 67, 71, 83, 123, 226, 243
 Nuffield science
 para-scientific   107–109, 122, 124, 131, 227, 229, 231
 taster   99, 106, 110, 111, 144
competency based education   232–233
curriculum
 core   19, 22, 108–109, 129, 131, 228, 236, 243
 development   139, 171, 230, 236, 243
 hidden   15, 230

Department of Education and Science
 statistics   2, 3, 26, 36–44, 48–53
difficulties with subjects   9

discipline 24, 109, 122, 131, 144, 227, 237, 243

economic factors 8, 10
Education Acts 18, 20, 235
educational philosophy 230–234
employers 2, 128, 129, 132, 160, 161, 162, 163, 167, 172, 209, 234
England 3, 4, 5, 7, 32, 129, 144, 240
Equal Opportunities Commission 1, 3, 11, 18–25 *passim*, 67, 82, 84, 93, 157, 225, 231, 234, 235, 238
examination boards 71, 138
examinations
  C.S.E. 7, 33–44, 65, 112, 130, 131, 133, 135, 143, 145, 146
  entries 2, 33–44
  G.C.E. 'O' level 7, 33–44, 111, 130, 132, 135, 150, 151
  results 7, 33–36
  systems 237

femininity 10
further education 48–52, 248–250
  colleges 7, 45, 72–73, 160, 244
Further Education Unit 230

goals of education 232, 238
good practice 2, 4, 22, 23, 24, 25, 67, 75, 76–78, 79–80, 83–84, 226, 237, 242–245
governors *see* schools
guidance system 161–163

Her Majesty's Inspectors 1, 9, 13, 82
  survey 1973 2, 6, 13, 14, 26, 32–33, 53, 72, 73, 83, 84, 129, 225
higher education 45, 48–52, 67, 203, 248, 251
hobbies of pupils 45–47, 250–252, 253–254

independent study 233

job opportunities 8, 154–155, 167, 173, 208

local authority associations 234, 235
Local Education Authorities 3, 18, 20, 71, 75
  political control 75, 77, 83, 135, 223, 234, 235
leisure activities of pupils *see* hobbies
linked courses 7, 72–73, 244
lower ability (pupils) 9, 27

management, schools 235–236
Ministry of Defence 153

National Association for Maternal and Child Welfare 136
neutrality
  option forms 123–124
  subject descriptions 135–136, 168–169, 229
  teachers' attitudes 173, 205–209, 228, 236

option
  blocks 101, 113–114, 123, 130, 134, 227, 243
  booklets 81, 82, 125–129, 135–144, 152–154, 156, 165–167, 168, 227, 229, 242, 256–263
  forms 101, 104, 105, 113–121, 122–124, 146, 151, 155, 227
  schemes, tests of 86–99, 226, 255

parents 2, 3, 22, 55, 65, 82, 102, 121, 135, 147, 148, 150, 155, 156, 157, 160, 163, 169, 203–204, 207, 209
parent-teacher meetings *see* schools
pilot studies 4
postal survey *see* survey, postal
pre-emption 11–12, 21, 23, 72–73, 120, 243
premature specialisation 11–12

Index 275

prospectuses 3, 58–60, 82, 225, 229, 242
punishment 3, 197–199, 214–215
  corporal 15, 60, 198
pupil attitude scales 210–224, 265–266
  sample 210
  agreement with EOC policy 212–213
  boys and girls in school 213–217
  family and home 222–223, 265–266
  jobs and careers 218, 220, 265
  men and women 220–222, 266
pupils
  allocation by sex *see* schools: quota systems
  attitudes 5, 7, 107, 147, 167, 228–229
  friends 65, 102, 121
  interviews 4, 99–104, 154–155
  isolation of 171, 234, 243
  lower ability 86, 107–109, 116, 122, 129, 131–133 *passim*, 144, 145, 151, 160, 167, 209, 227, 231

questionnaire 3, 66, 82

race 10
registers 15, 71, 83, 242
relationships, sexual 15
resource
  allocation 11, 111, 147, 242
  argument 124, 170
  level of 75, 77, 83, 84, 114, 116, 227, 233, 234, 239
  rotational craft timetables 14, 59, 67, 72, 75, 80, 82, 83, 84, 99, 106, 109–113, 116, 120, 121, 122–123, 124, 139, 143, 144, 147, 150, 151, 156, 226, 227, 231, 243

schools
  age-range 4, 77, 239

balancing intake 61
case studies 2, 4–5, 44–66, 99–121, 129–135, 144–152, 227–228
catchment 21, 77
club and societies 63, 245
comprehensive 7, 14, 77, 240, 241
financial provision *see* resources
geographical location 4, 77, 239
governor's meetings 66, 82, 225, 229, 235, 242
grammar 7, 14, 241
links between 67, 73, 135, 163
parent-teacher meetings 57, 66, 75, 82, 83, 225, 229, 242
playgroups 69, 71, 197–198, 214–215, 242
policy on equal opportunity 56–67, 99, 145, 168, 197, 225, 226, 229, 242
primary 1, 16, 82
quota systems 64, 69, 75, 83, 134, 225, 243
selective 75, 80, 84
single-sex 4, 7, 11, 12, 14, 15, 21, 27–31, 32–33, 45, 62, 63, 66–67, 73–74, 84, 93, 99, 120–121, 129, 134–135, 145, 150–152, 170–171, 226, 239, 240, 241, 245
staff meetings 57, 66, 75, 82, 83, 225, 229, 242
uniform 71
school leavers 45–52
  survey 5, 26, 36–44, 48–52
Schools Council 155, 233
Schools Council Integrated Science Project 128–129
science laboratories 11, 134, 135, 150, 245
Scotland 3, 4, 11, 32, 240
  schools in 4, 161–163
Secretary of State 235
separation of pupils *see* classes
setting 107
Sex Discrimination Act 1975 1, 2, 18–25 *passim*, 26, 32, 33, 53,

Sex Discrimination Act – *contd.*
  54, 58, 61, 72, 82, 83, 106, 111, 142, 144, 157, 161, 225, 226, 231, 235, 243
skill based education   230–231, 232
social class   9, 207
Society of Education Officers   235
special request systems   19, 22, 23, 64, 150, 206, 242
staffing   3, 17, 21, 153, 242
subjects
  availability   10–17
  Cinderella   154, 233
  compulsory   14, 24, 31, 38, 53, 73, 86, 87–88, 93–94, 99, 101, 108, 110, 130, 145, 150, 153, 187–189, 227, 237, 243
  influences on choice   99–124, 129, 227
  linked   105–107, 124, 227, 229–230
  links with jobs   165–167
  take-up   2, 6–10, 11–14, 26–53 *passim*, 61, 78–81, 84, 93–99, 121–122, 130, 133, 225, 226
Sun, the, page 3 of   61
survey, postal   3–4, 72
  sample, cluster   3, 27, 58–79 *passim*, 127–129, 143, 177, 213, 239–241, 256–263
  sample, nominated   3, 27, 58–79 *passim*, 127–129, 142, 152–154, 157–158, 213, 239–241, 256–263
  representativeness   4, 239–240
  response rate   4, 239

teachers
  attitudes   2, 5, 15, 82, 99, 101, 175–209, 236–238
  promotion   66
  responsible for equal opportunities   3, 57–58, 61–68, 75, 83, 128, 225
  see also subjects, influences on choice
teacher attitude scales   175–209, 212–215, 264
  basic beliefs   179–181
  commitment to equal opportunity   181–185
  encouragement of non-traditional choice   192–197
  physical sciences and technical subjects   187–189
  role of careers education   185–187
  role of parents   203–204
  sample   175
  school organisation   197–203
  stereotyped subjects   189–192
teacher training   238, 242
timetabling   21, 114, 116, 124, 155, 227, 229, 233, 243
trousers
  girls not wearing   15
  girls wearing   71

Wales   3, 4, 5, 7, 32, 240
work experience   154, 160, 161, 162, 174, 234

Youth Employment Programme   163